THE ELECTION GAME *and How to Win It*

THE
ELECTION
GAME
and How to Win It

JOSEPH NAPOLITAN

ECHO POINT BOOKS & MEDIA, LLC
BRATTLEBORO, VERMONT.

Published by Echo Point Books & Media
Brattleboro, Vermont
www.EchoPointBooks.com

The Election Game and How to Win It
ISBN: 978-1-63561-781-8 (paperback)

Cover design by Adrienne Núñez
Cover photographs: Cecil Stoughton,
courtesy John F. Kennedy Presidential Library and Museum, Boston

PREFACE

Perhaps I should start by saying what this book is and is not.
It is *not* a textbook on how to run a political campaign.

It is *not* an exposé.

It *is* a personal book relating some of my experiences in managing political campaigns and counseling candidates in the United States and foreign countries for the past fifteen years.

Because it is a personal book, I use the vertical pronoun frequently, without resorting to any editorial subterfuge or euphemism.

Not everyone is likely to find all the chapters equally interesting. Several, such as the use of electronic campaign techniques or political polls, may appeal primarily to persons with special interests. A longish chapter on the Pennsylvania gubernatorial election of 1966 is the most thorough case study of any campaign I have been involved in, and may be too technical and detailed for most palates.

This book came out of my head. I interviewed no one, embarked on no vast research projects. It tells what I know about the art of winning elections as simply and succinctly and factually as possible.

Some people's feelings may be hurt, but if I am to write this at all, I feel impelled to tell it as it is, and that's what I shall do.

Joseph Napolitan

ACKNOWLEDGMENT

First of all, I am grateful to my candidates through the years, paricularly those who, knowing full well their political careers were on the line, allowed me to experiment with new techniques.

I am indebted to Tony Schwartz for his painstaking reading of the manuscript and for his suggestions and criticisms, particularly in the field of electronic communication. Only those who are familiar with Tony's personal audio environment will appreciate the extent of this effort.

This book could not have been written without the assistance of my long-time secretary and No. 1 assistant, Dorothy Sajdak. There are those who say my business would continue without interruption if I left it, and collapse if she did, and they may be right.

Michael Rowan, Pauline Stuart, and Priscilla Caudle all made important contributions of ideas and effort.

But none of this would have been possible without the forbearance of my wife, Mary, and my children, who tolerate long trips, extended absences, and grumpy returns in order that I may persist in this esoteric calling.

Basically this is a book of ideas and opinions, and, while I am grateful to all who helped, the opinions, mistakes, faulty memories, and other errors are mine alone.

Joseph Napolitan
September 1, 1971

Contents

1

THE POLITICAL CONSULTANT—
What Is He?

I AM A POLITICAL CONSULTANT. My business is helping elect candidates to high public office. I don't see anything particularly sinister about that, but some people do.

It's always been difficult for me to understand why the press and other observers, inside and outside of this country, believe that people like me pose a threat to our political system.

Politics is big business in this country—and in most countries that have free elections. In the United States the major parties spend anywhere from ten to twenty million dollars every four years, trying to elect a President. In the larger states it costs a million or more to run a respectable campaign for governor or United States senator or mayor of a large city, and I'm not even considering here the extraordinary expenditures of a Nelson Rockefeller.

If someone were going to erect a building that cost a million dollars, he'd undoubtedly hire an architect to help him design the building, or at least a skilled contractor to build it. State and local regulations wouldn't even allow him to proceed unless the blueprints were prepared by a competent engineer.

If you were going to the hospital for even a simple operation, such as having your appendix removed, you'd want a doctor to do it, not your golfing partner or your brother-in-law, and not just any doctor, but a surgeon, a man who specializes in slicing people open and sewing them back together again. If it were a more serious operation, for you or a member of your family, you'd scour the country or the world to find the best possible person, the most eminently qualified specialist.

Even if you were moving from one house to another you'd probably want an experienced mover to do the job, rather than two husky fellows with a pickup truck.

Why, then, is it so unusual for a political candidate who is spending several hundred thousand dollars, or a million or more, to want to hire the best talents available to help him achieve that office? Damned if I know. But there is reluctance, even resentment, about this emerging business.

Maybe we'd better try to define what a political consultant is and what he does.

To me, a political consultant is *a specialist in political communication.*

That's all there is to it, and I don't think it's anything very macabre or Machiavellian.

So far as I am concerned, there are only three steps to winning any election, here or abroad:

First, define the message the candidate is to communicate to the voters.

Second, select the vehicles of communication.

Third, implement the communication process.

Or, put another way:

Decide what you want the voter to feel or how you want him to react.

Decide what you must do to make him react the way you want. Do it.

Sounds very mysterious, doesn't it? But it's not. Of course, it doesn't always work—sometimes because of the consultant, sometimes despite him, often for other reasons (including the possibility that the guys on the other side may be doing the same things and doing them better than you are).

A campaign can break down on any one of these three steps, but more likely it will break down on the first one: defining the message. Candidates often are unclear in their own minds precisely what it is they want to say to voters, or even why they are running. Or they may have so many things they want to say that they are unable to select and clearly articulate the ones that are most important, those that will have impact, be persuasive, motivate voters to cast their ballots for them instead of their opponents.

Selecting the vehicles of communication usually depends on the campaign. In national elections—presidential elections—every means of political communication is available: television, radio, print advertising and brochures, billboards, direct mail, computers, professional telephone campaigns, rallies, meetings, speeches, and the junk: buttons, streamers, nail files, shopping bags, and ball-point pens.

In most statewide elections you also have a full range of options, although some states may be more difficult than others. New Jersey is a problem for television, because you must buy New York and Philadelphia stations and pay for reaching more people who can't vote for you than can, even if your message is the most persuasive possible. Alaska is another problem, because great chunks of the state cannot yet receive television. Where discrimination really is important is in those Congressional campaigns in which the geographic makeup of the district makes electronic media impractical, usually because of the cost. And even in states and elections where you have all the communications resources available to you, unless you also have adequate financial resources as well, you must be selective and concentrate on the forms of communication that will permit you to achieve maximum impact within the limits of your budget.

Implementing the message often is a question of money. You may have honed your message down beautifully, you may have prepared exquisite television spots, but if you don't have the money to buy the time to show those spots, you might just as well not have them.

I intend to refer to these three steps frequently throughout the book, but that's the basic premise we function on: *defining the message, selecting the vehicles, implementing.*

Questions often are raised concerning the ethics of political consultants. I can't speak for everyone, but the people I know in this business have high ethical standards—higher than those of most businessmen, doctors, or academicians. If they are going to continue in business, they have to.

If we were to work on just one campaign for just one candidate and felt very strongly about it, we might be more tempted to pull out all the stops and win at any cost. But when you know that you've got to come back the next year, and the years after that, you know that you must survive on your reputation, and if the reputation stinks you're not likely to get clients, or at least the kind of clients you want.

I happen to be a Democrat. In the United States I work only for Democratic candidates I like, and the last part of that description is as important as the first part. Life is too short to work for candidates whom you don't like, or with whose political philosophies you strongly disagree. This isn't to say that other consultants may not strike a rapport with candidates whom they have no feeling for and do a superb job for them, but I can't work that way.

By being this selective, I invariably establish a good working relationship with my candidate. This good working relationship, based on mutual trust and respect, enables us to win more campaigns than we lose. And political consultants don't often get favorites. A candidate, incumbent or challenger, who feels he is far ahead and won't have any difficulty winning, usually does not retain an outside consultant, for the very good reason that he doesn't need to. Sometimes a clear favorite will hire an outside consultant anyway, simply because he doesn't want to take any chances. I can't say I've had many candidates like this; the only one who comes to mind immediately is President Ferdinand E. Marcos of the Philippines, who hired me in 1969 to help him in his campaign to become the first President of the Philippines ever re-elected. Sometimes a candidate *becomes* a clear favorite as the race progresses and continues to retain a consultant because of an agreement entered into before the outcome was so apparent. This happened to me in Maryland in 1970, when I was engaged to help Governor Marvin Mandel in his campaign. Early in the year, when it looked as though former ambassador to France and Peace Corps director Sargent Shriver would be a formidable opponent in the primary, Mandel was seriously concerned about his chances of winning. When Shriver decided not to run—with a little assistance from us, which I describe later—then it was clear that Mandel was going to win and he didn't need me or anyone else.

But, most of the time, people like me are retained by the under-dog, the man with a chance of victory who really doesn't know how to put it all together. Often these are newcomers to politics, men who have made their mark in business and now want to try their hand at politics. Occasionally they are senators or governors who have been in office for a while and for one reason or another are in trouble. This was the case with Governor John Burns in Hawaii in 1970, who was completing his third four-year term and wanted to run again, in the face of formidable opposition. He ran and he won, and I think I contributed something to the campaign.

The American Association of Political Consultants, which I founded, and the International Association of Political Consultants, which I cofounded with Michel Bongrand of Paris, have wrestled for years with the idea of creating and formalizing a code of ethics for political consultants. Eventually we will come up with a standard set of rules, but until then we probably will continue to follow the suggestion of Martin Ryan Haley, an astute government-relations and political consultant, who observed that he saw nothing wrong with the Ten Commandments.

It's hard to regulate morality or the ethics of candidates or con-sultants. But more than any other field I know of, the work we do is subject to scrutiny by the public and the press. Consultants themselves may remain in the background—the best ones always try to, although not always successfully—but their work is public.

The media are accepting the importance of campaign managers and consultants. The New York *Times,* for example, now actively tries to find out and publish the names of a candidate's manager and consultants in state elections, items that no one paid much attention to a few years ago, and which you would have difficulty getting printed if you sent in a press release with all the details.

Maybe this is the place to describe the difference between a campaign manager and a political consultant.

A manager, and he may go under any other title—director, chairman, administrative assistant—is a full-time worker who should have day-to-day control and decision-making authority in a cam-paign, subject only to the veto power of the candidate. He also should have complete control over the expenditure of campaign funds.

Consultants come in various breeds. Some are expert campaign managers in their own right; others operate in fields more esoteric and would be total disasters as managers. The general consultants usually are people with broad political backgrounds, often including years of experience managing campaigns, who are available to consult on virtually every phase of the campaign. They may specialize in one area or another—media or organization, usually—but have some knowledge of all campaign operations.

Other consultants are real specialists, some with a great deal of knowledge about over-all campaign operations and some with very little. These include film and radio producers, advertising agencies, time buyers, graphics designers, lighting experts, makeup men. Perhaps the most innovative political communicator I know is Tony Schwartz of New York, a specialist in the use of sound, but I'm sure Tony would be aghast if anyone suggested he manage a political campaign.

Sometimes a consultant's primary function in a campaign is to hire other consultants. A media consultant, for example, may assemble a team that will include a television producer, coach, lighting expert, and makeup man; a radio producer and announcer; a graphics designer; a time buyer associated with an advertising agency or working independently; and a pollster. By knowing who the competent people are in all these fields, and what their services are worth, he can put together a high-powered package for a candidate, and usually save several times his own fee in doing so. (This doesn't always mean that the candidate pays less for these services than he thinks he is going to; candidates often have unrealistic views about the cost of television or radio production, for example, and a qualified consultant can soothe his brow and reassure him that the fees requested are reasonable for the job to be performed.)

I once saved a United States senator fifty thousand dollars in a single afternoon, plus more for time buying, by suggesting that he switch from the television producer advocated by his advertising agency to an independent producer (who also happened to be much better, as well as less expensive) and by sharply curtailing his time buys. He won easily—there was hardly any way he could lose—and he was being taken for a ride by people who either didn't know what they were doing or else were deliberately trying to milk the account for all it was worth.

My experience with advertising agencies in political campaigns has been, to be polite, mixed, as I note in the following chapter, in which I describe releasing Doyle Dane Bernbach from the Humphrey campaign in 1968 and hiring Lennen & Newell instead.

Let me start by saying that in most campaigns I think advertising agencies are useful but not essential. It is possible to assemble independent specialists who can perform the same functions as an advertising agency, sometimes for more than what the agency would cost, sometimes for less, but most of the time it's not worth doing this if you can find a compatible agency to work on the account.

I share the fear expressed by some political observers about turning politics over to advertising agencies—but for different reasons. They are worried that the slick agencies are so super-efficient, so extra-competent that they will remove the human element from the election. My worry is that many agencies are so incompetent and inefficient that they can easily destroy a good candidate.

Good political campaigns are basically task oriented rather than program oriented. A political manager uses research, for example, in a different way from most advertising agencies: the political man uses it to learn what needs to be done to win; agencies often use research to *justify* what they already have done, or to test the impact of what they do. First they make the spot, then they test audience reaction to it; the campaign manager does his research first, and by the time he makes the spot he's pretty certain that it's on target.

In 1969, at a seminar sponsored by the American Association of Political Consultants, I was astounded to hear Gene Case, whom I consider a bright and creative advertising man (he was largely responsible for the superb Nelson Rockefeller television spots in 1966 while with Jack Tinker & Partners), say that in his opinion political advertising had no effect on elections. That comment still puzzles me, because I can't imagine why Case stays in the political advertising business if he really believes what he said; maybe he just had an off day. Anyway, his comment compelled me to make the observation, which I believe, that we had just seen a living example of why political advertising is too important to leave to advertising agencies. Case also got involved in the question of morality and ethics. Defining truth remains one of the elusive goals of our time, and, as Tony Schwartz notes, fact is a function of print, while electronic media are concerned with effect.

You do run into some good agencies. The best I've ever worked with is a small agency in Honolulu, of all places: Lennen & Newell/Pacific, an independently operated subsidiary of the big, New York-based agency. In my first exposure to the Honolulu agency I was told by its director, Jack Seigle, and the account executive assigned to Governor John Burns's campaign for re-election, Chuck Heinrich, that while they thought they knew something about advertising, they didn't feel they knew too much about politics, and if I could provide them with some political inputs they felt they could turn out useful advertising material. What a refreshing attitude! And the whole thing worked beautifully.

Most agencies feel a compulsion to be creative, whatever that is, whether or not their creations bear any relevancy to the campaign. I have seen agencies show candidates full-page newspaper ads (totally inappropriate to the campaign in question anyway, because we never used a full-page ad in the entire campaign) at their initial meeting with him, before they even had the slightest idea what the campaign was about.

Twice in one year I had advertising agencies get the date of the election wrong in making their presentations. In one humorous instance the agency assured the candidate that they had a lock on some beautiful prime-time television spots on Sunday night, May 5, and Monday night, May 6. When I questioned the value of using spots on those particular nights, one of the agency partners snapped, "Well, it's clear you don't know much about advertising," a charge I readily conceded, but I also noted that while I might not know much about advertising I did know a little about elections, and I failed to see how spots scheduled to run on Sunday and Monday nights were going to do the candidate much good when the election was being held on Saturday, May 4. We happened not to select that agency in our campaign.

My chief complaint about advertising agencies is that they don't make the effort to really try to understand the problems of the campaign and the candidate. They often ignore the research obtained through surveys, or fail to act intelligently on the material that the polls uncover. And their general air of superiority is an insult to the intelligence of any reasonable candidate or consultant.

These criticisms aren't true of all agencies or all professional advertising men, obviously. But to find a really top-flight agency outside of New York or one or two other large cities is unusual, and even in New York there is a reluctance for agencies to accept the idea that an independent producer who specializes in political work and who reports directly to the candidate (and thus is paid by him, eliminating the 15 per cent agency commission) can do a better job than the man they had in mind. In most, not all, campaigns, I strongly favor the use of independent film and radio producers, men who are used to the deadline problems of a campaign and the foibles and whims of candidates, who can seize upon and utilize the information revealed in polls, and who can adapt experience gleaned from other campaigns to the particular campaign in question.

There is a basic difference between product advertising and political advertising. An election is, in the words of my London colleague Tom Murray-Watson, like a one-day sale. You can buy that Volkswagen or can of soup or gallon of gasoline today or tomorrow or next week or next month; you can only vote for a candidate once. If you peak your campaign too soon or too late, you are in trouble. What good does it do to attain maximum voter acceptability on Labor Day if the election isn't until November 7 —or to project your campaign so that it will peak on Thanksgiving Day, two weeks after the votes have been counted? Not much.

If you can achieve a happy marriage of advertising agency and consultant, then you may have a formidable communications team, particularly if the agency (and the consultant) is willing to admit that it may not know everything there is to know about politics or political communication. Agencies often operate at a slower pace than independent producers geared to and familiar with the needs of a campaign. (I'm excluding presidential elections here, because in those contests the agency of record always tools up, adds extra people, and usually can perform with reasonable speed and efficiency.) By the time time the agency goes through its "creative" meetings, discusses and regurgitates ideas, prepares storyboards, and goes through the multiple and often redundant steps that agencies seem impelled to take, then a good independent producer will have the television or radio spot in the can or on the air.

The good agencies do have resources that are helpful to a candidate and his staff—an art department, for example, that can quickly turn out designs for stationery and bumper stickers and posters, layouts for brochures, and signs for headquarters. They usually know the best photographers around and can arrange for one to obtain the still photographs of the candidate that are necessary in every campaign. If they are buying time and space, they usually have rapport with the television and radio stations and newspapers. (If they don't, they shouldn't be involved in the campaign on this level anyway.)

And, despite my criticisms, agencies occasionally do come up with superb ideas for campaign materials and spots. If agencies would only accept the idea that they are *part* of the creative unit of a political communications team and do not have a monopoly on talent or ideas, then they would get along better and so would the candidates and consultants who work with them.

Political consultants, unlike advertising agencies, and many producers, tend to work for one party or the other. I refer here to general consultants, not the ultra-specialists such as those who offer canned telephone messages or services such as lighting or makeup, or who specialize in direct mail, or who represent computer service centers. These are essentially technicians whose contributions can be valuable indeed but who have very little direct input into the message that is to be communicated by the candidate to his constituents.

There are good generalists on both sides of the political fence. One of my close friends is F. Clifton White, who works only for conservative Republican candidates (or, thinking of his success with James Buckley in New York in 1970, with Republicans who run as Conservatives). Clif White also is a specialist in a highly esoteric field of presidential politics: organizing conventions and lining up delegates. His crowning accomplishment in this field, perhaps the best performed by anyone, was organizing Barry Goldwater's convention victory that gave him the Republican nomination for President in 1964. I once asked Clif what would have happened if Nelson Rockefeller had defeated Goldwater in the Republican primary in California in 1964, a few weeks before. the Republican convention.

"By the time of the California primary," Clif replied, "we had enough committed delegates so that Goldwater could have stood on his head in Times Square and shouted, 'I am an idiot,' and we still would have won the nomination." I believe him.

While White and I may disagree on political ideology—I work only for Democrats, and they tend to be liberal—we agree almost completely on tactics and strategy. We both approach a campaign the same way, and I am sure that Clif won't work for any candidate he doesn't personally like and feel rapport with any more than I will, although the candidates we eventually select may have very little in common.

The good people in this business aren't hustlers or con men. For the most part they are bright, politically aware people who possess the essential ingredients for any campaign consultant: ability to make decisions, willingness to work long hours and travel almost constantly, a knowledge of the media and the availability of top-flight specialists in various areas of political communication. Few of them have held or sought office, or have any great desire to do so. I, for one, would no more think of running for office than I would of becoming a professional sky diver; in fact, sky diving looks pretty good by comparison. If I were to run for office, the worst thing that might happen to me (and the people who voted for me) is that I would be elected.

I tell people I have no interest in government and don't know anything about it and they think I am joking, but I'm not. My interest is in the political process, the challenge of trying to elect a man to office, with a preference for taking on a candidate who isn't supposed to win and winning with him. Few experiences I know, save perhaps having an orgasm, equal the feeling on election night when the vote reports start coming in and it looks as though you are going to spring an upset. That makes the whole thing worth while.

College students in particular express disbelief when you tell them you only work for candidates you like, that you have no interest in government and no desire to seek office yourself. One night at Yale, where I was a Poynter Fellow and delivered a series of lectures on political campaigning, I appeared on a platform with Jack Newfield, biographer of Robert Kennedy and an editor of *The Village Voice,* among other accomplishments. It was billed as a debate but didn't turn out to be one, because we agreed on most things, but during the course of the evening one of the students expressed strong disbelief when I told him that I would turn down a wealthy candidate I didn't like, that I worked only for men I liked (I've never had a woman candidate; that would be interesting). My wife was in the audience and apparently felt so strongly about the attack that she had to rise to my defense; it's fortunate she hasn't been at some meetings at which I and others of my ilk were really subjected to much sharper criticism for our chosen role in life.

Sure, there are some whores in our business—I could name one or two, but no more, and probably many fewer than in any other semiprofessional service industry. Once in a while someone will come along who will try to take a candidate for everything he's got, promising much and delivering little. If the candidate falls for this kind of pitch, that's his hard luck. I know of one instance in a major state where a Senate candidate spent seven hundred thousand dollars with one self-styled expert, who failed to deliver what he promised, and what he did deliver was late and inferior. The candidate happened to finish third in a three-man race that he could easily have won, although, admittedly, there were other errors in his campaign, including formulation of his message, which I would have said was about 180 degrees, or at least 175, out of kilter with the constituency he was trying to reach.

Don't get the idea that seven-hundred-thousand-dollar fees are run of the mill; that's the only one I know of. I really don't know what other consultants charge, but I've never charged more than twenty-five thousand dollars for an election, and in most cases considerably less, sometimes as little as nothing if I had a special reason for wanting to help a candidate. Nor do I solicit candidates; anyone I work for comes to me, and we turn down more than we accept— not necessarily because I don't like them, but because they have come to us for the wrong reasons, or are in the wrong kinds of elections for my type of operation. I usually consult in nothing below a statewide election, although I will occasionally help in a Congressional or large-city mayoral contest. But if a candidate is in an election in which precinct organization work is likely to be much more important than media, I'm likely to refer him to someone such as Matt Reese, who specializes in organization.

Suppliers of political materials or time or space feel candidates are a bad risk; I don't. If we are taking on someone new and unfamiliar to me, I may ask for part of my fee, or half the poll cost if we also are doing a poll, in advance, but seldom more than that. If we extend a candidate credit the first time and he is slow to pay, we may ask for money in advance on a second go-around, but clients whom we have worked for before and who have paid their bills when they said they would, can pretty much set their own timetable for payment. In fifteen years of running political campaigns, taking polls, and serving as a consultant, I have had only one candidate, who was seeking the gubernatorial nomination in Alabama, fail to pay his bill. In one other campaign, an eight-hundred-dollar check bounced and never was made good. And we're still trying to collect the balance for some poll work in Iowa, but that probably is collectible. Except for current bills, everyone else we've ever worked for, candidates and Democratic committees, always have paid. That's a much better record of collection than I had when I was doing commercial public-relations work.

I've been involved in one campaign in which the candidate, a wealthy man, didn't ask my fee and never even knew what it was until after he had won the contest. When I told him what it was— ten thousand dollars—he said, "That's not enough." It was for me, because it was a campaign in which I was trying to prove something, and did.

Two things a campaign consultant can't function without, if he operates on the national or an international level, are jet airplanes and long-distance telephone calls. For the past five years I've averaged two hundred thousand miles a year by air. In 1970 I made seven trips to Europe, two to Asia, five to Alaska, ten to Hawaii, and one to the Caribbean, all on politically related business. My particular brand of counseling may take me abroad more than many consultants, except possibly Martin Ryan Haley, whose specialty is government relations (i.e., what happens *after* a candidate is elected) rather than political campaigns, but most of the consultants I know spend as much, or nearly as much, time as I do on airplanes and on the telephone. Airplanes, particularly long flights, are good places to work: no telephone interruptions, and five or six hours of clear time to work and (something we need to do occasionally) think.

In one not-untypical two-week stretch in 1971 I spent Sunday in Massachusetts, went to Los Angeles on Monday, Anchorage on Tuesday, San Francisco on Friday, back to Massachusetts on Sunday, Louisville on Monday, Washington on Tuesday, Baltimore on Wednesday, New York on Thursday, back to Massachusetts on Friday, and to Europe on Sunday—all on campaigns or political business.

Seldom have I used the telephone to such good advantage as I did in the Humphrey presidential campaign in 1968, particularly in my working relationship with Tony Schwartz. Tony's estimate is that we consulted for a total of three and a half hours in that campaign, most of it by telephone. Our modus operandi was simple: I would describe the problem to Schwartz on the telephone, send him any reference material we might have on it—polls, position papers, statements of the candidates, newspaper clippings—and ask him to come up with a radio or television spot, or both, that would propose a solution to the problem or convey the effect that we desired. After Schwartz's ingestion of the material we provided, he would call me with one or more concepts, sometimes within a few hours, never longer than a few days. I'd say yes or no or maybe, and we'd move from there. We happened to be a couple of hundred miles apart—but it could have been two thousand as easily as two hundred.

And when I was working in the Filipino presidential election in 1969, Tony used to read me radio spots over the telephone, ten thousand miles away, for me to accept, reject, or modify.

On one occasion Frank Licht, governor of Rhode Island, called me in London to discuss a tax problem. His call reached me at midnight London time (6 P.M. in Providence). In the morning, I drafted my ideas, put them on a telex in my London office, and they were on the governor's desk when he got there the following morning. That's the kind of instant communication and information transferral that would have been impossible not many years ago.

A good campaign consultant often is no more effective than the director of the campaign in which he is engaged. If the campaign manager is competent, the consultant's role is easier, and his effectiveness maximized. Good managers know how to use consultants.

They call them on the telephone, review problems, discuss solutions, listen to ideas which they may accept or reject, and implement those they feel will be useful.

The ingredients for a competent campaign manager, in my book, are general intelligence, loyalty to the candidate, the trust of the candidate, ability to make decisions, and a knowledge of the media. If he happens to know something about politics as well, that's so much to his advantage, but there is no way you can buy loyalty or trust or intelligence or the ability to make decisions. Campaign managers, incidentally, are poor candidates to win popularity contests—even, maybe particularly, among staff people. The manager is the one who says no when a negative is needed, and often this means pleasing one person and offending three others. But if you win, everyone loves you, and if you lose, what difference does it make?

Napolitan's inflexible rule for campaign managers is this:

If the candidate wins, it is because of his charm, intelligence, and appeal to the voters; if he loses, it's your fault.

There may be exceptions to this rule, but I've never happened to run into any.

Some campaign managers are poor because they are indecisive and procrastinate so long that the effectiveness of what they do is blunted. (In the long run, who really cares if the ink on the brochure is blue or green?) Or sometimes they feel they need a consensus before they can act, so they consult everyone in sight or reachable by telephone, or call a meeting to discuss the problem, instead of making a decision.

Some campaign managers are bad because they are too aggressive, so egotistical they assume there is only *one* right way (theirs), and inherently suspicious and doubtful of any suggestions coming from an outsider. These are the fellows most likely to be so insecure in their own jobs that they feel compelled to tear everyone else's ideas down because they see them as threats to their own position.

This syndrome is particularly acute in presidential elections, in which all are so concerned with jockeying for and protecting their own position that they lose sight of the fact that the main objective of the whole campaign is to win the election.

Probably the worst kind of campaign managers, though, are those who are basically nice guys, but won't act, and tell lies besides. These are the people who assure the time buyer that the check for the television spots has gone in the mail that morning, when they know damned well it hasn't, or will promise a producer he'll be paid on Friday, then on Tuesday, then on the first of the month, and never deliver. The disservice they do to their candidate is incalculable, and all the while they believe they are functioning in his best interests. If money isn't available to pay a bill when it's due, the best thing is to simply say that—and never to promise that a bill will be paid by a specific date unless you are absolutely certain that it will be. What happens in cases like this is that the consultants and producers and time buyers spread the word, and if the candidate ever decides to run again he has the option of paying in advance, if the best people agree to work for him at all, or accepting second-raters.

Sometimes even candidates of demonstrably superior intelligence do strange (and if you wish you can read stupid for strange) things. In 1970 Morris Abram, a man of superior intellect and accomplishment, resigned as president of Brandeis University and announced his candidacy for the Democratic nomination in New York for United States Senate. Then, *after* he had announced he was running, he started to try to find a campaign manager and put together a staff and do all the things he should have done before he announced. Inevitably the effort was abortive, and Abram soon dropped out of contention. A shame, because he was a capable candidate, and while he might not have won I am sure he would have contributed meaningful ideas to the campaign.

My advice to candidates is to look long and hard before selecting a campaign manager, and when you do settle on the person you want, to give him the authority to do the job properly, and this includes expenditure of funds. In any campaigns that I manage I insist upon absolute control over all expenditures; most first-echelon managers I know insist upon the same authority. That's the only way you can maintain control of the campaign.

The campaign manager also should have final say over the schedule, because, especially in the final days of an exhausting campaign, candidates are often poorly prepared to make sensible decisions. In 1960, for example, Richard Nixon made an ill-advised promise he would visit every one of the fifty states during the campaign. This caused him, virtually on the eve of the election, to make a flying trip to Alaska. He won Alaska and its three electoral votes—but the thirty-six hours he spent on this trip could have been much more profitably spent in a state such as Illinois, where he lost by a handful of votes.

It is imperative that the candidate and the campaign manager develop a close personal relationship if one does not exist before the campaign. The manager will be closer to the candidate during the campaign than anyone except the candidate's wife. (It's not unusual for the wife to look upon the campaign manager as a competitor for her husband's time, particularly if she feels he is being run ragged by some insensitive soul who really only is trying to get him elected.)

The candidate and his manager may not agree on everything; often they may disagree, and there's nothing wrong with this. But once a decision is made, both parties should stick to it. If a manager has a serious disagreement with his candidate, he has two choices: he can give in or he can get out.

The worst choice any candidate can pick for his campaign manager is himself. No one—repeat, no one—can do a competent job in a major campaign if he tries to serve both roles. One job suffers, and usually both. My standard advice to candidates who want to be campaign managers is to drop out of the race and go find themselves a candidate to manage. And good campaign managers don't always, or perhaps even usually, make good candidates. Ken O'Donnell was a powerful campaign worker for John F. Kennedy, but a disaster as a candidate in two tries at the Democratic gubernatorial nomination in Massachusetts.

While campaign managers may choose to go into government if their candidate is elected, campaign consultants seldom do—except, possibly, following a successful presidential election. Most consultants are in their chosen business because they like the excitement of the campaign and the cutoff date: win or lose, they know by the end of the first week in November they can seek new challenges.

Consultants often are in conflict with established party organizations, partly because they have replaced organization regulars in making important campaign decisions. And the advent and broadening of mass media has meant the slow demise of party organizations.

Really the only major function of the political party structures these days is to nominate the candidates for President, and my personal feeling is that we'd all be better off if this responsibility also were placed in the hands of the people. Straight party voting is passé; yet state and county organizations still get upset if a candidate doesn't slap VOTE STRAIGHT DEMOCRATIC (or REPUBLICAN) on his billboards, stationery, and television spots. People vote for people, not parties.

And the regular party organizations often see the consultant, or professional manager, as a threat to what they consider their rights of patronage. I find this attitude shortsighted. First of all, few consultants I know of are interested in postelection patronage, and if the candidate doesn't win there isn't going to be any patronage for anyone anyway.

When I noted earlier that I am neither knowledgeable about government nor particularly interested in it, I perhaps should have added "except as it relates to politics." My interest in the official functions of candidates whom I have helped elect extends basically to how they handle themselves in office so far as their own political future is concerned. The best rule, by far, is that the best government makes the best politics. If a man is a good senator or governor, re-electing him will be easier. Candidates who are elected and joy-ride for the first two thirds or three quarters of their terms under the assumption they can make it all up later during the campaign may be opening themselves up for sharp disillusionment, which is another way of saying they might well be bounced out of office the next time voters get a chance to express their opinion at the polls.

One other thing to remember about political consultants: they've always been around. It's just in the past few years that we've begun to be identified and labeled as such. But candidates always have had advisers, and while these may have been volunteers instead of professionals, they were consultants nevertheless. (And I don't know of any professional consultant who at one time or another doesn't volunteer his services if he feels there is a good reason for him to do so.)

Only lately have we developed a breed of peripatetic advisers who earn their living from giving political advice to seekers of high office all over the country or the world. If they spend their lives doing this, it only makes common sense that in the course of doing so they should acquire skills and experience not necessarily possessed by people in the candidate's regular circle of friends.

And if a consultant has been around for a while, you can be reasonably certain he's pretty good: there's nothing like a consistent string of losses to send race horses or political consultants into early retirement.

2

THE 1968 PRESIDENTIAL ELECTION

EVEN MARGARET MEAD tried to get into the act.

The famous anthropologist would call me every two or three days during the closing weeks of the 1968 presidential election with suggestions on how Hubert Humphrey could improve his appearance on television.

Most of her suggestions were sound: Humphrey should be crisper, briefer, low-key, cool. I didn't have the heart to tell her that we had been trying to get Humphrey to do those things since the campaign started, with an appalling lack of success. But the experience is typical of what happens in presidential campaigns—the most unwieldy, chaotic, sloppy, wasteful operation known to man, except possibly waging war.

Presidential campaigns are too big to be efficient, have too many people involved to be effective, and by their very nature exclude the simple, tough, quick decision-making, decision-implementing forces that characterize much-more-effective if much-less-publicized campaigns for lower offices. The Humphrey campaign might have been a little worse than most at the start, but not much, and from what I know about it, the Nixon operation wasn't a hell of a lot better.

I really didn't have much interest in getting involved in the 1968 presidential election, even though running campaigns and counseling candidates is my business. My intention was to concentrate on a few Senate and gubernatorial campaigns that I had a real interest in, and stay out of the mad hullabaloo of the presidential test. This was an early decision, arrived at when it appeared that Lyndon Johnson would be a candidate for re-election. I wasn't totally isolated from the presidential process; as early as the summer of 1967 Larry O'Brien, who undoubtedly is the only man in history to be campaign manager for three presidential candidates in the same year, had asked me to put together some thoughts on the thrust of the 1968 campaign, and I did. O'Brien was Postmaster General at the time, and it was assumed he would be running Johnson's re-election campaign. Or, more precisely, it was assumed that Johnson would be running for re-election and O'Brien would be managing the campaign. One trouble with the Johnson campaign was that there were about three times as many people involved, at least, than could be used effectively, and the man in the White House was making the decisions anyway.

This is stupid, no matter who the candidate is. No one can be a good candidate and a good campaign manager at the same time, even if he's good at running campaigns, and I don't think Lyndon Johnson was. As noted earlier, if a candidate wants to be a campaign manager he should withdraw himself and go find somebody's campaign to run.

Johnson was a master, among the best this country has ever produced, at maneuver and manipulation within government. No one understood the Congress the way he did. I also happen to think he was an underrated President, and that his mark on history will be more lasting than most. But I've never seen any evidence that Johnson understood much about getting people elected to office, and I've seen a lot of evidence to the contrary.

If he really had been a skillful politician he wouldn't have done the things that made it virtually impossible for Hubert Humphrey to win in 1968. Two of Johnson's decisions were so incredibly bad that in and of themselves they cost Humphrey enough votes to lose the election.

One was the decision to hold the convention in Chicago; and the other, to hold it late in August.

There was no political reason in the world to hold the convention in Chicago, except to please Mayor Richard Daley. Ironically,

Daley is a good politician, not to mention the toughest man I've ever met in politics, and if he had been in some other state instead of Illinois I'm sure he would have fought to keep the convention out of Chicago. The convention should have been held in Miami for many reasons, and in the summer of 1971 the Democratic National Committee site-selection committee sensibly selected Miami for its 1972 convention.

And so far as the timing of the 1968 convention is concerned, look at it this way: the convention coincided with Lyndon Johnson's birthday. All I can say about that is that I wish the President had been born on the Fourth of July. The last previous comparable convention was in 1960, when John F. Kennedy, a non-incumbent, was nominated to run against the Republican candidate, Richard Nixon, also a non-incumbent.

The convention that nominated Kennedy was held in Los Angeles early in July. Considering Labor Day to be the traditional start of the active campaign for President, John F. Kennedy had seven weeks to get ready between the end of the convention and the start of the campaign. In Chicago in 1968 the convention ended on a Saturday morning. The next Monday was Labor Day. That gave Hubert Humphrey forty-eight hours instead of seven weeks. Quite a difference.

And when you consider that the Humphrey staff had done so little post-convention planning that it's not worth mentioning, then you get some appreciation of how devastating the late convention was to Humphrey's chances. Sure, the convention dates and site were picked long before it looked as though Humphrey would be the candidate, but the President had an ideal opportunity and a perfect reason to shift the site, and the date: the telephone strike in Chicago.

The television networks would have been happier, the Chicago cops would have been happier, and Hubert Humphrey might have been President today.

But I'm getting ahead of my story.

I was as surprised as most people when Johnson made his famous I-will-not-run speech on March 31, 1968. I was interested, but not particularly concerned, because I wasn't planning to get involved in the presidential election anyway.

Eugene McCarthy already was in with both feet, Robert Kennedy had completed his tortuous self-examination and decided to go after the big prize, and it was a certainty that with Johnson out Humphrey would be in.

None of which really affected me. I had worked for John Kennedy in his Senate and presidential elections, for Ted Kennedy in his 1962 Senate race, and had played a late and insignificant role in Bobby Kennedy's 1964 Senate election in New York. In the parlance of politics, I was what is called a "Kennedy man." But I envisioned no role for myself in Robert Kennedy's campaign; he had people climbing over the walls, good people, too, and I felt I could be of more help to candidates such as Mike Gravel in Alaska and Jack Gilligan in Ohio than I could to Bobby. They needed me more than he did.

I even had some conversations with the McCarthy people; they were the most disorganized of all. I explained that I would not accept any role in the campaign, but that I would be glad to sit down with them and give them my ideas, for whatever they were worth, on what I thought the senator should be doing. We had a couple of meetings, I made some suggestions, and that was the end of it.

So far as Humphrey was concerned, I had always liked him, particularly since 1966, when he was the one candidate of national stature to stick his neck out for Milton Shapp in Pennsylvania. (A favor not reciprocated by Shapp when the time came for evening up.)

I knew that Larry O'Brien held an extraordinarily high opinion of Humphrey, and he knew him much better than I did, so I was willing to accept that Humphrey was a competent man well equipped to lead the nation. But I knew that with Johnson out O'Brien would be with Kennedy, and I didn't have any desire to go knocking heads with an old friend, even if anyone were asking me to help Humphrey at that time, which no one was.

I had no doubt that Humphrey would be nominated, so long as the candidate was nominated at a convention and not in an open primary.

Convention politics differs drastically from election politics. It is a highly specialized field. There are a few good people around who understand it—O'Brien among the Democrats and Clif White among the Republicans, in particular—but most people, including a lot of them in this business, don't really understand the difference.

Convention politics requires one skill: the ability to count.

In a presidential convention you're not concerned with two hundred million people, but three thousand or less. And even as Kennedy and McCarthy were picking up handfuls of delegates at primaries, Humphrey was adding more than that in state conventions.

Convention politics represents the last stronghold of party political machinery. This is where the so-called party pros really do have some power—and basically their support was for Humphrey. (I have more to say about the difference between convention and election politics in a later chapter.)

Kennedy and McCarthy were getting the press; Humphrey was getting the delegates. He picked up 18 out of 22 in Wyoming, 111 out of 130 in the Pennsylvania caucus, 63 in Michigan, 57 in Missouri, globs here and globs there.

It's impossible for any candidate to win the nomination solely on the basis of delegates acquired in states with binding presidential primaries. Pennsylvania's meaningless presidential preference primary went for McCarthy; Humphrey walked off with three quarters of the delegates. I'm not defending the system; to the contrary, I think it is archaic and atrocious. But those were the rules we were playing under in 1968, and Humphrey was winning.

At the time of his murder, Bobby Kennedy needed something like 80–85 per cent of all the uncommitted delegates to win the nomination on the first ballot, and there didn't seem, to me, to be a chance in the world that he would get them.

Of the states still not counted, Humphrey had a lock on more than enough delegates to put him over the top on the first ballot.

I have heard the argument that if Kennedy hadn't been killed he would have been able to sway enough delegates away from Humphrey to win. This I doubt, but it's a question we'll never have answered. And when Kennedy was struck down on that bleak night in Los Angeles, there was no conceivable way Humphrey could have lost that nomination.

Everyone seemed to realize this except Humphrey and his staff.

In a way, they were right: win the pennant before going into the World Series. But they concentrated so much on winning something they couldn't lose that they lost track of something they probably were going to lose but could win: the presidency. And with the convention held so late, and no advance planning, and no time, Humphrey started off with a disadvantage that has never been fully presented in the press.

Anyway, I had no intention of participating in the campaign, or even of going to the convention: the Alaska primary was taking place smack in the middle of the convention, and I looked forward to being at Mike Gravel's house in Anchorage when the returns came in showing (hopefully) that he had scored a stunning upset over Senator Ernest Gruening in the Democratic primary for United States Senate.

But the second week in August I had a call from O'Brien's office asking if I could meet with him in the Executive Office Building in Washington. By this time O'Brien, who had resigned as Postmaster General to become Bobby Kennedy's campaign manager, was running Humphrey's campaign. His agreement with Humphrey, as I understood it, was to handle things until the convention; he had no arrangement to do anything after that. This was O'Brien's idea, not Humphrey's, because Humphrey wanted him aboard all the way.

I said, sure I'd meet with O'Brien in Washington.

He, his top aide Ira Kapenstein, and I were there.

We chatted about the campaign and how fouled up it was. O'Brien asked if I was planning to go to the convention. I said no, that I was planning to be in Alaska to wait out the primary with Mike Gravel.

"Look," O'Brien said, "you can't do any good up there, win or lose. But you can be of some help to me in Chicago."

"How?"

"By taking a look at the media and the postconvention planning. The advertising agency is supposed to make some presentations, and Orville Freeman has some things he wants me to go over, and I simply am not going to have the time to get into that sort of stuff while the convention is going on."

"What are your plans for after the convention?"

"I don't have any," O'Brien said, and I believe he was telling the truth.

"Okay," I said, "I'll go. Can you get me a room somewhere?"

"It's all arranged," O'Brien said wearing his big Irish grin.

I went to Chicago from Des Moines, where I had been helping Harold Hughes in his campaign for United States senator, and wondered what the hell I was getting into.

The Secretary of Agriculture, Orville Freeman, a tough, smart, two-fisted ex-governor of Minnesota, had been asked to collect all of the postconvention planning materials from the various Humphrey entities—Citizens for Humphrey, United Democrats for Humphrey, and God knows what else. I became fond of Freeman during the campaign, although late in the campaign we had one of the most violent clashes over the use of television that I've ever had with anyone, but the papers he had assembled as a post-convention plan indicated only one course to me: start all over again.

Apparently everyone had been so busy worrying about delegates that none of them were concerned about voters.

Teddy White, working on his third "Making of the President" book, stuck his head into my hotel room one day during the convention. I was pounding a typewriter.

"What are you doing—writing a speech?"

"No, I'm writing the campaign plan."

"You're kidding," White exclaimed. "You mean that this hasn't been done yet?"

"Well," I said, "if it has, I haven't seen it, O'Brien hasn't seen it, and I don't think the candidate has seen it."

On August 25, Ira Kapenstein (who died in 1971 at the age of thirty-five) and I attended a media presentation made by Doyle Dane Bernbach, the New York advertising agency that had been selected by the President to do his campaign when it appeared that he would be running, and which stayed on to handle Humphrey's advertising.

A lot has been written about how and why I dismissed Doyle Dane and picked another agency in the Humphrey campaign, most of it wrong, because I was the only one who knew and no one who was writing about the big schism ever was interested enough to ask me, and I'm not big at issuing press releases.

But on that particular morning I had no ax to grind with Doyle Dane, for a couple of pretty good reasons: based on their reputation, I had a lot of respect for the agency, and because I was not planning to work in the campaign I really didn't care a hell of a lot about what they were going to do. I'm just irritated by inefficiency in a campaign, and was trying to protect O'Brien's (and Humphrey's) interests while I was in Chicago.

Rather than speak from memory, let me quote from a memorandum I prepared for O'Brien immediately after the meeting. The full text of this memorandum is reproduced on pages 283–285.

"It was a disappointing showing. We saw storyboards on 12 60-second spots and one 20-second spot. Two or three were good enough to go into production at once, two or three others are useable with revisions, and the rest range between mediocre and terrible.

"Not all of this is the agency's fault (although I believe their basic approach is wrong . . .). For some reason known only to themselves the Humphrey research people have not let the agency have access to polls and surveys in their possession. . . .

"The agency had made no provision for any anti-Wallace material, and conceded they were not aware of the political nuances of the campaign. (Two of their spots for example had Negroes as narrators—an insane thing to do.)

[Note: Later, after Doyle Dane was dismissed, someone in the agency said I was anti-black because of my criticism of these spots. "Napolitan wanted no black faces at all," the anonymous agency spokesman said. Bullshit! The first Humphrey television spot ever to go on the air after the convention had a black face on it. So did the second one. So did many of the others. So did the two thirty-minute films, the half-hour Q-and-A programs, the election-eve telethon. But the two spots that DDB presented that day would have alienated both the Black Panthers and the Ku Klux Klan, one hell of an accomplishment in sixty seconds.]

"My basic criticisms of the spots are these:

"1. They lacked warmth and conviction.

"2. With one or two exceptions, they fail to indicate that Humphrey is tough and decisive.

"3. They lack emotional appeal.

"4. They are burdened with statistics and figures; this is fighting emotion with logic, and it just won't work.

"5. Some were slick, and these may be useful, but I got the feeling that they might be too slick."

. . . . . .

"The approach, incidentally, was typically Madison Ave.: there must have been 20 people there, all set 'to go to work,' and none of them having the vaguest idea of what the hell they are supposed to be doing. (And I don't think there were three Humphrey votes in the whole crowd.)

"I criticized the spot I had seen the other night [a dreadful pull-out from a Humphrey speech]. Predictably, they said they had been ordered to run that by the Vice-President's staff. (I tried unsuccessfully to find out who was giving this kind of order, or approving what was shown.)"

The presentation was made by Bill Bernbach himself. I had never met Mr. Bernbach before, and believe I have seen him only twice since, and I am sure he knows 1000 per cent more about advertising than I'll ever know, but it is possible I know a little more about politics than he does, and it's a shame we weren't able to pool our knowledge and work together, but it didn't work out that way.

The first storyboard Bernbach showed that day epitomizes the whole problem. The spot opened with a close-up of an elephant's head decorated with the letters GOP. Throughout the spot, the only visual is the elephant walking backward until it disappears, while a narrator is reciting a lengthy list of undigestible statistics on how bad the Republican party is, and closing with a big HHH.

"That's a terrible use of television," was my immediate comment. (Later someone in DDB was quoted as saying, "No one talks to Mr. Bernbach that way." Well, maybe he's right, but I'm not long on formality.)

I tried to explain that the statistics were difficult to digest, and I thought we should aim for warm, emotional messages in our television spots.

Later, before we parted ways—and actually one of the reasons why we did—I learned that DDB's production budget for that spot was fifty-seven thousand dollars. When you consider that Humphrey was dead broke, that's a lot of money, especially for a spot that simple.

I don't know how much it costs to rent an elephant, but it can't be more than one thousand dollars. So you put a big GOP on the elephant's head, film him walking toward the camera, run the film in reverse, add the narration and the disclaimer, and you've got the spot, if indeed you were silly enough to accept the spot in the first place.

That's worth fifty-seven thousand dollars?

Not to me.

This, too, reveals the cost differential between received and perceived media. DDB's "window on the world" style of commercials cost more than those which take the viewer on an inner trip and utilize information subconsciously stored in his mind. Triggering responses from stored material not only is more effective than giving the voter a mass of new material to learn (because learning is one of the most difficult of the brain's jobs while remembering is one of the easiest), but also is less expensive.

Appendix B is a memorandum I prepared for O'Brien on August 25, giving my ideas on what Humphrey's television package should include.

More on DDB, media, and the campaign in a moment. But now let's take a look at what was happening in Chicago, the Johnson/Daley choice for the Democratic National Convention.

Some Chicago city officials concede that the police "overreacted." If that's a euphemistic way of saying they beat kids over the head with clubs, then I guess they did.

I wandered through the crowds, and I tasted fear. I admired McCarthy and George McGovern for going into the crowds; I think Humphrey was wrong not to, and I don't care how many surveys taken in Tallahassee, Des Moines, Portland, or Worcester show that voters in America supported the police in their battle with the students.

This was a matter of personal courage and I was disappointed that Humphrey didn't show any. I'm not at all certain that he lacked the courage—as he said later in one of his speeches, "I used to be a pretty good bomb-thrower myself"—but I think he was listening to the omnipresent voices of caution who were urging him to play the safe, sensible role and stay in his hotel suite. Where he promptly offended the good taste of thousands by rushing to a television set and planting a kiss on a video image of Muriel Humphrey, in full view of an alert cameraman. I concede that Muriel Humphrey is an eminently lovable lady—but, my God, not that way.

The insanity of Chicago has been too well documented to need repeating here; all I can say is that it shoved Humphrey so far down the well that it was November before he could see daylight again. With friends like Johnson and Daley, Humphrey didn't even need Nixon, and the crowning irony came on Election Day, when he didn't carry Illinois.

Retrospective analysis plays tricks. Looking back on the summer and fall of 1968, most people, if you were to ask them, would tell you that Nixon always was ahead of Humphrey.

That's just not true. In June and July, after Robert Kennedy's assassination and before the Republican convention, both the Gallup and the Harris polls showed Humphrey running *ahead* of Nixon:

GALLUP

	June	*July*
Humphrey	42	40
Nixon	36	35
Wallace	14	16
Undecided	8	9

HARRIS

	June	*July*
Humphrey	43	41
Nixon	36	36
Wallace	13	16
Undecided	8	7

Four things happened between the end of July and early September that caused a decided shift in the polls:

1. Nixon was nominated at an orderly convention in Miami.
2. Nixon went on the air with good television and radio.
3. Humphrey went on the air with a series of preconvention spots that chewed up seven hundred thousand dollars of funds that were badly needed later, and the spots were terrible: they showed Humphrey at his worst. They were pull-outs from speeches, and Humphrey didn't look good or sound good.
4. Humphrey was nominated at the debacle in Chicago.

But at the hurly-burly of the convention, O'Brien was facing some difficult decisions. He had decided to leave government to re-enter the private sector, as he likes to call it, and was entertaining several attractive offers from large companies. O'Brien is not a personally wealthy man, although his unwillingness to accept compensation for his political work sometimes leads people to believe that he is.

He served without fee or salary in the Humphrey campaign, and when he returned as chairman of the Democratic National Committee in the spring of 1970 it was with the understanding that he would serve without pay.

At the convention there was a real question in O'Brien's mind about staying with the campaign, or accepting one of the attractive offers from business.

Humphrey, of course, wanted him to stay on and run the campaign.

In one of my memoranda to O'Brien, dated August 29, 1968, I said:

> "1. These are the requests I would make of the Vice-President as prerequisites to your accepting the position [Democratic national chairman]:
>
> a. Agreement to serve as National Chairman to Nov. 15, 1968.
>
> b. He calls the people on your list to obtain their approval of delaying your acceptance of contract offers until after the election.
>
> c. His notification of the staff of the DNC and his personal staff and campaign advisers that you are in complete and total command of the campaign.
>
> d. Complete authority to hire and fire staff at the DNC.
>
> e. Authority to determine who will do what in the campaign.
>
> f. Complete authority over expenditures of the campaign budget.
>
> g. Unlimited access to the candidate.
>
> h. The candidate's agreement that he will not make any major policy or political decision without giving you an opportunity to comment or criticize."

The problem with being in this business is that you become so emotionally involved with what you are doing that you just can't

walk away from it. While O'Brien, his wife Elva, his close and
trusted associate Ira Kapenstein, and I had hours of conversation
on should he or should he not take on the chairmanship, we
really were only kidding ourselves. Larry could no more have
walked away from the campaign at that point than I could have
if my conditions were met.

My conditions were simple:

1. Complete control of paid media.
2. A clear title in the campaign.
3. No salary or fee, but with the DNC to pay my expenses.

But, at the time, O'Brien was genuinely torn about what he
should do. At one time he had just about decided not to take the
chairmanship, and was meeting with Humphrey. Elva O'Brien and
I were in the O'Brien suite talking about it, and she said something
to this effect: "It's in his blood. He won't be happy unless he takes
it."

Whereupon I wrote and delivered a short memorandum which
I reproduce here in its entirety:

CONFIDENTIAL MEMORANDUM

August 29, 1968

To: Larry O'Brien

From: Joe Napolitan

Re: Your personal campaign activities.

1. I think you should take the chairmanship of the DNC
   and run the campaign through the election for these
   reasons:
   a. Whether you do or whether you don't you are going
      to be sucked into it some way, and if you go in it
      might as well be as the boss.
   b. The only way you could avoid it would be to walk
      away completely by leaving the country or otherwise
      making yourself inaccessible.
   c. If you do that only two things can happen to Hum-
      phrey:
      i. He can win and would have done it without you.
      ii. He can lose, in which case you cannot expect him
          to be particularly grateful to you.
2. If you were going to divorce yourself from politics

entirely, I would say get out and forget it. But I cannot believe that whatever you may choose to do will be entirely divorced from politics or the desirability of enjoying a pleasant relationship with the Congress and the Administration.

3. Elva has read this and she agrees.

I honestly don't think O'Brien was being coy about accepting the position Humphrey wanted him to take. He had had a hell of a year—starting off with the Johnson campaign, leaving the Cabinet, taking over the Kennedy campaign, seeing Robert Kennedy assassinated (Larry is one of the few, maybe the only, person who was with both John F. Kennedy when he was killed in Dallas and Robert F. Kennedy when he was killed in Los Angeles), deciding to go into private business, taking on the Humphrey campaign, and guiding the events at the convention. It is enough to boggle most minds; add a healthy dose of physical exhaustion and you get an idea why the decision was not easy.

At four o'clock on Thursday afternoon, August 29, Humphrey picked Senator Muskie of Maine to be his running mate; almost exactly twelve hours later, at four in the morning on Friday, August 30, O'Brien agreed to be national chairman and campaign manager, and I agreed to go along as director of advertising.

Not everyone was happy about these arrangements. Senator Fred Harris of Oklahoma, who had labored long and hard for Humphrey, was doubly disappointed: first, he wanted to be the candidate for Vice-President, and, barring this, the Democratic national chairman.

With all due respect to Fred Harris, whom I like and admire, I think Humphrey made the right decision both times in picking Muskie and O'Brien.

The Democratic National Committee met formally on Saturday morning, August 31, at the Conrad Hilton, and O'Brien officially replaced John Bailey as national chairman. Also important, Bob Short of Minneapolis was installed as national treasurer. The convention broke up after lunch, and we headed home for what was left of the weekend.

The next day was Sunday, and the day after that was Labor Day, kick-off day for the presidential election.

Talk about being unprepared for the big game . . .

I took stock of what we had and this is what I found:
1. No acceptable postconvention campaign plan.
2. No television spots in production.
3. No television films in production.
4. No usable television spots or films left over from before the convention.
5. No radio spots ready to go or in production.
6. No really good print materials available.
7. A very limited stock of money-wasting campaign gimmicks and materials, the kind of crap that candidates always insist upon but which isn't worth a damn in getting votes.
8. Some polls planned, but not in the field.
9. An advertising agency about which I had serious doubts.
10. No money. I mean no money—not a little bit, or a small balance, but zip. I'll say more later about the superb job Bob Short did in picking up enough dollars to get us through the campaign—a task for which he really never has received proper credit.

And although we didn't know it at the time, the devastation of Chicago and our own inability to come back because of lack of funds, material, and planning contributed to a massive deterioration in the polls: an immediate postconvention poll by Gallup showed Humphrey down twelve points to Nixon (compared with five points up in July); two additional Gallup polls in September both showed Humphrey fifteen points down: 43–28 on September 20–22, 44–29 on September 27–30.

So there we were on Labor Day: no materials, no money, and about to face a fifteen-point deficit in the polls.

And not only did the decision to hold the convention in Chicago cripple us, but now the late date was beginning to take its toll: we didn't have the time to properly recoup. If the convention had been held early in July, and we could have swabbed some wounds in the summer, then maybe we wouldn't have been looking straight into the eye of the cannon on Labor Day.

But there we were, and the question was: what are we going to do about it?

I spent the early part of Labor Day at a family picnic at my home in Massachusetts; by midafternoon I was on a plane to New York, and late in the afternoon I was on Humphrey's chartered

727 at LaGuardia Airport. As I waited for Humphrey and O'Brien to arrive from a rally in the city, I drafted on a yellow pad what was to become the media plan for the presidential campaign.

Since it helped almost elect a President of the United States, perhaps it is worth recording here. Maybe this will help everyone who thinks presidential campaigns are well organized get some idea of how flimsy the construction often is. Here is the plan, in memo form from me to O'Brien:

MEMORANDUM

To: Larry O'Brien

From: Joe Napolitan

1. Here is a brief report on media at this time:
   a. There are three people I consider indispensable to the success of the media campaign—Charles Guggenheim, Shelby Storck and Tony Schwartz.
   b. I have spoken with all three. Storck and Schwartz are aboard, with terms to be arranged.
   c. Guggenheim said he was at the point of exhaustion after putting the Kennedy memorial film together. [This film later won Guggenheim an Academy Award for the best documentary of the year.] I am to call him Tuesday. I think we can work this out; Charlie always needs to be wooed a little—but he is the best in the business.
2. Here is what I propose to do with these people and with Doyle Dane Bernbach:
   a. *With DDB:* meet with Bill Bernbach this week, tell him to proceed with the spots we found acceptable and to come up with any creative ideas they could for new spots. I also will inform them that we have other people working on TV and radio spots, and that we will select those we want to use from all that are produced. DDB will place all material. I will work with them on time-buy and placement schedules. I also want the agency to begin quickly preparing some print pieces for utilization by Democratic organizations through the DNC. There are a few good Humphrey pieces around; we need a greater va-

riety and more emphasis on specific areas (farms, minorities, etc.). Also need a superb general-purpose
picture piece. I'll worry about these with the agency.

b. *Guggenheim and Storck:* I want them to work on
these projects, either together or independently as they
wish:

1. A 30-minute *emotion-packed* documentary.
2. Some 5-minute and 15-minute programs (including one of each length about Mrs. Humphrey)
for off-prime TV time—particularly at times when
women watch. I also would envision a 5-minute
and 15-minute program about Muskie.
3. A spot package on Humphrey the Man. These will
be current and emphasize the candidate's positive
qualities. The package will include 60's, 30's, 20's
and 10's.
4. If it appears feasible—a 30-minute film on the
Democratic Platform. This has never been done
before, there is an awesome amount of good emotional material in the platform (if it is properly
visualized) and Humphrey and Muskie and other
Democrats—Franklin Roosevelt, Harry Truman,
John Kennedy, Lyndon Johnson—can be woven
through it. I think this kind of film would be a
new departure from conventional political rhetoric,
and could be extremely effective. There also is a
logistical reason: this film consists largely of *edit-
ing,* with a strong narration, and could be started at
once.

c. *Schwartz:* This guy is a true genius in his field. I
want him to work on *issues-oriented* spots, both
radio and television. He is best by giving him a
problem—Vietnam, crime, law and order, racial tension—and let him work out a solution. I would guess
we would get five or six television and maybe six or
eight radio spots from Schwartz. The best way to
work with him is give him the problem and let him
go.

3. I am going to make a determined effort to get every-

thing but the Humphrey documentary ready as quickly as possible, and work out a system for various state committees to get copies of prints, tapes or discs and get them on the air in their states—at their expense— as soon and as often as possible. This would supplement, not interfere with, our regular media program. So far as I know, no one has ever made maximum use of this procedure, although several candidates have made stabs at it.

4. At the moment I am contemplating only two kinds of newspaper ads for placement out of our budget: fundraising ads and film promotion. In addition, I think we should go into production at once on some ads for mats and reproduction proofs, and get these in the hands of state and local committees for placement.

   (Incidentally, advertising agencies resist such techniques because they do not receive the commission, but I really believe that the economic wealth of the agency is secondary to winning the campaign.)

5. If the Vice-President is going to be in Waverly for a few days, I would like to get a film crew up to shoot some stuff of him at home. We'll never get a better opportunity.

6. With any luck, I should have this program in motion by the end of the week.

That was it, the whole media plan. Amazingly, most of it worked out the way we had planned.

I passed the memorandum to O'Brien; he read it and passed it across the aisle to Humphrey.

The Vice-President read it, scrawled "O.K.—HH—Go!" on the bottom. That was my license to operate, and we went to work.

Ordinarily it takes about three months to produce a proper political documentary, and that is when the producer has ample advance time for planning and preparation. In this case we needed the documentary in seven weeks, at the outside, and were dealing with two producers already committed on other campaigns.

Guggenheim finally refused to participate, pleading exhaustion and other commitments.

Even Humphrey couldn't budge him when I got him on the phone from Humphrey's home in Waverly, Minnesota:

"I'd like to help, Mr. Vice-President," said Guggenheim, who admittedly sounded exhausted, "but I'm pretty busy right now."

"God damn it, Charlie," said Humphrey, "I'm pretty busy myself."

I wasn't angry, just disappointed. Guggenheim later volunteered his services and helped produce two half-hour studio programs with Humphrey and Muskie.

Shelby Storck was with us from the beginning.

Storck was one of the sweetest men I've ever known, and the most versatile film maker I've ever encountered. He could produce, direct, write, and narrate, all beautifully. His death in the spring of 1969 was a great personal blow.

In the first week of September Storck was busy revising the documentary he had made for Mike Gravel in Alaska, where Gravel had upset Senator Ernest Gruening in the primary, and also doing documentaries for Governor Winthrop Rockefeller in Arkansas and Smith Bagley, a Congressional candidate in North Carolina.

I don't know how he did it, but on Wednesday afternoon, September 4, Storck and his No. 1 crew, including crack cinematographer Art Fillmore, arrived at the Humphrey homestead in Waverly to begin working on the documentary that became, in my opinion, the single most effective weapon we had in the campaign. (An opinion, incidentally, shared by Joe McGinnis and expressed in his book *The Selling of the President, 1968*.)

Ironically, even though he had come on very short notice, the only people Storck found at the Humphrey home when he arrived were Muriel Humphrey and me; the candidate, O'Brien, et al. had left in the morning for Washington, where Humphrey was to attend a meeting of the National Security Council. This wasn't terribly important so far as Storck was concerned, because there was a lot of background footage of the house and the lake that they needed, plus some leisurely interviews with Mrs. Humphrey.

I had never met Muriel Humphrey before that visit to Waverly, and I must confess I quickly succumbed to her charm; she is one of the most gracious ladies I know.

After the Vice-President and his troupe had swooped off to Washington, leaving the two of us alone, she asked if I had had lunch. I said no, I hadn't. So we sat in the modest Humphrey kitchen, while the woman who in a few months could have been First Lady, made us each a bologna sandwich and a glass of milk, confiding that the Vice-President liked peanut butter on his bologna sandwiches. We had a long and amiable conversation, about everything except politics. What a joy Muriel Humphrey is, after all the women in politics who not only want to run their husband's campaigns, but give the impression they really believe they would make a better candidate than he would.

By evening I was in New York meeting with Tony Schwartz, and the media campaign was launched.

There were three big problems in the Humphrey campaign, from my point of view, and I list them in what I consider the order of importance:

1. Time.
2. Money.
3. The candidate's positions.

Of time, we had not enough.

Of money, we had none, at least to start with.

The candidate's positions, or, so far as I am concerned, the lack of certain positions, requires more explanation, but before we get into that, let's examine the Doyle Dane Bernbach episode.

DDB handled Johnson's advertising in 1964, and Johnson won big, but I have the feeling that Johnson might have survived the challenge from Barry Goldwater even if a small agency from Muskegon had been handling his stuff. This is not to denigrate the quality of the spots DDB did for Johnson; some of them were quite good—but what a target they had to shoot at!

(A matter of personal irritation to me was DDB claiming credit for creating the famous spot of the little girl plucking petals from a daisy. I know that Tony Schwartz was responsible for this, and can prove it. I also was a little surprised that DDB would telephone Schwartz from Chicago requesting that if I should ask him who did the creative work on the daisy spot to say that it was DDB and not himself. This seemed a bush-league stunt for a big-league agency.)

Much has been made of the fact that some DDB staffers were moonlighting for Gene McCarthy while the agency was officially designated to handle the Humphrey campaign, and this allegedly was one of the reasons why I recommended DDB be dropped from the Humphrey campaign.

The funniest part of that whole story is that I didn't even know about the McCarthy moonlighters until after we had replaced Doyle Dane, so that this situation didn't affect our decision at all. Apparently some of the people at DDB felt very defensive about their moonlighters, because the incident was mentioned often. I couldn't have cared less—but I wonder how the people who make Volkswagens would feel if they knew that some DDB staffers were moonlighting for Volvo.

The real reason that we parted company with DDB was:

1. I did not feel they were in tune with the campaign or really interested.
2. Another competent agency was.

In DDB's defense, they were given totally inadequate guidance and direction by the Humphrey staff, mainly because no one was making the tough decisions that needed to be made.

By nature, a good campaign manager or media director is a son of a bitch; he's not likely to win any popularity contests. But if the campaign is successful, everyone thinks he's a hero, and if it isn't, then he's a bum no matter how good he was.

The real qualities of a campaign manager/media director are general intelligence and the ability to make decisions. If you sat around trying to arrive at a decision by consensus you'd come up with mediocrity by majority, but nothing very effective. There's never any shortage of good ideas in a campaign; there's always a shortage of intelligent directors who will say, "Okay, we're going with this one, scrap those," and slam the door.

No one is going to be right all the time, and if you're wrong too often you are out of business, voluntarily or involuntarily, so to be any good you've got to click on a reasonably high percentage of your judgments. This means accepting responsibility, and before responsibility can be accepted it must be delegated. In my case in the Humphrey campaign, I had the delegated authority from Humphrey and O'Brien and I wasn't hesitant about using it. No doubt I made some bad decisions in that campaign—but dropping DDB was not one of them.

This isn't to say I wouldn't use or recommend DDB in another case. With the raw talent floating around that place working for a candidate or a cause or a client whom they were really enthusiastic about, I'm sure that, properly guided, they could put on a hell of a campaign. Hopefully, the candidate or client also would have a lot of money.

What really precipitated the split was two meetings late the first week in September. One was at DDB, and the other at the Manhattan office of a high-level Humphrey volunteer.

These meetings were attended by Jeno Paulucci and me. Paulucci has to be one of the most interesting, most successful, and most difficult men I've ever run across. One thing he doesn't lack is imagination. The son of Italian immigrants, he settled in Scandinavian country in northern Minnesota and began making Chinese food and putting it in cans. A few years later he sold his interest for $57 million, and has gone on to bigger things.

Jeno and I had our first argument over the telephone before we even met, but as the campaign progressed we developed a mutual liking and respect.

One of the storyboard presentations DDB made at the convention in Chicago showed a little old lady talking about why she was going to vote for Humphrey, why she couldn't possibly vote Republican. In the drawing, she looked like everybody's grandmother; we thought it would be a good medicare/senior citizen kind of spot, so we told DDB to go ahead and produce it.

Most *political* film producers—a Storck or a Guggenheim or a Bill Wilson or Bob Squier or Dick Heffron—would have gone out and found a real person and filmed her. But DDB, and I suppose this is common procedure in their sphere, hired a model. Instead of the sweet little old lady, we were shown an elegantly coifed, beautifully gowned woman wearing a string of pearls that looked as though it had just come out of Harry Winston's window, filmed against a brocaded chair in a lavishly appointed setting, acting for all the world as though she had to get through the spot quickly because she was keeping her chauffeur waiting. And I swear to God she spoke with at least a hint of an English accent.

I watched the film in disbelief. Jeno was more direct.

"Are you guys out of your fucking minds?" he demanded.

Now, it wasn't the fact that the woman had been miscast that bothered me—it was the fact that apparently no one at DDB who was working on this account *even realized* that she was miscast, that this was not the kind of spot that could possibly win Humphrey any votes.

We talked for a while, looked at a couple of other things they had in the works but that weren't ready to go on the air, and left for the other meeting.

Here I met for the first time Barry Nova and some of his associates from Lennen & Newell, a large agency with a square reputation. It turned out—and this was news to me at the time— that Lennen & Newell had also been working for Humphrey in the preconvention period. They had been working for Citizens for Humphrey while DDB was working for United Democrats for Humphrey.

I was asked to look at some things they had prepared at their own expense and merely because they were interested in helping Humphrey. The package included two spots that were virtually ready to go on the air immediately with very minor changes, and a series of newspaper ads that could go into production at once for distribution around the country.

More than that, the people from Lennen & Newell acted as though they *liked* Hubert Humphrey; those at DDB acted as though they *tolerated* Humphrey.

That was the big difference.

On the way back to Washington, Jeno Paulucci and I discussed the presentations and agreed for our purposes we would be better served by Lennen & Newell than DDB.

I made this recommendation to O'Brien, he agreed, and that was that.

Lennen & Newell created a subsidiary called Campaign Planners, Inc., to handle the Humphrey advertising. They set up shop in the Democratic National Committee headquarters with half a dozen people and went to work.

One of the people they brought along was Allan Gardner, who had been an account executive at Papert Koening & Lois, which had handled Robert Kennedy's campaign. Gardner is one of the most astute political advertising people I know, particularly in the logistics of getting the material on the air.

Seems like a small point, but let me give you an example: Another New York City agency wanted to make a five-minute program for Mrs. Humphrey. This wouldn't cost us anything, and I'm very big at accepting gifts like this.

The program was made, and it was pretty good—except for one thing: it was five minutes long. A five-minute network program actually runs four minutes and eighteen seconds, and you might assume that a top-flight advertising agency would have realized this. They didn't, and the spot had to re-edited to bring it to length. This is an area in which Gardner was spectacularly helpful in the Humphrey campaign, and he was the only person in the Lennen & Newell subsidiary who had any real political experience.

So we finally had our media team assembled:

–Shelby Storck, to do the thirty-minute documentary and some spots.

–Tony Schwartz, to do radio and some television spots.

–Bob Squier, who handled all unstructured television, coaching, production of some studio programs, arranging for Humphrey to be on shows such as "Meet the Press," Johnny Carson, and the network regulars, and also producing, beautifully, the Humphrey telethon on the night before the election.

–Bill Wilson, who served as an independent producer for the agency and turned out, among other things, two fine pieces, one with Humphrey and Ted Kennedy, and the other with Ted Kennedy and Larry O'Brien.

–Harry Muheim, a whiz at writing political radio spots.

–Sid Aronson, whose firm did the thirty-minute documentary on the Democratic party, and five-minute and fifteen-minute programs on Senator Muskie.

–Hal Tulchin, a fine videotape man, who produced Schwartz's television ideas, including an extremely effective five-minute program narrated by actor E. G. Marshall.

–And, at the end, Charles Guggenheim, who did a fine job on the programs he eventually did produce.

All in all, it was a powerful team—perhaps the best media team ever assembled for a political campaign.

If it had been assembled in June instead of September, if there had been a little more money, if the convention hadn't been held in Chicago, then probably Hubert Humphrey and not Richard Nixon would be President today.

Ironically, as good a job as the Lennen & Newell people did, an anonymous accountant in their agency may have blown the campaign.

Agencies take extraordinary steps to make certain they aren't left being owed any money at the end of a campaign. They overbill, cry, scream, stamp their feet, and do all sorts of things to get their money.

Bob Short, who really did an incredible job under extraordinarily adverse conditions, met the agency payments—sometimes not quietly, but he met them.

So what happened?

A few weeks after the election, the agency returned to the Democratic National Committee $318,000 in unspent funds. They weren't trying to steal anything; they just wanted to make sure they weren't holding the bag after the election.

If their accountants and time buyers had used a sharper pencil, and had not allowed so much for contingencies, we would have had another quarter of a million or three hundred thousand dollars additional to spend on media in the final week of the campaign.

When you consider the fact that if thirty-six thousand voters in three states—Alaska, Delaware, and Missouri—had switched their votes from Nixon to Humphrey the election would have been thrown into the House of Representatives, you have an understanding of what that three hundred thousand dollars meant to us.

Or if we could have pumped all that money into one critical state, such as California, it might have made the difference. If California had gone for Humphrey instead of Nixon, the race would have gone into the House, and if it had, I think Humphrey would have won it there.

But that's the kind of fruitless exercise that keeps you awake on winter nights long after the votes have been counted and the journalistic interpretations of what happened and why grow dusty in old newspapers piled in the cellar.

On September 14, I handed O'Brien a memorandum that, if it had been followed, I think could have won the election for us. But the Vice-President rejected it, and, after all, it was his campaign. The entire memorandum is reproduced on pages 288–292, but let me quote some pertinent portions:

"It is my strong belief that if this campaign continues as it has started we will lose.

"Even though our media program is shaping up, and we are seeing some signs of daylight in our organization, I don't see how we can make up a 12-point gap in the Gallup Poll in seven weeks using the same campaign tactics we are now using.

. . . . . .

"The tragedy is that we have it within our means to win!

"This campaign lacks bold programs.

"We are playing it straight, using conventional, orthodox programs —and making no gains.

"This would be fine if we were ahead. But we aren't.

"We have an advantage over Nixon that we are not exploiting. (Ironically, Wallace has the same advantage and *is* exploiting it.)

"The advantage we have is this:

"We have nothing to lose—and the Presidency to gain—by being bold.

"Let me put it this way:

"1. *If we continue as we are we will lose.*

"2. *If we try some bold plans and they backfire, we still lose.*

"3. *If we try some bold plans and they work, we may win.*

. . . . . .

"I believe three things are necessary to put the Vice-President in contention:

"1. A sharp break with Lyndon Johnson.

"2. An independent Vietnam policy that will win back votes that should be Humphrey's but which now are wavering.

"3. A policy on law and order that will separate him from Nixon/ Wallace and appeal to the conscience of the American voter."

My Vietnam plan went like this:

"1. HHH notifies the President he is going to Paris to personally meet with Harriman and Hanoi representatives.

"2. HHH announces this to the public.

"3. He goes to Paris and meets with [Averell] Harriman, et al.

"4. HHH returns, calls a press conference, and announces that based on his conversations in Paris he is convinced that the first step on the road to peace is an immediate halt to the bombing.

"5. We have people like Ted Kennedy, George McGovern, Mike Mansfield, Gene McCarthy lined up to enthusiastically endorse [the Vice-President's] position.

"6. Two days later Harriman resigns and announces that he agrees with [Humphrey], disagrees with the President, and intends to spend the rest of the time before the election persuading the country that [Humphrey's] position is right."

In context, it should be explained that it had been reliably reported to us that Harriman indeed was unhappy with the way the war was going, did favor a bombing halt, and had said he would do anything Humphrey wanted him to do to help win the election.

I listed the pros and cons of the idea:

"PRO

"This would be a dramatic breakthrough that would put the stamp of leadership on the Vice-President. Obviously, it requires a hard-nosed attitude to carry it off.

"But it would set to rest the fears of many persons that Hubert Humphrey does not have the courage to stand up to Lyndon Johnson.

"Harriman is important to the operation, but not essential.

"The biggest plus is that the move would bring back to Hubert Humphrey *millions of votes which should be his but which we cannot now claim.*

"CON

"The President will be unhappy. (While contemplating this, let me repeat a remark reliably attributed to Marvin Watson and made within the hearing of several persons this week: 'We may not be able to elect Humphrey President but we sure as hell can stop him from being elected.'

"Nixon will accuse us of gimmickry, but I am not sure this hurts.

"The superhawks will be upset—but I don't think we have too many of their votes anyway."

Later, in summarizing, I noted:

"The great unpleasantness is incurring the personal wrath of Lyndon Johnson—but if it comes to a choice between electing a President or getting a President angry, I know what I should do.

"This is a time for boldness, and I think the Vice-President must *act* boldly as well as talk that way."

In the words of a well-known political figure in America, let me make a couple of things perfectly clear: I am not a foreign-policy expert, I was not nearly as well informed on Vietnam as George Ball or dozens of other Humphrey advisers, and my personal feelings of opposition to the war did not enter into my decision to make the recommendations that I did.

Mine was purely a political judgment. I felt that Johnson was hurting Humphrey, that the war was hurting, that Humphrey was waffling. I almost would have preferred him to take an all-out hard-line militaristic attitude than to continue the indecisive role he had fallen into.

We needed something explosive, and I felt the war was the logical forum. And, who knows, the action might even have helped shorten the war. It always is difficult to recapture the mood of a country two or three years after an event, but in the fall of 1968, as the presidential campaign ripened, the war was the big issue and we were wobbling all over the place on it.

For Nixon, of course, the problem was different: he was running ahead, he was well funded, and all he had to do was avoid rocking the boat. (It was this hesitancy that, at the end, almost permitted us to catch him.)

So I submitted my bold plan to stop the bombing, split Humphrey from Johnson, inject something exciting into the campaign, and nothing happened.

Two weeks later, on September 30, in Salt Lake City, Humphrey delivered a half-hour television speech on the war that, while it hedged and hemmed, pushed Humphrey a little more toward the side of peace than the President. As weak as that speech was, it had an astounding effect, and, as much as any single event, was the turning point in the campaign.

So hungry were Americans, including Democrats who normally would have been Humphrey supporters, for a break with the existing policy on the war that they even opened their pocketbooks as a result of the speech.

Bob Short, the harried, hard-talking Minneapolis trucking and hotel man who had agreed to serve as national treasurer to help his old friend Humphrey, suggested that we time the Salt Lake City speech so that there would be twenty seconds or so left at the end for a fund-raising appeal. I doubted that such an appeal would bring in much.

"How much do you think we would get?" Short asked.

"I don't know—ten thousand dollars, maybe twenty thousand dollars tops."

"You have any other ways of earning twenty thousand dollars in twenty seconds?"

I admitted I hadn't, and as the time and production for the Salt Lake City speech was around ninety thousand dollars, if we could get twenty thousand dollars back, so much the better. So I wrote a twenty-second fund-raising pitch, O'Brien recorded it on videotape, and we tagged it on the end of the Salt Lake City speech.

The money began pouring in by the bagful—literally.

Most were five and ten dollar contributions—but one was for fifty thousand dollars. Fred Gates, one of Humphrey's closest friends, took charge of tallying the money. He would sit in a little office in a corner of the DNC, surrounded by mail sacks carrying letters of encouragement, cash, checks, beaming like a baby, ready at an instant to tote out the current tally.

Before the deluge stopped, more than three hundred thousand dollars had come in by mail as a result of the Salt Lake City speech.

I have heard and read since that President Johnson feels that Humphrey lost the campaign in Salt Lake City because he diverted from Johnson's policy on the war, if even so slightly. I tend to agree with the President, but for different reasons: he thinks Humphrey went too far, I don't think he went far enough.

Humphrey was sensitive to the use of Senator Muskie's name, and was concerned that we weren't emphasizing the Humphrey-Muskie team enough. In a memorandum on September 15, he wrote:

"The Democratic ticket is *Humphrey-Muskie*—and I want to underscore that. Both names are to be used in everything we do.

"Muskie is an asset. He is new. He is bright. He is convincing. And he has other assets that you know all too well.

"I would be willing to bet anything that had the recent Gallup poll phrased the question: 'Which ticket do you support, Humphrey-Muskie or Nixon-Agnew?' that we would have been two to four points better off. Muskie has an appeal to the ethnic groups, to Catholics, to university students and professors. He is my secret weapon. He is a wonderful man, and he has a wonderful family."

Humphrey's recognition that Muskie was a clearly superior choice to Agnew also was being utilized by Tony Schwartz in the preparation of his radio and television spots.

One of our earliest and controversial spots was what we called the "20-second laughter spot."

The spot opens on a television set that on its screen has a card reading AGNEW FOR VICE-PRESIDENT. The audio is a man laughing, raucously. Finally the message: "This would be funny if it weren't so serious."

We did the same thing in a radio spot, and as the media began to hit—that is, as we began accumulating enough money to get on the air—it was clear that the anti-Agnew material was having some impact. Schwartz came up with another that we used both on television and radio.

The television version showed the bobbing line and bleep-bleep-bleep of an oscillograph recording a person's heartbeat. Then the message: "Muskie. Agnew. Who is your choice to be a heartbeat away from the presidency?"

We did the same spot on radio, using only sounds instead of pictures and lettering.

I facetiously referred to these as my anti-Muskie spots. Certainly there is nothing in the content of the spot that is any more anti-Agnew than anti-Muskie. This is where the environment, and personal involvement, comes in. A man from another planet might not have been able to tell whether those spots were anti-Muskie or anti-Agnew—but not many people in America had any doubts. Television provided the stimulus, but personal reaction was the real content of the spot.

Our media people began churning out films and spots, some of them superb, many of them extremely good. And from whatever sources, Short was coming up with the money to pay for production and for air time, not as much as we wanted, but more, frankly, than I was afraid we might have to settle for.

The half-hour Storck film was a masterpiece. It opened with Jimmy Durante singing "The Young at Heart," moved into a sequence with Hubert and Muriel Humphrey and Ed and Jane Muskie out bowling, just as people do in Waterville, Maine, on a Friday night, except that the Humphreys and Muskies happened to be in the alleys of the Executive Office Building in Washington. But the men were in shirtsleeves and looked like natural human beings.

Humphrey is, indeed, one of the warmest human beings I've ever met, and to reveal this was the major purpose of that film.

Another was to remind people of Humphrey's record. Humphrey has been criticized by many, including me in this book, for failing to act as decisively as they would have liked at the Chicago convention—but not many remember that it was Humphrey who almost caused a riot and did cause a mass walkout at the 1948 Democratic National Convention in Philadelphia in his famous speech in which he declared it was time for the Democratic party to "walk out of the shadow of states rights and into the sunshine of human rights." It was a moving speech; Storck worked it into the film beautifully. We also reminded people that it was Humphrey who pushed for the nuclear test-ban treaty, and that gave us an excuse to use a good picture of President Kennedy and Humphrey at the ceremony of the signing of the treaty.

The most controversial element of that film, however, involved a sequence in which the Vice-President talks about his retarded granddaughter.

I have been accused of injecting this into the film as a blatant piece of emotionalism totally irrelevant to the presidency.

Well, let me say this: had I *known* of the situation, I wouldn't have had any hesitancy about putting it into the film, but I *learned* about Humphrey's retarded granddaughter when I saw the rough cut of the film in St. Louis.

Nobody making the film knew anything about the retarded granddaughter in advance.

Like so many other instances that I could cite, this incident in the film evolved from long conversations and patient research. One of the sequences showed Humphrey and his wife playing with their grandchildren at Waverly; the other was a straight head-on interview of Humphrey filmed in San Francisco. The children were filmed several weeks before the interview, and at the time, no one in the film crew even knew that one of the children was retarded!

Humphrey began talking about his family in the San Francisco interview, and said some extraordinarily moving things about how he had learned, on election night 1962, that his daughter's baby girl, born that day, was retarded. His comments were eloquent, his reactions warm and human.

Is this irrelevant to the presidency? I don't think so. I think that if a man possesses the simple qualities of warmth, humanity, and affection, that the American people should know it, even if they are turned off by such sentiments. We weren't trying to create an image of Humphrey here, we were trying to reveal him as he actually is, because we believe, or at least I believe, that the real Hubert Humphrey is a much more appealing figure than the verbose political figure conjured up by many at the mention of Humphrey's name.

Humphrey, incidentally, never saw this film until midnight on the night before the election, at the home of Lloyd Hand in Los Angeles, where he had gone to a party following the coast-to-coast telethon.

And, like most other people, when he saw the section about the little girl "who taught me the meaning of true love," he cried.

The half-hour film was shown more than any other political documentary in American history, about fourteen hundred times on a per-station showing. It was aired seven times on network television, averaging about 175 stations, and another couple of hundred times in selected markets.

There is no doubt in my mind that this film did more to help Humphrey begin his climb in the polls than any other single thing we did in the campaign. Other things were good and useful, and I am not discounting them—but I can't think of another single incident, speech, program, film, statement that had the impact on the American public that film had.

In Paris, a few weeks after the presidential election, at the organizational meeting of the International Association of Political Consultants, we showed both the Humphrey film and a half-hour biographical documentary about Nixon that had been provided by the Republican National Committee.

After both films had been shown, there was silence. Then a man from Holland asked: "But I don't understand—how did Nixon win the election?"

Schwartz, Hal Tulchin, and E. G. Marshall combined their talents to produce a superb five-minute program. The script was written by Tony's wife, Reenah. Marshall stood on a set that contained huge blowups of the heads of the three presidential candidates— George Wallace, Richard Nixon, and Hubert Humphrey.

He started with Wallace, then went to Nixon, and finally to Humphrey. Marshall was halfway through talking about Nixon before it was possible to tell which candidate he was for. It was a masterful performance, a brilliant idea, and I'm only sorry we didn't have an opportunity to run it more often.

There is a direct correlation between the amount of money we spent on media and Humphrey's rise in the polls. As we began getting money in, and putting our stuff on the air, we began moving up.

We also had opportunities that we muffed. For instance, the debate that never came off.

It was clear that Nixon didn't want to debate Humphrey, but I also had the distinct feeling that Humphrey wasn't terribly keen on debating Nixon, either, because he never allowed us to go all out after Nixon.

Bob Squier summed up our feelings pretty well in a memorandum on September 23, when he wrote:

"1. Television debates will benefit the Vice-President, not Mr. Nixon.

2. The inclusion of Mr. Wallace in the format is devoutly to be wished.

3. We want at least one Agnew/Muskie debate."

While we made some noises around the National Committee about debates, and tried to get Congress to do something about relaxing section 315b of the Federal Communications Commission code, governing equal time for political candidates, we never pushed as hard as we could have for the debates.

As a matter of fact, Humphrey never really challenged Nixon to a head-to-head debate, with the candidates sharing the cost, or even with us putting up all the money if necessary. Why he shied away from this one I'll never know. We were behind, we had nothing to lose that I could see, and it looked as though we were beginning to get Nixon on the run. Maybe we just had more confidence in Humphrey's ability to take Nixon than he did himself.

I liked Jeno Paulucci's idea for full-page newspaper ads that would read:

HOW DOES NIXON

EXPECT TO STAND UP TO HO CHI MINH

AND MAO TSE-TUNG

IF HE IS AFRAID TO FACE

HUBERT HUMPHREY

ON AMERICAN TV?

In a memorandum to O'Brien on October 7, I wrote:
"I think it is time we zeroed in on the debate as an issue. . . .
This should be a multifaceted operation, including but not neces-
sarily restricted to the following elements:

> "A. A clear, direct demand for a two-man debate by the
> Vice-President, first in a statement and subsequently
> in every speech and public appearance. The thrust
> here should be along these lines:
>> (1) The American people have a right to know where
>> the candidates for President stand.
>> (2) If Nixon will not appear in a three-man debate
>> then Humphrey challenges him to appear with
>> him in a two-man debate with the costs to be
>> shared.
>> (3) If Nixon won't buy the time Humphrey will pay
>> the cost of the debate (or debates.)"

Later on I said:
"a. If Nixon is qualified to be President why won't he debate?
b. Humphrey thinks we should have government in the sunshine,
not in the shade; that the American public should not be
expected to accept a candidate whose cards are face down
on the table.
c. Nixon apparently has made deals with private interest groups
that he does not want made public. (See today's NY Times
editorial.)"

For whatever his reasons, the Vice-President wouldn't go along
with the debate plan. Maybe he thought it had been overdone,
maybe he believed that people were fed up with debate challenges,
maybe he was hesitant about debating Nixon. I don't know the
reason, but I think it was a mistake for us not to go after Nixon
on this issue. In the five-minute E. G. Marshall program, Reenah
Schwartz used a line that summed it up pretty well: "In 1960 Mr.
Nixon lost an election because he debated; in 1968 he thinks he
can win an election by avoiding a debate." She was right.

No one, including Humphrey, was going to stop the irrepressible
Jeno Paulucci from carrying on his own debate challenge. On one
occasion he hired a skywriter to paste in half-mile-high letters in

the sky over a Nixon rally, "WHY WON'T NIXON DEBATE?"
Another time, he hired some pretty models, dressed them as chickens, and hung signs around their necks indicating that they were
Nixon and a little timid about debating Humphrey.

Fun, but no cigar.

Talking about fun—without doubt the funniest spot produced in
the campaign, at least by our side, never got on the air. Even I
drew the line at this one, although it breaks up viewers whenever
they see it.

The spot was prepared and produced by Schwartz and Tulchin
after a long night of producing serious spots; I guess it was their
form of therapy.

It's a twenty-second spot that opens on a black screen on which
is written the words "Political Announcement."

The screen pulls open with the distinctive sound of a voting-
booth curtain being pulled back, and inside the booth are levers
marked with the names of the three candidates for President.

A man's hand appears, and he is mumbling something about
how some people take all night to vote, ah, here's the lever I want—
Wallace and General LeMay.

He pulls the lever and—BOOM—everything explodes and dissolves into a nuclear mushroom.

I remember showing the spot to Ed Muskie one day when we
were taping a Q-and-A program in Washington.

His first response was guffaw laughter; then he went aghast.

"My God," he exclaimed, "you aren't going to show that on the
air, are you?"

I assured him we weren't.

In some ways, Humphrey was a very good candidate to work
with; I also grew to like him very much as an individual, and I'm
willing to concede that on some of the things we disagreed on, he
may well have been right.

But like so many candidates, he really had very little appreciation of what television could do for him—or to him. I think he
may have had a better understanding of this after the campaign.

One incident stands out in particular:

Late in September we desperately needed some footage of Humphrey to fill some gaps in our spots and films. Bill Wilson laid on
a remote video control unit to do some taping of the Vice-President

when he was to spend a day at his home in Waverly. Shelby Storck had his film crew there. The remote video unit cost us twenty-two thousand dollars, whether we used it or not, and when you are scraping for pennies that's a lot of scratch.

First we got word from the Vice-President's staff traveling with him that he was too tired to spend a day taping and filming. Then, a few hours later, we heard that he had accepted an invitation to speak to the Minnesota Democratic-Farmer-Labor Party and a Minnesota AFL-CIO meeting on the day we were supposed to do our filming and taping. He also was planning to hold a press conference, and suggested that we have our crews there to film him at the press conference, and, ergo, our problem would be solved.

Angry, I fired off this memo to Orville Freeman:

"Obviously we cannot make the Vice-President appear for a film session if he does not want to appear. But let me make these points which I hope you will see fit to relay to him:

a. We have complete control over every foot of film or tape our people shoot. Obviously we are not going to let anything get on the air that we do not approve.

b. If he is too tired to appear in a *controlled* film session then under no circumstances should he appear at a press conference. An exhausted candidate should *never, repeat never,* hold a press conference where he is subjected to hard questioning and might commit a slip of the tongue that could be damaging if not fatal.

c. There may be other good reasons for having a press conference at this time, but he certainly should not do the press conference in preference to our controlled shooting.

d. We desperately need certain small segments of film for some spots.

e. Every television spot we make will be seen by 50 to 100 million people. It seems to me that if he can go to a Minnesota AFL-CIO meeting he would better spend the time in a controlled film and tape situation.

f. Although this is not the primary factor, the fact remains that we are committed to paying the crews if they work tomorrow or not."

I didn't bother to add that if Humphrey couldn't carry the Minnesota AFL-CIO and the Minnesota DFL we might as well all pack up and go home anyway, because the election was down the drain.

But we made no impact. Humphrey refused to let us get the shots that Wilson and Storck desperately needed, held a boring press conference that produced not one foot of usable footage for us, blew twenty-two thousand dollars, and maybe made a few people in Minnesota happy.

But while we were making little headway with the candidate, so far as getting him to devote more time to preparing and spending time at film sessions was concerned, we were having some impact on the electorate.

The agency produced a sixty-second gem called "What has Richard Nixon ever done for me?" The Schwartz spots were probing nerve ends of the Nixon/Agnew team. The thirty-minute film on the Democratic party, while not what I would call a howling success, wasn't bad, and, surprisingly, received a much more favorable response from younger voters than older people. I had assumed that the shots of Franklin Roosevelt in some of his famous speeches (". . . we have nothing to fear but fear itself," etc.) would bring back memories and be appreciated by the middle-aged and older voters. Actually, the documentary apparently had more appeal for young voters who had never seen Roosevelt and barely remembered Truman. I'll say this for that film: it had a hell of a cast of characters—Roosevelt, Truman, John F. Kennedy, Robert Kennedy, Ted Kennedy, Gene McCarthy, Lyndon Johnson, George McGovern, Ed Muskie, Humphrey, all wearing white hats, while the black hats included Wallace, Nixon, and, not linked to them but illustrative of certain problems in other countries at other times, people such as Hitler and Mussolini. It was a real potpourri, and almost made it big.

Terry Sanford, the astute former governor of North Carolina and chairman of Citizens for Humphrey in the campaign, and a shrewd and intelligent politician in his own right, put his finger on the flaw the first time he saw the film: "It doesn't have an upbeat ending."

He was right. We showed Democrats in control for a long time, and left voters with a feeling there still were a lot of problems to be solved. Our time schedule on this was incredibly short, and we simply didn't have time to correct the flaw before the film was distributed, but Sanford was right on target with his comment.

Money continued to be the big problem. When we had it, and

were able to get on the air, we were having impact: a Gallup poll late in October showed we had narrowed the gap to eight points, still a long way to go, but a lot better than the fifteen-point deficit we had faced a month earlier.

Here are some comparisons of network time buys published in the magazine, *Broadcasting Advertising* on October 14, listing political time buys as of October 10, for Nixon and Humphrey; even these figures, lopsided as they may be, are misleading, because Nixon, wisely, was pumping a lot of money into regional, state, and local buys, concentrating on specific markets with targeted material. This makes sense, and we were not unaware of its value, but our problem here was not only money but time. Regional and specific market buying requires planning and time; we were so rushed, because of our late start, we simply didn't have the time to do this job properly.

This gets back to a point I made earlier: the lack of post-convention planning.

Anyway, here are the network buys as of October 10:

NIXON	HUMPHREY
ABC-TV	
12 one-minutes (Summer Olympics)	2 prime-time five-minutes
2 prime-time five-minutes	1 prime-time half-hour (Nov. 4)
1 prime-time one-hour	
ABC RADIO	
109 minutes	None reported
124 half-minutes	
CBS-TV	
10 daytime five-minutes	7 daytime five-minutes
14 nighttime five-minutes	14 nighttime five-minutes
2 NFL football minutes	2 NFL football minutes
28 regional NFL football minutes	1 prime-time half-hour
8 prime-time minutes	
1 prime-time half-hour	
CBS RADIO	
3 fifteen-minutes	None reported
1 twenty-five-minute	
139 minutes and half-minutes	

NIXON	HUMPHREY
NBC-TV	
4 daytime minutes	1 daytime minute
18 prime-time minutes	19 prime-time minutes
1 late fringe minute	2 late fringe minutes
1 five-minute	1 prime-time five-minute
1 two-hour (Nov. 4)	3 AFL football minutes
	1 prime-time half-hour
NBC RADIO	
30 five-minutes	4 fifteen-minutes
2 NFL football minutes	6 five-minutes

Note particularly the disparity between Nixon and Humphrey on radio. We had some exceptionally good radio spots, but, until the last three weeks, were unable to get them on the air, whereas Nixon started his radio broadcasts—and they were good—early in August, right after he won the nomination.

Some months after the election, Teddy White called me to check some facts for his *Making of the President, 1968.*

"Joe," he said, "I've got some information on time buys from the Vice-President's office, but there seems to be a mistake in dates here. They say that you didn't start your radio broadcasts until September 14. That can't be right, can it? Shouldn't it be August 14?"

"It's wrong, all right," I said, "but not the way you think it's wrong. It wasn't September 14, or August 14, but October 14, when we started our radio."

And that was the case. We had these lovely radio spots in the can, and I played them for anyone who wandered into my cubbyhole at 2600 Virginia Avenue in Washington. Unfortunately, the vast majority of the seventy-odd million people who voted in the presidential election never found their way into my office, and most of them never had a chance to hear the radio spots.

We were pleading with our own people in the field—maybe begging would be a better word—to try to raise funds locally for radio, television, and newspaper ads. Some of our people responded pretty well, others weren't as effective. So while Nixon's electronic media were gushing forth, ours were trickling.

Toward the end, however, the situation improved considerably.

I don't know where Short was getting the money from, and to tell you the truth I didn't care, but in the last couple of weeks we were able to match Nixon dollar for dollar, right up until the final weekend, when I had to cancel a scheduled network showing of the thirty-minute documentary on Humphrey and a couple of NFL football spots we had ordered. For those not well informed about costs of television advertising, those three items represented more than $200,000—approximately $87,000 for the half-hour, and $57,000 for each of the football spots. A hell of a lot of money!

Late in the campaign we produced a couple of half-hour question-and-answer sessions with antagonistic questioners firing questions at Humphrey. Let me explain how these were done:

We recruited questioners who indicated they weren't very happy with some of Humphrey's positions. Some were young, some were black, some were Republican. We sat Humphrey on a stool, put the questioners around him, as close as they could get, in a semicircle, and told them to fire away. This wasn't live, it was on tape, so we did have control of the situation. But no one interfered, there were no planted questions, and we deliberately encouraged the audience to ask Humphrey the toughest questions they could, and to follow them up if they were dissatisfied with his answer.

It usually takes about twenty minutes for the questioners and the candidate to warm up in a situation like this, but after they got going, some of the stuff was great: sharp, penetrating questions, some of which visibly angered Humphrey. But, like most good candidates I've known, Humphrey reacts best when the pressure is greatest. As the questions got tougher, his answers got better, and some of them were even reasonably short. While we couldn't possibly use all of the material we taped—the sessions usually ran for two hours—we never interfered with the thrust of a question, or edited either the question or the gist of the response.

These came off pretty well, and we also did one with Humphrey and Muskie in a dialogue. Some people thought this was the best thing we did in the campaign; I happen not to share this view. I thought it was all right, and that it served a real purpose in showing Humphrey and Muskie together, but on the whole I thought it faintly boring when compared with some of the other half-hour materials we had available, such as the film. But this is a matter of personal, subjective judgment, and it could be that I was prejudiced, maybe even blinded, by the film, which I liked very much.

As the campaign moved into the final days, it was clear that we
were gaining. Nixon was sticking with the same old stuff that he
had been using, and I appreciated his position: his aides were
telling him to stay calm, not to rock the boat, that he had a big
lead, that it was too late for Humphrey to catch up, not to take a
chance on making a mistake, that the only way he could lose the
election was to blow it.

Maybe they were right; at least, Nixon won, and it's pretty
hard to quarrel with success.

But we were flying at the finish. Two days before the election,
Gallup showed us down only by a point, 43–42, and Harris had
us down by two, 42–40. (Harris actually took another poll, on the
day before the election, which showed Humphrey ahead.)

Money was beginning to come in; we were getting enthusiastic
reports from our people in the field.

On the morning before the election I was awakened by a phone
call in my Los Angeles hotel room by the New Jersey state chairman.

"Hey," he said, "I think we've got a chance here."

"We've been trying to tell you that for six weeks," I said. "I'm
glad you finally realized it."

"Well, we're really going to get to work on it. I think we can pull
it out."

They didn't. We lost New Jersey, which, to my mind, was inexcusable. We won New York, Pennsylvania, Massachusetts, Connecticut, Rhode Island, Maine, Maryland—virtually every state in
the Northeast except New Hampshire and Vermont—but not New
Jersey. It will be a long time before anyone gets me to believe that
a real effort was made on Humphrey's behalf in New Jersey.

Our final media effort was a two-hour telethon the night before
the election. This was Bob Squier's baby, and he handled it beautifully.

Television ratings after the telecasts indicated that something like
sixty-three million Americans had watched part or all of the telecast,
but we had a hell of a time getting one of the stars of the show
even to appear—Senator Muskie, the candidate for Vice-President.

Muskie explained that he traditionally concluded his campaigns
with a speech in Waterville, Maine (population: 18,143), and that

he didn't want to break tradition then. I pleaded with him, to no avail. Squier was equally unsuccessful. We finally had to get Humphrey to put it to him personally, and that was the only way we got Muskie even to appear on the show. Another example of an intelligent candidate failing to recognize the importance and the uses of media.

Muskie's appearance was important for a lot of reasons, not least of which was the contrast between him and Agnew. Nixon also had a two-hour telethon the night before the election—but Agnew was nowhere to be seen. (Maybe he went to Waterville to fill in for Muskie; I don't know.)

But for viewers who flipped channels and watched parts of both the Nixon and the Humphrey telethons, the contrast was clear: there were Humphrey and Muskie on one channel, and Nixon and Bud Wilkinson on the other.

The telethons rather crystallized the differences between the Humphrey and Nixon campaigns. Ours was loose, relatively uncontrolled ("organized chaos," Squier calls it), with lots of people wandering in and out; Nixon's was highly structured, formal, unemotional, and dull.

Paul Newman, who did a tremendous job for Eugene McCarthy early in the year, rather reluctantly consented to serve as moderator, and, after a few sessions with Humphrey, became impressed.

"This guy's really got something," he said to me. "I never realized he had so much depth before I began talking with him."

It was also a make-up-and-let's-be-friends session for Democrats who had been through some rough-and-tumble clashes early in the year. Gene McCarthy telephoned in to wish Hubert well. Ted Kennedy appeared in a moving sequence with Larry O'Brien videotaped at the Kennedy compound in Hyannisport a few days earlier. This was Teddy's own idea, and he carried it off well. He reminisced about being in his brother Robert's house eight years earlier, when Jack Kennedy was running against the same man Humphrey would face. It was a good moment, and it helped.

After the telethon (we—and Nixon—actually had to put on two each to cover the various time zones across the country), everyone in our camp adjourned to Lloyd Hand's house for a party, and I couldn't help but think that even if we lost it the next day, wasn't it great to at least have come this far, where we were laughing and dancing the night before the election, instead of moping about, talking about what might have been.

Reality came on the following night, of course, or early Wednesday morning. We came pretty close—within 250,000 in the popular vote, and seven tenths of a percentage point between us and Nixon, quite a difference from the fifteen-point spread of six weeks earlier.

We won one state we didn't figure to win—Washington—probably because of the serious economic condition the state was in, and lost one we thought we would win—Missouri—which eventually went to Nixon by about twelve thousand votes.

We also lost a few where we thought we had a chance: New Jersey, California, Illinois, Delaware, Alaska.

A win in either California or Illinois would have thrown the race into the House; and, as noted earlier, the switch of thirty-six thousand voters in Alaska, Missouri, and Delaware would have had the same effect.

Could we, under the existing circumstances, have won it?

I'd have to say yes, I think we could. When you come as close as we did, it wouldn't have taken much extra effort to make the difference.

We probably should have spent our media money differently. We had a list of twenty-four states we had written off, and lost twenty-three of them—all except Washington. And there were a few others on the list that we really didn't have much chance in, but which we included on our possible list for a variety of non-pragmatic reasons —places such as Virginia, Kentucky, South Carolina, Tennessee, and Ohio.

If we had diverted some of our television dollars from network, for which we were paying to reach a lot of places where we had no chance to win, and made more intelligent media buys on a regional or state basis, I think we would have got a bigger bang for our buck and might have swayed a few of the states where we lost: Missouri, Delaware, Alaska, California, Illinois, New Jersey (although this is a tough media state), Nevada, New Mexico.

This would have required sharper time buying than we enjoyed, and more-intelligent planning and direction, and I accept the responsibility for not having insisted on doing this.

And, of course, if we had taken some bolder steps—come out for stopping the bombing before Johnson made his speech late in the campaign (a speech that I, for one, felt played no major role in the outcome of the election), pressed the debate issue harder, taken some bold and innovative steps that were suggested and rejected—then perhaps the outcome would have been different.

But we all have 20/20 vision in hindsight, and, on the whole, we had to be satisfied. At least Humphrey came out of it as a noble warrior who had waged a hell of a fight, and not as a battered and bruised candidate who had been buried by Richard Nixon.

And we all had the satisfaction of knowing that we had caused more than one person in the Nixon camp to tremble a little as the results came in.

I've got to give Humphrey credit for never losing the human touch, which I firmly believe is real and not put on. One of his dearest friends, since deceased, was Freddy Gates. I went to bed about five o'clock on the morning after the election, couldn't sleep, got up at seven to shave and shower, and walked out of my hotel room around seven-thirty. By that time we were gone, even if we weren't admitting it.

In the hall outside of my room I ran into Humphrey. He was on his way to Freddy Gates's room, a few doors away, to personally tell him that we had lost, before he heard it on the tube. I think Freddy took the loss harder than Humphrey, and it was really Humphrey consoling Gates, rather than the other way around.

Humphrey also paid me the greatest compliment of any candidate I've ever worked for: A few months after the election I was having lunch at the Madison Hotel in Washington. Humphrey walked in, saw me, came over to the table.

"I'm sorry you weren't out in Minnesota the other day," he said. "I was giving a speech to a group of college students, and one of them asked me what I could have done to win the election, and I told them, 'Get hold of Joe Napolitan sooner!'"

I don't know if the story is true or not—but it was nice of him to say so.

3

ELECTRONIC CAMPAIGNING

THE FIRST TELEVISION SPOT I ever conceived in a political campaign was in 1957. It was my first campaign, and my candidate was a young man named Tom O'Connor, who was running for mayor of Springfield, Massachusetts, against an incumbent who had served six consecutive two-year terms and was considered unbeatable.

The spot featured an exploding bomb like the ones they always draw in cartoons, a black ball with a long fuse, that blows up and the pieces form the words "New Leadership—Tom O'Connor." (God, can you imagine a candidate today using an exploding bomb in a mayoral election? Environments change.) We made the spot in a local film studio, sticking a wick on a bowling ball and filming it as the fuse fizzed. The studio added a little razz-ma-tazz, and there was our ten-second spot.

I doubt that that commercial had much to do with Tom O'Connor's victory (he defeated his opponent in the Democratic primary in every one of the city's sixty-four precincts), but it was the first of many experiments I was to make with television as a medium to elect candidates to office.

(Four years later I ran a campaign against O'Connor with another candidate, and we beat him. That's when I began to believe that maybe the campaign manager really did have something to do with winning elections. And fourteen years later O'Connor turned up in my office again, wanting to run for mayor, which he was prevented from doing by a legal technicality.)

Political consultants, like political campaigns themselves, break down into two major groups: those who specialize in the use of media and those who specialize in organization. I happen to be media oriented, and have spent the past ten years trying to find new ways to win votes via the various electronic tools available to us—television, radio, computers—as well as by more-traditional methods: newspapers, brochures, signs. Maybe now it's time to start drawing some conclusions, and the only prediction I'll make about those conclusions is that they won't be very conclusive: things are changing too fast, more tools are available than we know how to use or can afford, guys on the other side are coming up with bright ideas, too.

Some observers call this the new politics, but you hear so many things being called the "new politics" these days that you wonder if any two people agree on the same definition. For example, I think the splendid effort made by youngsters on behalf of Senator Eugene McCarthy in his 1968 presidential bid was just the opposite of what I consider the new politics; it was straight, and effective, organizational politics, the old politics.

Everyone has his own definition; let me give you mine:

The new politics is the art of communicating a candidate's message directly to the voter without filtering it through the party organization.

And the best way to do that, in a major election, is through the electronic media (and I should note that in this book I am concentrating entirely on the big campaigns—for President, senator, governor, and mayor of large cities; smaller campaigns can more effectively utilize other techniques).

In his recent (and excellent) book *The Information Machines,* Ben Bagdikian observes that electronic machines are amoral. The computer and the television tube can transmit good information or bad, fact or fiction, truth or lies.

Cynics frequently express doubt that television actually influences votes. They are wrong. It does. Of course, what some candidates fail to realize is that you can lose votes on television as well as win votes, and that many times ballots wind up being cast for the "least objectionable candidate," to paraphrase a term used by Paul

Kline to describe why viewers select one commercial television program over another.

Let me quickly cite two examples from personal experience on how television, and really only television, influenced elections in which I was involved; both instances are covered in more detail in other chapters.

The first took place in Pennsylvania in the Democratic primary for governor in 1966. My candidate was Milton Shapp. We didn't have enough organization in the primary to fill a telephone booth; we did have a first-rate half-hour political documentary. It was produced by Charles Guggenheim and directed by Shelby Storck. For years Pennsylvania politicians had told Shapp, "You can't beat the organization in the primary." Three weeks before the primary, polls showed Shapp with 6 per cent of the vote, the organization candidate, Robert Casey, with 29 per cent, another candidate, Erwin Murray, with 2 per cent, and a horrendous 63 per cent undecided. (This was a campaign that at the time was not generating much interest in Pennsylvania.) We ran a nine-day media campaign, emphasizing the half-hour film. Strictly through the use of media we were able to achieve this result on primary day:

Shapp	550,000
Casey	500,000
Murray	100,000

Not only did media make Shapp a winner, but it also succeeded in increasing voter turnout in the primary by 15 per cent over the last comparable election, in 1962.

Perhaps an even more-dramatic example occurred in the Alaska Democratic Senate primary in 1968. We were taking daily straw polls in Anchorage the final twelve days of the campaign. On the twelfth, eleventh, and tenth days, the polls showed Senator Ernest Gruening running ahead of challenger Mike Gravel in Anchorage about 2–1. The ninth day before the primary was a Sunday and we didn't poll—but that night we ran a simulcast of a half-hour documentary about Gravel on all three Anchorage television stations. The *next day* the poll showed Gravel running ahead of Gruening in Anchorage 55–45. He maintained this lead and went on to defeat Gruening in Anchorage and the state to achieve the greatest upset in Alaska political history. Nothing happened between the Saturday and Monday polls except the simulcast. Never before, or since, to my knowledge, has it been possible to isolate the impact of a single television program so dramatically.

Media divides into two categories, paid and unpaid, or, if you prefer, as I sometimes do, controlled and uncontrolled.

Paid, or controlled, media is what you produce and place yourself. Unpaid, or uncontrolled, media includes things such as press conferences, interviews, news spots, debates, and other televised or broadcast activities over which the candidate and his staff do not have direct and complete control.

It is not unusual to find a candidate who appears very slick and smooth in his paid material, and not so slick and smooth in his uncontrolled media. Some candidates handle both equally well, but all candidates are human (at least as of this writing) and all are subject to normal human frailties. We all have our good and bad days. If a candidate has a bad day when you are filming a documentry or a televison spot, you merely scrap it; if he has a bad day on "Meet the Press" or in a debate, he can blow the election.

Sometimes your candidate has a tendency to overanswer questions, to tell you more than you possibly want to know about the subject. In uncontrolled television this can be deadly; in controlled television you merely cut the answer at a reasonable time.

Television consultant Bob Squier, of Washington, tells how he had briefed Hubert Humphrey before Humphrey appeared on a panel-interview show taped one morning during the 1968 presidential election.

"I knew we had to get Humphrey to tighten up his answers," Squier said, "and I thought one way to do that would be to halfway insult him. We were taping a 'Face the Nation' show from Minneapolis, and I went into his dressing room before the show and said, 'Mr. Vice-President, I think you should answer the first question they ask you today "yes" or "no," no matter what the question is or even if it makes no sense.'

"I figured this would get him angry and it did. We argued about it for a few minutes, and then I left.

"Humphrey got on the show and he was beautiful—he answered 33 questions in 28 minutes, and really looked good.

"When he walked off the stage he gave me a big wink.

"I thought we had solved our problem. Then the next morning

he appeared on the 'Today' show. They asked him the first question and had to interrupt his answer after 20 minutes because his time was up."

Electronic campaigning is not anywhere near as sinister as its critics make it out to be. Let's consider in turn the three major instruments of electronic campaigning: television, radio, computers.

The biggest complaint made about television is that it is too expensive, a rich man's toy, that unless a candidate is very wealthy or sells his soul to various unspecified unsavory types he can't use television properly and will lose.

There's a germ of truth in all of this—but just a germ. Money helps in a campaign, but it by no means assures election. (Or, as advertising man Gene Case said in a New York *Times* article, "If you don't believe that, just ask President Rockefeller.") In 1968 I was involved in two campaigns, in each of which one of the candidates had literally unlimited resources. In one case I was working for the man with the money, and in the other I was working against him. In both cases the man with the money lost. There were other factors—and there always are.

Occasionally a candidate may lose simply because he is outspent by a wealthy opponent and can't match his television dollars, but what is more likely to happen is that a candidate with limited funds doesn't spend his money wisely.

I have seen candidates spend twenty-five or thirty thousand dollars on billboards early in a campaign, and poor-mouth in the final three weeks because they don't have any money to go on television.

In terms of background, experience, and ability, one of the best-qualified candidates I have ever worked for is LeRoy Collins, former governor of Florida who ran for the United States Senate in 1968. Collins had everything you could want in a candidate, including looks, charm, and intelligence. He had been an outstanding governor, a consultant to two Presidents, undersecretary of commerce, head of the National Association of Broadcasters.

But Collins insisted on spending a lot of money early in his campaign on piddling little things such as newsletters and feathers and gimmicks that were sent around to people who should have been with him from the start, and probably were, and then he kept chopping away at his media budget. Coupled with this, Collins had a real distaste for raising money; he simply wouldn't get on the telephone and make a hard-nosed effort to raise funds for his campaign. Trimming his media budget in the primary caused him to win by a handful of votes instead of the majority he should have had, and forced him into an expensive runoff. He won that but never really recovered, and blew the election in the fall.

You'll never meet a more likable person than LeRoy Collins, and from many aspects he was the ideal candidate. But his insistence on spending money for unnecessary items at the expense of his media budget may well have cost him a seat in the United States Senate.

In the 1968 presidential election, when I was serving as director of advertising for Humphrey, I enraged several state chairmen by refusing to honor (i.e., pay for) commitments they had made for billboards—usually to the tune of twenty or twenty-five thousand dollars a state.

"But we've *always* had billboards," they insisted.

"Well, we're not going to have them this year, unless you get up the scratch," I said. "I think billboards are good for one thing—name identification—and if the people in this country don't know by now that Hubert Humphrey is running for President we're down the drain anyway."

Had I honored their requests we could have spent somewhere between a hundred fifty and two hundred thousand dollars for billboards, money that was crucially needed to finance our television campaign.

So while television is costly, it also can be potent, and the candidate with limited funds in a campaign that may be won or lost on television squirrels his money away early in the campaign and saves it until it is really needed. This, in more academic terms, is called budgeting, a subject every candidate and campaign manager should know something about.

Then there are the candidates who want to buy a lot of television time but want to cut down on production costs. This is a peculiar form of insanity, but a reasonably prevalent one. What these cats are saying, if they ever stopped to think about it, is, "I don't care how I look or sound, just so long as people see a lot of me."

Doesn't make much sense, does it? Yet, in campaign after campaign, candidates will pass over the good television producers for the cheapest one. That's like a manufacturer losing a little on each item but trying to make it up in volume.

Picking a *cheap* producer, however, is different from selecting the *least expensive* among several *competent* producers. We have been able to save our candidates considerable sums of money—into the tens of thousands of dollars—by inviting three or four *good* producers to bid on a campaign and selecting the one with the most advantageous price. You can't do this all the time; it works more effectively in off years, when there aren't as many campaigns. And, most important of all, you've got to know who the good producers are before you go shopping around.

We've learned a lot about television—and we're still learning. Sometimes I doubt if we've even scratched the surface. The advent and common use of cable television may well revolutionize political as well as commercial television.

In the fall of 1967 I was in Rio de Janeiro to give a talk on political campaigning at the triennial world conference of the International Public Relations Association. I was anxious to get back to New York to attend a communications conference, "Vision '67," at New York University. My plane was late and I finally arrived in New York in the wee hours of the morning on the day the conference was to begin. I dragged myself out of bed to go to the morning and afternoon sessions, planning to skip the evening meetings, which appeared to be geared more toward entertainment than information. But one of the evening sessions was on using lasers to communicate, and the other was a demonstration of sound by a man I have mentioned earlier, Tony Schwartz.

My decision to sit in on the evening sessions has had a profound effect on my career. I still don't know much about lasers, but I have learned a lot about Tony Schwartz. I sat transfixed through Schwartz's presentations; it wasn't only the best presentation on the use of sound I had ever heard, it was ten times better than any other.

After Schwartz finished his session and was leaving, I cornered him in the lobby, introduced myself, and asked if he had ever done any political work.

"No," he said, "I really haven't. Wait a minute, I did do one spot in the 1964 presidential election for President Johnson. Maybe you saw it—it was a little girl picking petals off a daisy."

I had seen it. This perhaps was the most controversial television spot ever made—not for what was in it, but for what people read into it.

Tony and I had several meetings in the fall of 1967 and through the early months of 1968. At that time, he was working out of a basement in his home at the corner of West Fifty-sixth Street and Tenth Avenue in New York (since then, he has purchased a small church next door and converted it into a studio). While our friendship ripened, we never worked on anything together until the Humphrey campaign of 1968.

When I agreed to take on the job of director of advertising for Humphrey nine weeks before the 1968 election, I listed Schwartz as one of three people I considered indispensable in preparing our television and radio. I flew from Humphrey's home, in Waverly, Minnesota, to New York to have dinner with Schwartz and told him I wanted him to work on the campaign.

"What do you want me to do?" he asked.

"I want you to think," I replied.

For the next eight weeks I fed problems to Schwartz and he turned them into solutions. Unfortunately for Humphrey, we never did get maximum benefit from Schwartz's radio products in that campaign, because we didn't have enough money to go on the air until the final three weeks of the campaign, and I think radio needs some time to build. But Tony, working with Hal Tulchin, did produce some extraordinary television materials.

Since then, Schwartz and I have worked together in more than twenty campaigns. His perception into the uses of sound is extraordinary.

Schwartz is one of the few men I have met whom I can say is an unqualified genius in his field. This isn't to say everyone likes him; he can be short and abrasive with people with whom he feels no rapport, and one or two clients have been unhappy with the material he produced because they felt it did not accurately project the message they were trying to get across.

And Tony has some personality quirks—as, he won't travel. Anywhere. In all the time I've known him I've never known him to go farther from Fifty-sixth Street than the Lincoln Center campus of Fordham University in one direction and Washington Square in the other. And he won't visit candidates or clients. They come to his place if they want him to work for them. That obscure corner on Tenth Avenue has seen an interesting parade of distinguished visitors in the past four years, including senators, governors, congressmen, mayors, candidates for these offices, and the curious—people such as the Marchese Emilio Pucci, of Italy, who was fascinated by Schwartz's grasp of sound in television and radio.

My colleague Michael Rowan calls Schwartz "a pragmatic Marshall McLuhan."

McLuhan happens to be one of Tony's close friends—not surprisingly—and one of the interesting things Schwartz did in the 1968 campaign was pull from all the tapes he has of McLuhan those comments that he thought would be relevant to political campaigning.

One of the most useful bits we culled from a McLuhan tape, unfortunately not in time for the 1968 campaign, was a four-word declaration that may well change the whole concept of electronic campaigning: "instant information creates involvement." More about that later.

In addition to his own creativity, Schwartz, like all the good people in this business, is a master at adaption. A small example:

The Federal Communications Commission requires that political radio and television spots be identified as such. This is called a disclaimer. The FCC establishes no precise format for the disclaimer, and the networks and local stations often have their own rules.

The best disclaimer, by far, that I have ever heard, came from a Boston advertising man named Mal McDougal, who was working on Boston Mayor Kevin White's campaign for governor of Massachusetts in 1970. The disclaimer was, ". . . paid for by a lot of people who want Kevin White elected Governor." Beautiful. To make it effective, and legal, we formed a committee in Massachusetts called "A lot of people who want Kevin White elected Governor."

Schwartz was doing White's radio spots. I told him of the disclaimer; he seized upon it and made a slight change: after the radio pitch, the announcer would say, ". . . *and that's why* this message was brought to you by a lot of people who want Kevin White elected Governor."

We used the disclaimer in seventeen different elections in 1970— sometimes with humorous aftereffects: in Alaska, our opponent,

Governor William Egan, further changed it to read: "This message was brought to you by a *whole lot more* people who want Bill Egan elected Governor."

The message was adaptable to television as well as radio, and we used it in both places.

Following the 1970 campaigns, two candidates filed protests with the FCC about the disclaimer, and early in 1971 I wrote to the FCC asking for a written ruling on whether we could use the disclaimer, provided an actual committee called "A lot of people who want _____ elected _____" were formed.

The FCC has written me saying that we could not use "a lot of people" as a disclaimer, because it is too vague, but we are pursuing the matter. Personally, I don't believe that "a lot of people" is any more vague than "Citizens for Nixon," which the FCC accepts.

Television is there. Everyone can use it. Some use it more effectively than others. And I don't think the ones who are imaginative enough to use it effectively should be penalized.

In 1968 Richard Nixon successfully employed the "man in the arena" technique developed by Roger Ailes. It apparently worked pretty well; Nixon survived. It wasn't the kind of thing I might use, because I thought it looked staged, but I realize that I probably was viewing it with more-sophisticated eyes than the average voter, and to many people it really looked as though Nixon was in the arena, playing the role of the Christian martyr.

We've played around with some gimmicks on television, and we're constantly experimenting with new techniques.

As far back as 1960 we scheduled a five-minute news-style telecast on behalf of Endicott Peabody, candidate for the Democratic nomination for governor in Massachusetts. Our press secretary at the time was a young man named George Berkeley, a former newscaster. For the two weeks preceding the primary I bought a five-minute time segment the same time each night, 6:25 to 6:30 P.M., just before the local news. In those days, Boston newspapers sold front-page ads, so we ran a small ad on the front page saying:

POLITICAL ROUND-UP
ALL THE LATEST POLITICAL NEWS.
TONIGHT AND EVERY NIGHT UNTIL THE PRIMARY.
6.25—CHANNEL XX

We used a straight news format, and included straight news items—about Senator John F. Kennedy meeting with his aides at Hyannisport, and Vice-President Richard Nixon scheduling a campaign tour, and Senator Leverett Saltonstall speaking in Worcester, and an announcement by Saltonstall's opponent, Thomas O'Connor.

This happened to be a seven-man primary fight, and the favorite was the secretary of state of Massachusetts, Joseph Ward. Naturally, on any given day one or more of the other six candidates was giving Ward the zing one way or another. So on our "Political Round-up" we found time to use a couple of items critical of Ward—quoting the candidate who made the statement—and also managed to find room for some comments highly favorable to Endicott Peabody, including, according to our plan, the final item of each program.

Well, all hell broke loose. The station ruled us off the air, even though we had complied with federal (and local) regulations by placing a disclaimer before and after the program. Their argument was that the program "looked too much like a regular news program." My answer to that was, "So what?"

We finally persuaded another station to use the program, but they insisted upon running a crawl across the screen every sixty seconds that said PAID POLITICAL BROADCAST, and that took the edge off our little scheme.

In the 1966 election for governor of Pennsylvania, the Republican candidate, Raymond Shafer, used a device (I believe concocted and executed by producer David Wolper) that was patently phony, but worked.

On the week before the election, Wolper's crews filmed some footage inside a television station, and from various easily identifiable locations throughout the state: a dock in Erie, a steel mill in Pittsburgh, a coal mine in Scranton. Then pseudo news announcers would tell how much strength Shafer had built up in that particular area, how popular he was, what a swell fellow he actually was, and how he was going to win.

On election eve, Shafer had an hour-long program, and interspersed within the program were these segments "on location."

"Now we switch you to Erie, where our correspondent has a report on the status of the gubernatorial election there. . . . Come in, Erie."

Phony as hell, but effective.

Okay, those have been gimmicks; now let's return to the real world. Or as real a world as television can be.

Television is a tool. It may be the best of the tools we have available to us in politics, but it's not the only tool, and in some cases it can't be used at all. A saw is a very useful tool, too, but not if you're trying to build a stone wall.

There are some campaigns in which television is totally inapplicable. Take a Congressional election in Brooklyn, for example. The primary is likely to decide the election. If you try to use television, you find that only about 5 per cent of the people who watch the message you are beaming over the airwaves live in your Congressional district. And many of those who see it aren't eligible to vote in the primary, because they are too young, not registered, or not Democrats. What you eventually get is something like a 2 per cent return on your television time-buying dollar. Not worth it, of course. So when you get in a situation like this you forget about television and use other media: newspaper advertising, direct mail, possibly a little radio if you have a black or Puerto Rican constituency, because these minority groups often have great loyalty to particular radio stations on which time can be purchased inexpensively.

New Jersey and Delaware are difficult states in which to use television effectively. The northern end of New Jersey is a suburb of New York, the southern end a suburb of Philadelphia. To reach people in those areas you need to buy New York and Philadelphia television, expensive as hell when you consider the return. Delaware doesn't have any television; you have to buy Philadelphia to reach Delaware voters. Again, in these cases you are better off spending your political dollars in other media.

In some other states television can be a problem, but you've got to use it anyway, despite the waste. In Kentucky, for example, you have to buy time on television stations in five states—Ohio, Indiana, West Virginia, and Tennessee, as well as Kentucky—to blanket the state. The rates charged by these stations, however, are low in comparison to those in New York or Philadelphia.

Most of the time you can use television; how effectively you use it depends on the candidate, his campaign director, his television producer, and his time buyer.

Some candidates are comfortable on television, others are not.

If you have a candidate who is uncomfortable with the medium, you probably won't be able to change him (I don't really think you can ever change a candidate, or even his image, in a short campaign), but you probably can help him a little: a television coach to make him more at ease, a top-flight producer who will bring out the best in him. The campaign director puts this all together; the time buyer makes certain you get the biggest bang for your buck.

We hear a lot about "packaging candidates." Television, used properly, does precisely the opposite: it unpackages candidates. If anyone is "packaged" it is the voter, because he becomes enveloped in media, which becomes environmental as the campaign progresses.

Most candidates, honest to God, are better than their image. There are some fakers in the business, some crooks, some charlatans —but probably not nearly as many as there are in medicine, the law, or academia. The higher the office, the more likelihood that the candidate will be a reasonable, straightforward person.

A thieving doctor or businessman, if he's clever, can stay out of the spotlight; candidates and elected officials can't. By the very nature of their business they are exposed to the public day in and day out. And to the press.

As an ex-newspaper reporter, I don't have a lot of sympathy with columnists and commentators who criticize people in my business because we show the candidates in their best light. That's our job. If the candidate has warts, it's their job to reveal them, not ours. I don't knowingly work for candidates who lie—but neither do I insist upon my candidates' sliding knives into their own bellies so they will slowly bleed to death during a campaign. If a candidate has had a drinking problem or a messy divorce or was involved in a fracas earlier in his career, it's not my job to trot these facts before the public. If he's asked about them, tell the truth—but don't expect us to require a candidate to bare his flaws unilaterally.

A candidate running for office is a man looking for a job. Not many job seekers in private industry tell *everything* about themselves when they apply for a new position. They tell the good things. If their prospective employer asks if they have ever been arrested, or why they were fired from a previous job, they answer. It's the same with candidates: his job, and that of his advisers, is to call public attention to the good things about him, the reasons why he, and they, believe he is better suited for the office he seeks than his opponent.

I believe the press has an obligation to dig into a candidate's background and to reveal to the public anything they believe shows him to be less qualified for the office than he claims to be. I do believe, however, that the press has an obligation, not always fulfilled, of giving the candidate an opportunity to tell his side of the story in the same article or air time in which the criticism is made. Too often I have seen a charge against a candidate on Page 1, and his rebuttal to that charge on Page 15 three days later.

(After his defeat in the 1970 gubernatorial primary in New York, Howard Samuels was appointed director of New York City's Off-Track Betting Corporation. In an interview with the New York *Times* one day, he wryly observed that when he was a candidate for governor he had difficulty getting his positions or even his name in the paper, but "now that I've become a bookie I get my name in the paper all the time.")

Just because a candidate's position is different from yours or mine doesn't necessarily make him evil. I don't happen to agree with President Nixon or Senator Stennis on lots of things—but they put their head on the line every time they run, and if the people elect and re-elect them, that's their problem.

I don't happen to work for candidates I don't like personally, or whose political philosophies are alien to mine; that happens to be a matter of personal preference, and I can afford to take this independent position. But I'll be damned if I am going to make television spots or radio commercials revealing the *weakest* of my candidate's characteristics; I'm going to play hell out of the best of his characteristics.

There has been a lot of criticism about short television spots—30- and 60-seconds, in particular—with the claim that they give voters an unfair picture of the candidate.

What many people don't realize is that television stations are under no obligation to sell candidates anything, and often will not sell anything longer than thirty or sixty seconds. In a campaign I am working on as I write this book, stations refuse to sell prime-time spots longer than thirty seconds—and there's not a damned thing we can do about it. If we want to get on prime time (and who doesn't?) we've got to make thirty-second spots. This doesn't mean there isn't a proper place in campaigns for the thirty-second, or even the ten-second, spot: if the message you are trying to convey takes only ten or thirty seconds, why should you be required to use a longer spot? This is a problem we sometimes have with advertising agencies: the material we want to get on the air fits beautifully in a ten-second or a thirty-second frame, but the agency resists using these because their time buyer has purchased only sixty-second spots, paying no attention whatsoever to the content of the material or the message we are trying to get across. If the message, for example, is one of simple name identification, you don't need five minutes to accomplish this; once a candidate becomes known, then you can begin associating him with positions, but name identification comes first.

In 1970 Bob Squier produced a thirty-minute film for Governor Marvin Mandel of Maryland. There are two television markets in Maryland: Baltimore and Washington. The Baltimore stations sold us a limited number of half-hour times; the major Washington stations refused to sell us any. So there we were, sitting with a good half-hour film, and no way to show it to the 40 per cent of Maryland residents who live in the Washington area. (Some of the UHF stations in Washington would show the film, but none of the more-powerful, VHF stations.)

In Hawaii in 1970, Medion made a half-hour film for Governor John Burns. The most powerful television station in Honolulu re-fused to sell us even one half-hour segment to show the film.

Five minutes is a nice length for a political telecast—long enough to reveal useful information about a candidate, short enough to make it economical to produce and hold the viewer's attention.

But again we run into trouble with television stations: some refuse to sell any five-minute segments, and I know of none that will sell five minutes of prime time, except in presidential elections, when the networks make available five-minute units by reducing the length of some of their network programs.

In Massachusetts in 1970, one of the two television outlets in the western end of the state point-blank refused to sell anything longer than sixty seconds to political candidates. The other station sold us a few fringe five-minute programs. When I protested, they agreed to sell us a package of ten more five-minute programs, all between six-fifty and six fifty-five in the *morning*—not exactly what I would call prime time.

When several candidates are seeking the same or different offices in the same campaign period, and all of them want to get on the air with five-minute programs, obviously the number of showings each can receive is small. Stations (and networks, for that matter) are not required to sell you anything; all they are required to do is sell Candidate B the same and equivalent amount of time that they sell Candidate A. If they sell A nothing, they are under no obligation to sell B anything either.

Candidates often are forced into the unenviable position of laying out large sums of money to produce good television material and being left with no place to show it because the stations won't sell them time even if they have the money to pay for the time. In such a case, the incumbent has an advantage, because he can usually command more exposure through the forum of his office.

Political television programs come in eight conventional lengths: 10-, 20-, 30-, and 60-second spots, and 5-, 15-, 30-, and 60-minute programs. Occasionally, for a telethon or some special event, you might take ninety minutes or two hours, but this is highly unusual. The 20-second spot is fading, because stations now are trying to push 30s, which they can piggyback into a 60-second time slot. And unless a 10-second is produced with extraordinary skill, it can't be used for much more than name identification—a video billboard, so to speak.

The most common lengths now are thirty- and sixty-second spots and five-minute programs. Fifteen-minute programs have the same drawbacks as five-minute programs: unavailability of prime time, and greater production cost.

You can, in most places, buy a half hour of prime time, at least on some of the stations in any given market, but many candidates are unwilling or unable to buy half-hour segments. Some believe that it is impossible to hold the viewer's attention for thirty minutes, but, more often, they can't afford the expense of producing a half-hour documentary. (The cost of making a high-level half-hour documentary produced by one of the half dozen or so producers I consider capable of turning out this kind of product runs between $75,000 and $125,000—a lot of money.)

The cost of buying time for half-hour programs, incidentally, usually isn't as much of a problem as the uninitiated might believe; the cost of a half hour in prime time isn't much more than the cost of a sixty-second prime-time spot.

There are two basic ways of producing political television spots: the *cinéma vérité* technique, which usually involves shooting a lot of footage of the candidate doing various things in various environments (talking with the elderly, playing with children, deploring the polluted river, answering questions, shaking hands, examining a school, etc.), and the structured spot, similar to most of the product commercials you see on television every night. Most independent producers lean toward the *cinéma vérité* technique; most advertising agencies seem to favor the structured spot. This is not to say that either can't do both, but some producers tend to do some things better than they do others. A pleasing mix was accomplished in the Hawaii gubernatorial campaign in 1970, when Lennen & Newell/Pacific, in the early stages of the campaign, when the attempt was being made to acquaint voters with the accomplishments of Governor John Burns, depended heavily on the scripted, storyboard, structured spot to emphasize issues-oriented material, and then, after two waves of structured issues spots, switched to Medion for a third wave of highly personal spots featuring the governor himself. Medion undoubtedly could have produced the structured spots, and Lennen & Newell the *cinéma vérité* spots, but I am certain that by using different producers who were specialists in different techniques, the agency succeeded in doing the best possible job for its client—and played a major role in re-electing him to a fourth term in a race he entered as a decided underdog.

Sometimes producers resist doing what they do best. In recent years Charles Guggenheim has resisted producing longer political documentaries and has concentrated on five-minute programs and shorts. A half-hour documentary can tie up a producer for a long period of time, and despite the cost of the film to the client, the profit margin to the producer isn't overwhelming. I'm not suggesting that Guggenheim doesn't make as many thirty-minute films as he used to because he can make more money producing spots, but I do know he has discouraged some candidates who wanted half-hour documentaries from using them. I think this is too bad, because some of the longer films he has produced are political classics.

I think there is a definite place for the half-hour film in political campaigning, particularly for two kinds of candidates. The first is the unknown candidate making his first try for office, who needs the depth of exposure that a half-hour film will give him and which he can't ordinarily get through the use of short spots. And the other is the candidate or officeholder who has been around a long while and whose earlier accomplishments may have been forgotten by the electorate. A splendid example of this second candidate was Hubert Humphrey in 1968. Everybody knew who Humphrey was, but a lot of people, particularly the young, the poor, and the black, had forgotten, or never known, some of Humphrey's epic struggles in his early days as a senator, or even his racket-busting record as mayor of Minneapolis. His film, done by Shelby Storck, brilliantly re-created his earlier career, and I doubt that it was pure coincidence that Humphrey began climbing in the polls as the film got national exposure.

I believe a half-hour political documentary needs three assets to be successful:

1. It must have an engaging opening; it must grip people in the first minute, or they'll switch off.
2. It must be entertaining as well as informative, because it is competing against the best that commercial television has to offer. (I'll make no comment on what that might be.)
3. It must be properly promoted.

Promotion is important for a half-hour film, because you've got to get viewers to tune in for it. Spots are viewed accidentally; you try to place them in time slots where the kind of people you want to reach probably are watching, and it is wasteful to promote a spot schedule, because usually it means attracting only the committed, whether to you or your opponent.

Some of the best promotional ads for half-hour documentaries that I know of give no indication of whom the film is for. In Mike Gravel's Senate campaign in Alaska in 1968, our ad said simply:

TONIGHT

AN IMPORTANT DOCUMENTARY FILM
ABOUT THE 1970 ELECTION FOR
UNITED STATES SENATE IN ALASKA.

That was an attempt to bring non-committed viewers to the television set.

The Humphrey half-hour in 1968 was promoted through an ad that read:

TONIGHT
SEE A SIDE OF HUBERT HUMPHREY
YOU'VE NEVER SEEN BEFORE.

That could mean anything, pro or con, and again was aimed at attracting voters who had not made up their minds.

There are other uses for the half-hour length other than documentaries. They can be used for straight-on, eyeball-to-eyeball speeches, something I don't recommend often, unless the candidate really has something important to say and can carry off the half-hour without difficulty. I keep reminding candidates it took John F. Kennedy only twenty-two minutes to explain the Cuban crisis to the country in October 1962, and filling up thirty minutes with straight talk, and holding your audience, is not easy.

Of course there are uses for this style. One of the turning points of the 1968 presidential election was Humphrey's half-hour talk from Salt Lake City in which he explained his position on the war in Vietnam. But this was an exceptional case: voters around the country were waiting for Humphrey to make a major policy statement on Vietnam, and interest in the program was built in. In the course of an ordinary campaign for senator or governor, there aren't many times when the candidate has something that important to say, or is physically capable of staying on camera for half an hour and holding his audience.

Then there are question-and-answer programs, and, properly handled, these can be effective and informative. The format I prefer is to sit the candidate in the middle of a bunch of hostile questioners, up very tight, almost knee to knee. This is to keep the candidate talking in a conversational tone of voice and prevent him from raising his voice to answer questioners far away, as he might in a hall. We usually do these in studios, on videotape, and let them run for ninety minutes or so, cutting that down to a usable thirty-minute segment. Usually it takes twenty minutes for the questioners and the candidate to get into the swing of things. Having hostile rather than friendly questioners makes for a better program, because most good candidates respond better to tough questions than they do to easy ones. And if the questioners obviously are friendly, or the program looks staged, it turns viewers off, and in turn they turn you off.

Sure, we use the segments of the program in which our candidate looks the best. If he fluffs an answer, or mops his brow with the camera on him, or stumbles over his words, or is garrulous, or mutilates his syntax, we'll cut that out of the finished product. But we never try to change the sense of a question or lift parts of any question or answer out of context—outside, perhaps, of shortening an answer that is too long. Questioners are told to ask the candidate anything they want, and often lively debate develops between the candidate and the questioners.

If the whole thing turns out bad, we dump it, but that doesn't happen often. What is more likely is that we'll get enough for a couple of good shows, maybe a five-minute or a fifteen-minute show as well as the original half-hour we had planned.

Candidates sometimes like to have live telecasts of rallies and things like that, but I oppose, almost always successfully, such efforts. First of all, the conditions for presenting the program often aren't as good as they would be in a studio: lighting, sound, and all the other variables that make a program look good. And then there always is the big risk that you face whenever you go on live— that the candidate may make a big blooper. Remember, I'm talking now about *paid* media, television programs that we pay out our money to show on the air. Later I'll discuss candidate appearances on unpaid programs of this nature, which present a different set of problems. But when we are paying to put something on the air, I want to make damn sure it looks as good as it can.

You also have things such as the trite press-panel interview, in which members of the local press are invited to ask questions of the candidate. Frankly, these don't work as well as when you use real people, not because the press questions are tougher, but because the format is stilted. Many times, the questions are easier, because they are the same ones the press has been asking in the campaign right along, and a good candidate can pretty much anticipate what he'll face on a program of this type. But the format is old and dull, and most of the shows produced in this manner turn out that way, too.

The candidate can sit with some "experts" on various problems in his state, such as pollution or unemployment or the cost of living, and discuss ways of solving the problems, but, for one reason or another, this doesn't make for exciting television. Worst of all is when the candidate and the rest of his ticket sit around discussing the campaign. That's instant dullsville, and should be avoided at all costs short of mutiny of the bountiful.

Hour-long segments usually are used only for something in the nature of a telethon, an interesting creation that can sparkle or be deadly dull, often depending upon who produces it. Bob Squier, who did the Humphrey telethon in 1968, is sharp and imaginative. On the Republican side, Roger Ailes, whose style is entirely different from Squier's, does a good job. Democrats tend to be livelier than Republicans (personal observation) and hang looser on television. This usually makes for a more stimulating program.

A concept of paid telecasting that you'll be seeing more of is something I have dubbed telenews, although other people use it and call it something else. This consists essentially of feeding television stations brief news clips of your candidate in action. If you're running for President, you probably don't need it, but if you're running for governor or senator, this can be a useful device indeed. Most television stations, particularly small ones, simply can't afford to send camera crews around the state following the candidate. Even the big ones seldom go out of their own viewing area, unless the event is something special. But almost all these stations occasionally, if not every day, will use a high-quality film clip sent to them by the candidate's film producer, provided, of course, that it meets their standards, gets to the station in time, and is properly identified. All we're really talking about is transferring the mimeographed press release onto film, with the chances of its getting used substantially increased.

Telenews is a fairly expensive operation. You need an able crew, skillfully directed, to turn out the material, and some solid logistical support to make sure the film is quickly processed and distributed to the stations in time. Videotape cuts down the time but shoots up the cost, because mobile videotaping is much more expensive than filming.

Television news programs are well watched, and if a candidate can hit the local news with regularity, then he is going to get exposure that he would not otherwise have received. Of course, the event to be filmed should be newsworthy in itself; television news directors can spot junk pretty quickly, and they dispose of it the way it should be disposed of—in the scrap heap. And a continuous flow of junk may mean that when you provide a legitimate piece of newsy film it will be treated with suspicion. But if you happen to be campaigning in a state with fifteen or twenty television stations, and have the resources to film and distribute your candidate in action, and two or three times a week are able to provide a film clip to stations throughout the state, you are going to get more exposure than your opponent (unless, of course, he is doing the same thing).

Curious and contradictory arguments develop over thirty-second and sixty-second spots, with the critics in white hats claiming that these aren't long enough for voters to become acquainted with a candidate. These same white hats criticize (a) spots that are not issues-oriented and (b) spots in which the candidate does not appear.

Most of the good issues-oriented spots I've seen are those in which the candidate does not appear, not because anyone is trying to hide him, but simply because there isn't enough time to define an issue *and* propose a solution *and* have the candidate appear in the spot, all in thirty or sixty seconds. And why is it necessary? If a candidate wants to do a spot showing that industry in his state is polluting streams and rivers, is it better for him to appear on camera and talk about it, or better for the camera to go to the polluted streams and show how they are being polluted? I'll opt for the second choice every time. If the subject is bad housing, or the lack of good housing, isn't it more effective, and perhaps more honest, to show dilapidated dwellings and slums than to have the candidate talk about these? I think it is. And faced with the time restrictions that many stations place on candidates, it's hard to put everything into one spot.

We use television essentially as a positive medium. If it can be avoided, except in special circumstances, I never let one of my candidates use television to deliver negative personal messages. Let him rip his opponent apart in speeches, if he feels so compelled, but we think television works best if it is low-key, soft-sell, and positive. I think it can be demonstrated, if anyone ever wants to make a real effort to do so, that the "nice guy" on television is more likely to win the election than the man with a hard line, or the mudslinger.

Television can be the most emotional of our media, and I see nothing wrong with using emotions. More people vote with their hearts than with their heads anyway. Elections are won and lost on emotion, not on logic. I'm not saying this is good or bad, that I'm for it or against it, just that it is a fact. And I'll be damned if I'll try to answer my opponent's emotional appeals with logical dissertations. I've tried this a couple of times, and now I know how it feels to lose. It doesn't feel good.

The most emotional sequence from any television production I've ever been part of was in the Shapp half-hour *Man Against the Machine,* produced by Charles Guggenheim in 1966. Shapp, in a voice-over film, was telling about how his army unit released prisoners from a Nazi concentration camp in Austria at the close of World War II. As he was talking, the camera showed rather gruesome concentration-camp footage: bodies of victims heaped like cordwood, a hollow-eyed man with broomstick legs being carried out on a stretcher, a rabbi praying. Powerful stuff! There was good reason for using this footage, and creating this emotional impact. Milton Shapp is Jewish. He was the first Jewish candidate for governor in Pennsylvania history (and now is its first Jewish governor). There was, perhaps still is, a fair amount of anti-Semitism in some sections of Pennsylvania, and we knew this was hurting Shapp. We capitalized on this liability to show what it meant to be a Jew during World War II. I'm sure a lot of people voted for Milton Shapp after seeing that film *because* he is Jewish, a sort of reverse discrimination.

There's nothing wrong with emotion—so long as it is honest. What is bad, is the dishonest use of emotion. An example: In the Indiana Senate campaign in 1970, the Republican candidate, Congressman Richard Roudebush, ran a sixty-second television spot in which he virtually accused incumbent Democratic Senator Vance Hartke of putting guns in the hands of the Viet Cong. The spot claimed that Hartke had voted for legislation that helped provide arms for the North Vietnamese. It was a dirty spot, because it wasn't true. It turned out, incidentally, that Hartke had voted *against* the bill in question and Roudebush had voted *for* it!

The Republican National Committee's 1968 sequence that showed flashes of a smiling Hubert Humphrey interspersed with bleeding and dying American soldiers in Vietnam is another use of dishonest emotion. Both these spots, the one in Indiana and the Vietnam spot, were quickly pulled off the air.

I don't mean to imply that Democrats produce only clean, honest spots and Republicans only dirty, dishonest spots; I'm sure the tally would be about even, if anyone were to bother to keep score. It doesn't make any difference who does it; if it's dishonest it shouldn't be produced, and if it's produced it shouldn't be used.

I personally killed a half-hour film made for Hubert Humphrey by an independent producer in the 1968 campaign. The film took the worst of Richard Nixon, everything from his you-won't-have-Richard-Nixon-to-kick-around-any-more statement made the morning after he lost the California gubernatorial election in 1962 to his Checkers speech in 1952. It used material out of context and employed every low trick imaginable to portray Richard Nixon as a bastard. I'm sure Humphrey has never seen the film; he'd have a stroke if he did. It was repulsive footage.

The girl picking petals off the daisy that was used in 1964 is a different story. The visual part of the spot shows a little girl picking petals off a daisy, counting softly to herself, "One, two, three, four, five, six, seven, eight, nine, ten, eleven . . ."; then her voice fades out, and while the camera freezes on her eyes, we hear a strident military voice counting, "NINE, EIGHT, SEVEN, SIX, FIVE, FOUR, THREE, TWO, ONE, ZERO."

BOOM—the familiar mushroom cloud of an atomic explosion, over which we hear President Johnson saying: "These are the stakes . . . to make a world in which all of God's children can live . . . or to go into the dark. We must either love each other . . . or we must die."

Now there's nothing in that language that is inflammatory. Who could disagree with Johnson's remarks? What made the spot explosive and controversial was the environment in which it was played, what people read into the spot. Goldwater had made some foolish statements about nuclear bombs and defoliation in Vietnam, and viewers immediately concluded that the implication of the spot was that if Goldwater was elected we'd have nuclear war. That was *their* interpretation of the spot, based on what was in their own minds. Nothing in the spot suggested this. Tony Schwartz says that if he had been Goldwater, instead of condemning the spot he would have endorsed it and said he agreed wholeheartedly with what Johnson was saying. I guess some people feel differently about this one than I do.

This really is the difference between *received* and *perceived* media, between *inner-directed* and *outer-directed*. Effective political communications today is based on recall, of calling forth from within the listener or viewer information that he already knows, which can be triggered by an electronic catalyst.

Each of us is a vast storehouse of information, much of it buried deep in our subconscious, but which can be released by the right code, whether that code is a word or a sound or a few bars of music, an odor, a change in the weather, a special color, the passing glimpse of a person on the street.

Skillful use of electronic media permits us to unlock some of the information we all have, and adapt it to the particular situation we are concerned with. This means you do not have to put as much *into* a television or radio spot if you structure it in such a way as to unleash the emotions and intellectual attitudes already within us.

Some people stumble on this rather sophisticated technique and try to use it negatively: in 1966, George Mahoney won the Democratic nomination for governor of Maryland by campaigning on the slogan "Your home is your castle." And in 1967 Louise Day Hicks worked her way into the runoff for mayor of Boston with the theme "You know where she stands." The citizens of Maryland and Boston saw fit to abort the candidacies of Mr. Mahoney and Mrs. Hicks, respectively, which attests their good sense, but in both cases it was eminently clear to the voters just what these candidates meant, because their slogans, harmless in themselves, triggered emotional responses from their subconscious storehouses.

We're also learning a lot more about radio, including something we're just now accepting: radio has become part of the environment. People don't even realize they are listening to the radio, or how it affects them, or how many minutes or hours a day they spend within listening distance of a tuned-in radio. When we ask voters in a poll, as we often do, a question that goes something like this: "Where would you say you receive the most accurate and honest information about politics and government—from television, from radio, or from newspapers?" radio invariably finishes last. If you ask someone how often he listens to the radio, he often replies that he doesn't listen at all. But if you probe, you'll find that he has a radio in his car, and usually the radio is on when he is driving. Or if it is a housewife she may have the radio on for "background music" while she is doing her chores. And in many offices there is a radio playing quietly all the time.

People may not tune in to radio for special programs, as they once did—no more Amos 'n' Andy or Fibber McGee and Molly or Edgar Bergen and Charlie McCarthy—but radio is so accessible now that we take it for granted. It has become part of the environment. We sit in it, and don't even notice it. (Tony Schwartz tells of the survey in which respondents were asked to list every item they consumed or used up during the day. Everyone mentioned food, water, even shoe leather and gasoline. Hardly anyone mentioned air, because air is there, it's taken for granted, no one pays any attention to it. Tony also tells the story of Father John Culkin of Fordham, a pioneer in communications theory, who says that he doesn't know who discovered the ocean but he's pretty sure it wasn't a fish.)

Not only is radio there and listened to, but there are patterns that can be utilized with extraordinary efficiency by skillful candidates and their media advisers. Radio, for example, is a much better medium than television to zero in on an audience you want to reach with a particular message. Television, with a few exceptions (such as Spanish-language programs in New York) is shooting with a shotgun most of the time, while with radio you can fire a rifle directly at the voters you want to reach. Television does allow some flexibility through buying spots adjacent to programs appealing to specific groups (women's shows in the afternoon, sporting events, Lawrence Welk and other programs that attract an older audience), but the parameters of radio-station listening are defined far more precisely.

Black radio stations, for example, have predominantly black audiences—and any whites who regularly tune in are in rapport with some aspect of the station's programing, perhaps the type of music that is played. All-news radio stations attract the kind of audience that is receptive to the news-style radio spot; that's what they are used to listening to. FM stations that regularly devote all or most of their programing to classical and semiclassical music usually attract a particular type of listener, who is more likely to be better educated, and in a higher income category, than the average voter, although more and more FM stations now are devoting a large share or all of their programing to popular music. Much of FM radio also is stereo now, offering unparalleled opportunities for advanced communications techniques. Rock-n-roll radio stations appeal to younger listeners. Irish, Italian, Polish, and other foreign-language programs obviously are directed to these ethnic groups. And stations that devote most of their music programing to Frank Sinatra, big bands, and the songs popular in the '30s and '40s invariably attract a middle-aged audience.

Radio stations, much more than television stations, command listener loyalty. Viewers flip the channels on their television sets with much greater frequency than they push the buttons or twist the knobs on their radios. When I turn the ignition on in my car, the radio goes on at the same time and is invariably tuned to a favorite FM station. But when my teen-age daughter is with me, she immediately switches over to AM and her favorite rock station.

Armed with some knowledge of listening habits, the clever campaigner can make certain that his messages are beamed specifically at the audience he wants to reach. If he is concerned about registering new voters, for example, to take advantage of the eighteen-year-old voting privilege in federal elections, he's wasting his money if he buys FM radio. But if his message concerns problems relating to rising real-estate taxes, or some cultural project he is advocating, then FM is a superb outlet. FM actually is a separate medium now and should not be considered just another facet of AM radio.

The farm audience is another that can be reached effectively through well-placed radio—something Richard Nixon's media people did effectively in 1968. Farmers are early risers and depend on the radio for essential information: weather, crop and egg prices, other items important for people in their business to know about. A five-minute political speech by a presidential candidate can have impact at six o'clock in the morning, and its audience would be seriously diluted if the same program were aired at 2 P.M.

Radio has another extraordinary advantage over television, and that is the short length of production time. This gets us to McLuhan's theory of "instant information creates involvement." Let me give just two quick examples of how we have used the speed of radio to capitalize on reaching voters while the subject matter was current.

In Alaska in 1970 I attended a hearing at the State Capitol in Juneau on the proposed construction of an arctic highway that would run parallel to the proposed trans-Alaska pipeline. The Republican governor of Alaska, Keith Miller, had proposed that the state use its funds to build the highway. My candidate, Larry Carr, opposed the expenditure of state funds to build the highway, and felt that the oil companies, who would be the primary beneficiaries of the access road, should put up the funds for its construction. At the hearings a member of Miller's staff conceded under questioning that the idea of the state spending its own money for the road had originated with the governor; the oil companies hadn't even asked that the state spend any of its own money for the highway. The meeting broke up about 5 P.M. I drafted a sixty-second radio spot in my hotel room following the meeting and telephoned it to our campaign headquarters in Anchorage, where Walt Davis, a former radio announcer on Carr's staff, recorded it. The commercial was fed to stations throughout the state on a special telephone radio line. The next morning on our way to the airport we heard a news report about the hearing the previous afternoon— *followed immediately by our paid spot outlining Carr's views on the subject.*

The same year, in Massachusetts, the Democratic candidate for governor, Kevin White, felt strongly about a statement made by his opponent late one evening. Again I drafted a commercial and telephoned it to Tony Schwartz in New York, who in turn telephoned it to the announcer we were using in that campaign, Bob Landers, who happened to be in Los Angeles at the time. Landers recorded the message in California, fed it back to Schwartz in New York, where duplicate tapes were made, and within hours they were being delivered to radio stations in Massachusetts.

Radio time can be bought quickly, and if you already are running a radio schedule, as are most candidates late in a campaign, then it's simply a matter of swapping a new spot for one already in the can and ready to run.

Sophisticated candidates are going to use a lot more of this instant radio, and sometimes long before they are officially in a race or their campaign is in full swing. In January 1970, for example, subway fares in New York City were increased from twenty cents to thirty cents. There were no announced candidates for governor at the time, but if any of the potential candidates had capitalized on the event and purchased a modest amount of radio time immediately to state his position *while the news was hot* and people were concerned, he could have begun to build up a rapport with the voters as a champion of their rights even though he wasn't officially a candidate for anything.

The best example I know to show how people become involved through the communication of instant information is not political, but beautifully reveals the concept:

In the spring of 1970 the Apollo 13 mission was aborted en route to the moon. The whole world held its breath while the astronauts reversed course and made it safely home. People on every continent were concerned for their safety—*because they knew about it instantly*. There have been other heroic rescues and returns by explorers, in the arctic and on the seas, but these created little involvement on the part of ordinary people, because it was months or years after the event before they heard about it. In the case of the astronauts, people were involved, in depth, because they were part of what was taking place.

Here is what McLuhan said that caused us to restructure our thinking on radio/television news and spots and begin utilizing his instant-information theory:

"One of the major changes that has come into the world with the electronic environment as a total surround is that instant information creates involvement. Slow movement of information creates detachment. Instant information creates involvement in depth.

"One of the hidden factors in our environment today is this: when you have an instant information structure, you put outside as your environment the human subconscious. We tend to talk about the increase of consciousness during the electric phase, but what is increasing enormously is the subconscious. That is our new environment. The subconscious is the world in which we store everything, not something."

This principle can be adapted to television, as with the telenews concept discussed earlier, but radio has a clear edge in speed and flexibility.

So far, we have concentrated on *paid* electronic media; now let's shift over to unpaid, or uncontrolled, electronic media.

In many respects, this is much trickier and more difficult to handle than paid television or radio. When we produce controlled media, we have the option of using it or not using it; on uncontrolled media—news clips, interviews, debates, talk shows, guest appearances—we have no such control. While it is the campaign director's desire to make his candidate look and sound as good as possible, this concern is by no means shared by television or radio news directors. I'm not implying that these fellows go out of their way to make a candidate look bad; for the most part, they are pretty decent guys who will do what they can to help a candidate, any candidate, on either side, unless the candidate has given them some reason to dislike him. But there are lots of reasons why a candidate might not look as good in a news spot as he does in a paid commercial. Some are very simple and mechanical—equipment, for example. Except for the networks and a handful of major stations across the country, most news departments are understaffed and ill-equipped. There is likely to be a two-man crew: the interviewer, and a cameraman who also doubles as sound man and lighting expert. Obviously the conditions aren't conducive to the highest-quality production, even if everyone is trying to be as helpful as he knows how. (I've seen some stations that send one man out to interview a candidate: he sets him up, lights him, hands him a microphone, tells him the questions he wants answered, and then scurries back to run the camera. Admittedly, most stations aren't this primitive, but some still are.)

Panel interview shows, particularly on a national network level, can be traps for the unwary candidate—although any candidate who attains the level on which he is being interviewed on "Meet the Press," "Face the Nation," or some similar program damn well ought to be able to handle the situation; if he can't, maybe he shouldn't be there. But the panelists on these programs, knowing the competition is fierce, and conscious of making a name or reputation for themselves, are likely to be tough on the candidate (or any other guest, candidate or not). They are better-informed than local newsmen, bone up on the candidate and his positions before the program, and try their hardest to pose difficult or embarrassing questions. More than one candidate has blown his chances for election to high office on programs like these. In 1968 George Romney, the early front-runner for the Republican presidential nomination, wilted in the face of fierce questioning by the press and dropped right out of contention. And, again, maybe that's all right, too; if a candidate can't cope with a group of newsmen, no matter how tough, then maybe he isn't qualified to run the country or his state.

(The classic story of low blows on these programs is about the panelist who stopped a candidate just as they were entering the studio to begin the program to ask him if there was any area he especially did not want to be asked about. The candidate unhesitatingly mentioned one, and bang, you guessed it, that's the first subject raised by his "considerate" interviewer.)

In my campaigns, I insist that the candidate be subjected to a full-scale dry run before going on any difficult interview show. We try to fire at him questions as tough or tougher than he is likely to be asked on the air. If he stumbles, we try to help him work out phrases and decisive answers. Most of the time, in a panel interview program or a televised debate, what the candidates actually say is much less important than the impression they leave in the minds of the viewer. The candidate who answers firmly and decisively, who appears to be in command, whose phraseology is taut and whose composure is cool, usually leaves a good impression. The candidate who bumbles and stumbles, appears unsure of himself, draws his answers out to unbearable lengths, may actually know much more about the subject than his quick-hitting opponent, but will suffer for it. This is a particular difficulty with really well-informed candidates, who know that complex questions require more than simple answers, but, under pressure, aren't allowed to spend sufficient time to develop their answers properly.

The first Kennedy-Nixon debate in 1960 is such a good example that it has been used by almost everyone who has written about these things. Practically everybody who saw the program agrees that Kennedy "won" the debate—but who can tell you today anything that either of the candidates said? Who had which position on Quemoy and Matsu? (And who cares?) It's also been documented that those who heard the program on radio, as contrasted to those who saw it on television, gave Nixon a much higher rating than televiewers. And if you were to read the transcript in the newspapers with the names of each man blacked out, you'd have difficulty telling who said what, and no way of awarding a clear verdict to either man.

While on the subject of debates, the standard rule in our business is that if your man is ahead you try to avoid a debate, and if he is behind you try to get your opponent to engage in one. If you are better known, you dodge debates; if you are not as well known, you issue challenges, because you need the exposure.

I personally would like to see mandatory television debates in all elections for President, senator, and governor, and perhaps congressman as well. For all their faults, debates do have a tendency to bring out a man's character. You always run the risk of committing a mistake, or looking bad (sometimes for reasons totally beyond your control—a tough schedule, a head cold, a family emergency), but it's a risk I think candidates should be willing to take. I think there should be more than one debate—at least two, possibly three. And I think the networks or the local television stations should offer the time free to the candidates. Some now do, but there is no rule saying they have to.

And if my candidate is ahead going into the debate and can't cut the mustard, then he has a problem.

I am notoriously unsympathetic to complaining candidates: no one is drafted to run for office, and if they want the glory of the office then they ought to be able to stand the gaff that goes with winning it.

Even with all these noble ideals of mine, until the rules are changed, if I have a candidate whom I think would do poorly in a debate or who has a lead and has nothing to gain by a debate and much to lose, I'll do everything possible to keep him out of a television debate.

Joe Anastasi, campaign manager for Governor Marvin Mandel of Maryland, was astounded, upon picking up the Baltimore *Sun* one morning, to learn that his candidate had agreed to a series of televised debates with his Republican opponent, Stanley Blair. Mandel had done this unilaterally, without consulting his campaign manager. This may show independence, but it also reveals a lack of understanding of what a campaign manager is supposed to do. If Mandel had determined that he was going to debate even if Anastasi and I and others in his campaign felt it was wrong, that certainly was his privilege. But his campaign manager is the person who should work out the best deal, who should negotiate the arrangements for the debate. And he certainly is entitled to learn about the decision from the candidate and not from the newspapers.

Anastasi, not a man quick to anger, really hit the roof when he learned of Mandel's decision, and I don't blame him a bit. In honesty I must admit that Mandel did a superb job in the debates and eventually won the election by the biggest margin of anyone in Maryland history, and had a higher percentage of the vote than any candidate for governor in 1970 in a contested election. Even so, our polls showed him much better-known than Blair, running far ahead, with a lot more to lose than he had to gain from engaging in a debate.

Bob Squier has a whole routine that he has developed for prepping candidates for their appearances on panel interviews, debates, and other presentations with similar formats. This includes rest periods, eating at a certain time, showering, proper makeup, the right clothing.

Candidates are a strange breed. Sometimes they resist the obvious. I've recited several examples of candidates who failed to properly utilize their own camera crews when they were available. Candidates will concede the importance of television, paid or unpaid, but won't devote the proper amount of time or effort to getting ready. My favorite apocryphal story is about the candidate who is invited to speak to the Rotary club in a city seventy miles from where he lives. He, or someone on his staff, drafts a speech. He goes over the speech with his staff. He drives for an hour and a half to the city where he is to give the speech. He sits through an hour of rubber chicken and civic-club gibberish, then gives his talk to an audience of one hundred people (most of whom already have decided how they're going to vote). As he is leaving the hotel he is collared by a local television newsman who wants to interview him. The newsman asks a difficult question: "What is your plan to end the war in Southeast Asia?" or "How do you think tension between blacks and whites in the United States can be reduced?" and right off the top of his head the candidate answers, and that night 250,000 people see him give his answer on television. He has spent a lot of time preparing a speech and making a trip to reach a handful of voters probably already committed for or against him, and virtually no time at all preparing for an appearance that will be seen by hundreds of thousands of uncommitted voters.

Television producers with whom I have worked have a universal complaint: difficulty obtaining access to the candidate, even though the quality of their product may be what causes him to be elected. There is some magic yet in the personal appeal—being able to see and feel and maybe smell the people you are trying to get to vote for you.

Hubert Humphrey was particularly difficult in this regard in 1968. Our own crews, whom we were paying large sums of money from a skimpy budget, had difficulty getting Humphrey to spend time they needed to do the best possible job for him. I keep reminding candidates that more voters will see them on one prime-time television spot than they can possibly see or meet in person during the entire campaign, but we still meet resistance. Candidates would rather go to a rally of committed voters than spend the afternoon resting or preparing for television. On numerous occasions I've seen candidates rush through a filming session so that they can run out to make a walking tour or address a small group of voters somewhere—and often act as though it is an imposition to ask them to schedule enough time with our own television producers. Milton Shapp in Pennsylvania in 1966 wanted to go on a handshaking tour. I explained that there were only 150 days to the election, that if he shook hands with one thousand different voters every day, a somewhat difficult proposition, he'd succeed in reaching about 3 per cent of the voters who would cast ballots in the election. Kevin White of Boston, a fine candidate in some respects, also found it hard to understand why he should spend so much time with his television people when he could be "out campaigning."

But candidates are becoming more sophisticated. For all the talk of the people-to-people campaign style of Senator Eugene McCarthy in 1968, the fact remains that McCarthy used unstructured and unpaid television very effectively. In the California primary, for example, an important segment of his strategy was to schedule a "television event" every morning. This might be a walk along the beach where he would be mobbed by young people, a visit to the elderly—anything that was visually interesting. In reminiscing about the campaign, one of McCarthy's key operators in the California primary expressed amazement that the press really never caught on to what McCarthy was doing—not that there was anything wrong with it, but it was "organized spontaneity" and not the garden-grown variety.

The television event has become an important part of political scheduling. The ideal time is late morning. The event should have some newsworthiness, it should be accessible to television stations, and it should be visual—i.e., more than the candidate merely giving a speech or reading a statement. By scheduling it in the morning, you give the stations plenty of time to process their film or tape and slot the event in the early-evening news programs. This is a type of unpaid television available to all candidates for major office. Some take greater advantage of the opportunities it offers than others, but this really shouldn't be held against those who do capitalize on their opportunities.

Radio, too, should be used to full advantage. One way is to feed stations tape-recorded messages from the candidate, sometimes two or three times a day. The candidate can record a message and have this message placed on an instrument attached to a telephone. Radio stations can call in, toll-free, and pick the candidate's message off the instrument without the necessity for anyone in campaign headquarters even answering the phone.

It's an easy way to operate, but it puts the initiative on the stations to make the call. Some of the more aggressive and alert stations will call every day, just to see what's on the wire even if they decide not to use it. But these are the same stations that ordinarily would provide good coverage of what a candidate is doing anyway. The lazy or indifferent stations, lax in their news coverage, also fail to take advantage of the prerecorded statements available; they just won't make the effort to call in.

A much more-effective way of accomplishing the same objective, although it takes more work on the part of the campaign staff, is to have someone call each of the stations in the state or in the district every day, or every other day, or to transmit special information they believe will have interest to that station's listening audience.

The staffer will call the station and say something like, "Our candidate spoke to the State Druggists' Association at their annual convention this morning and came out in favor of selling drugs by their generic name. This is a pretty controversial thing for him to do before a group of druggists. We have forty-five seconds of his speech on tape. Would you like to have it?"

Acceptance to offers like this runs between 75 and 90 per cent. Obviously, the message must be newsworthy, or at least interesting. It must be short enough to work into a radio news program. The quality must be professional. Usually in order to obtain this kind of material you must assign to the candidate someone with a quality tape recorder and the ability to use it, and have him follow the candidate wherever he goes, recording his speeches and interviews. If there is no formal speech on the day's schedule, the candidate can read part of that day's press release into the recorder, and this can be transmitted back to headquarters for referral to the stations.

This process puts the initiative on the campaign organization instead of the radio stations, and often stations that simply would not make the effort to call into headquarters to pick up the same message will accept it if the candidate's staff displays enough ingenuity to make the call.

The cost of such an operation is not high, and the potential benefits from it are impressive. Any messages that are picked up by the stations, and a lot of them are, wind up in the station's news programs and often are repeated four or five times before being dropped. This is better time than you can buy on radio, and it's free, except for the expense of making the recording and telephoning it.

The old-style political advance man, whose duties included everything from putting up posters along the candidate's travel route to organizing "spontaneous" demonstrations at his various stops, is being superseded by what we now call media advance. This is a specialized area requiring skills that are, if not more advanced than those of the traditional advance man, certainly different.

As his title implies, the media advance man knows something about the use of media. Often he has had experience in television or radio, sometimes but not always in the news department. Less often he is a former newspaperman, because many ex-reporters tend to be print-oriented and dubious about the real impact of the electronic media, or lack intimate knowledge of how they function. The media advance man's primary assignment is milking the maxi-

mum amount of media exposure out of a candidate's visit to a
certain area.

The theory behind this is simple: more people will see or hear
the candidate on television or radio than he can possibly hope to
see in person.

But obtaining maximum exposure requires some planning. You
might start by taking an inventory of all the television stations in
the area that have programs on which the candidate might be
interviewed, including women's programs that might take him and/or
his wife. Then you try to make arrangements for the candidate to
appear on as many of these programs as possible during his visit.

You find out who the news directors of the television stations are
and make arrangements for an interview either at their station
or in the field. You schedule a television event. If the situation
warrants it, you may schedule a press conference.

You find out where the radio station is and who the news
director or station manager is and trot your candidate around to the
station to shake hands with the staff and be interviewed for a few
minutes, either live or on tape.

You make arrangements with local newspapers for the candidate
to visit the newspaper plant and have a chat with the political
reporter. He might also find time to talk with the publisher and
other editors while he's there, building future credits.

The media advance man is conscious of television/radio schedules
and requirements. A good one, for example, would never schedule
a press conference or a television interview in a room unsuitable
for such an event, or where the power facilities are inadequate for
the equipment. If a videotape remote is involved, for example,
the power requirements can be a real factor.

And the media man is extremely conscious of timing and getting
his tiger to the various stations and offices on time. He makes
certain that all media, print as well as electronic, are provided well
in advance with the candidate's schedule and with other information
they may need. If the candidate is to deliver a formal speech,
he makes certain that copies get to the right people in time.

If a station or a newspaper has a special request ("What is the
candidate's favorite meal when he's at home?" might be an inane
example; or it can be something pertinent to the particular area,
such as the candidate's attitude toward the proposed construction of

a nuclear power plant in the vicinity), then the media advance man makes appropriate arrangements. If a station can interview the candidate only between 3:45 and 4 P.M., the advance man makes certain the candidate is there on time.

He also follows up after the visit, checking to make sure the media people have everything they need. If they have any complaints, he listens to them and tries to resolve them. If thank-you letters are called for, he sees to it that the right member of the candidate's staff knows this and that they are written and mailed. If there are schedule conflicts, he tries to resolve them to his candidate's best advantage. If his candidate is going to be interviewed on a midnight talk show, he arranges for him to have enough sleep before scheduling the following morning.

And he knows if his candidate is a night person or a morning person, when he works best, when he looks and sounds best in interviews. Almost without exception candidates I have worked with perform better late than early. With some you have a difficult time getting them to go to bed—and as much trouble rousing them in the morning. I would add that good candidates have more stamina than most people. They operate on little sleep, and thrive on campaigning.

If the media advance man does his job well, everyone in the area who watches television, listens to the radio, or reads a newspaper is going to know his candidate has been in town. Those who neither watch, listen, nor read probably aren't going to vote either.

Media advance is important for all candidates in major elections, and particularly important for those with limited budgets, because it is an opportunity for them to get on the air free. Again, the opportunities here are available to all; the better the candidate, the more advantage he will take of these opportunities. And he will have the sense to realize that it is better to be interviewed on a women's talk show in the middle of the afternoon than to appear at a coffee hour or a reception for his workers in the local headquarters.

The real pro in the business develops excellent media contacts, so that if a hole suddenly appears on a panel interview or a talk show, the producer will tip him off and he can try to make arrangements to get his candidate, rather than his opposition, in the slot.

And he knows the FCC regulations pat. If a station is giving more time to the opponent, and appears reluctant to put his candidate on, then he can pull out a well-thumbed regulation book, point to the appropriate section, and demand equal time. This isn't recommended procedure, but once in a while you have to do it.

All this takes knowledge of how media operates, proper preparation and planning, and, above all, the co-operation of the candidate. Without that, even the best of the media advance men might as well stay in bed.

It probably is more important for a candidate to be adequately prepared for an uncontrolled media situation than it is for a controlled one.

In a controlled situation you have, as we know, the option of destroying or altering what is made. You have no such option in uncontrolled media. This is where the esoteric specialists come in —people who are experts in lighting or makeup, for example. Imero Fiorentino, acknowledged to be one of the best political lighting experts in the business, gave an interesting demonstration of his art at an early meeting of the American Association of Political Consultants. First he arranged the lighting so that a candidate's eyes were black hollows, his cheeks gaunt, his appearance unpleasant. Then he merely shifted a few lights, placing emphasis in one area instead of another, and the candidate suddenly looked like a movie star. In major campaigns, if there is to be a debate between the candidates, each team brings in its own lighting expert. As with makeup, candidates' requirements differ. And when so many voters make up their minds not on the basis of what a candidate actually says, but the impression he leaves with them while he is saying it, then obviously it is critically important that he look his best while he is on camera.

Makeup is another one of the arts politics has borrowed (rented would be a better word) from the theater. In a presidential election a candidate would no more travel without his makeup man than he would without his press secretary. I think this is fine—except when the candidate forgets who is who and starts taking political advice from his makeup man. The powerful lights of television studios can turn a living, breathing, red-blooded candidate into an instant zombie; makeup is a necessity. And good makeup doesn't show on camera; it just makes the candidate look natural.

One television actor put it this way: "The quality that really counted in acting was honesty, and once I learned to fake that I had it made."

It is an accepted fact in politics that the people who spend the most time with the candidate are the ones who ultimately have the greatest influence on his day-to-day actions and decisions, even if they are far less qualified than the people who stay home and mind the store. That's why you'll find a dichotomy of attitude in presidential elections between the coterie of workers who travel with the candidate and those who stay home and run operations out of headquarters. The travelers assume that they are the ones really running the campaign, while those at headquarters believe they are making the major decisions and the gadabouts who spend their time wandering around the country like gypsies are too close to the candidate to get an accurate overview of the campaign.

Another illustration concerns a former governor who shall remain nameless because I don't want to needlessly embarrass him. During his campaign for re-election he used to assemble his key advisers to discuss positions he should take on major issues or problems that were arising in the campaign. His driver sat in on these meetings, to be handy when the governor needed to leave. Invariably, after he had received inputs and ideas from the best political minds he could assemble about him, the governor would turn to his driver and say, "Well, what do you think, Eddie?" Often he accepted Eddie's advice over that suggested by others who were more knowledgeable. His campaign manager confided to me that he really didn't mind the governor asking his driver for ideas, "but I get the sinking feeling that he gives more weight to *his* opinion than he does to ours."

In Los Angeles, on the day before the 1968 presidential election, when Humphrey was soaring dramatically in the polls and for the first time looked as though he might catch Nixon at the wire, a national magazine editor told Bob Squier that if Humphrey actually won, it was the last campaign to which he was going to assign reporters to travel with the candidate. "If Humphrey wins," he said, "from now on my guys will stay home and watch television in their living rooms, because that's where the campaign is really won or lost."

He was right, of course, even though no national publication is likely to forgo the quadrennial presidential excursion. What the candidate was saying on the stump was not nearly so important as what was filtering through to the voter on his living-room screen. If a candidate delivered five powerful thirty-minute speeches on a hectic day of campaigning, the ninety seconds that were culled from one of them and shown on NBC or CBS that evening was all that 99.9 per cent of the voters had an opportunity to see, and they naturally had to draw their conclusions from what they saw. To show how television so often replaces reality, let me quote a few sentences from *An American Melodrama,* the excellent book about the 1968 presidential election written by three British journalists, Lewis Chester, Godfrey Hodgson, and Bruce Page, in which they describe the arrival of Robert Kennedy's body at the airport in New York following his assassination: "When Kennedy's body was brought back to New York from Los Angeles, one of us was at the airport to see it arrive. Standing with a group of reporters, he noted that they almost all watched the event on a specially rigged television screen. The actual coffin was passing behind their backs scarcely any further away than the small-screen version." Thus when even seasoned newspaper reporters had an equal opportunity to watch the real event or a television version of it, they chose to watch television—and let some anonymous director and cameramen decide what they were going to see.

I've never counted the minutes and seconds, but it was my clear impression, and maybe this is merely subjective recall, that for several weeks during the 1968 presidential campaign more time on television news was given to those who were heckling Hubert Humphrey than to what Humphrey actually was saying. I'm not criticizing the networks for this; they played the news as they saw it, and if it appeared to them that what the hecklers had to say was more important than what a candidate for President had to say, it was their privilege to devote their time to it.

But this brings back into focus the dangers of depending upon uncontrolled television to get your message across, and the necessity of using paid, controlled television to reveal the points *you* feel are important.

Whether you are producing paid television or helping your candidate appear his best on uncontrolled television, the producer or producers you select can be decisive. Some producers do some things better than others, and a skillful campaign manager or media adviser knows who can do what the best, and can utilize him for that purpose.

If I wanted a remote videotape production—that is, a videotaped sequence shot on location rather than in a studio—I'd be more inclined to go with Bill Wilson of Saturn Pictures in New York than most other producers. In the Humphrey campaign, among other segments that Wilson handled were an effective spot package, including a five-minute program, with Senator Edward M. Kennedy and Humphrey strolling through the grounds at Kennedy's home in Virginia, and another section used in the election-eve telethon of Kennedy and Democratic National Chairman Larry O'Brien discussing the presidential election in front of Robert Kennedy's home at the Kennedy compound in Hyannisport.

Bob Squier is great at television coaching, preparing candidates for uncontrolled television appearances on talk shows and panel interviews, and at organizing telethons.

Charles Guggenheim is fine for longer films and spots in which the candidate appears in natural settings talking with real people, particularly if you are trying to strike an emotional appeal. And, as I have noted, Guggenheim is superb at the half-hour documentary when you can get him to make one.

Fine half-hour documentaries now are being produced by Dick Heffron and Bert Decker at Medion in San Francisco. The best half-hour film done in 1970 was, I believe, the one they produced for Jack Danforth in Missouri. Titled *The Uphill Run,* it very nearly catapulted young Danforth into an upset victory over veteran Senator Stuart Symington. As it was, Danforth came within a percentage point of upending Symington, and this film had a great deal to do with it. They also did a good one for Governor John Burns in Hawaii that year, *To Catch a Wave,* directed by Eli Bleich. An unusual feature of the Burns film is that it is the only half-hour political documentary I have seen that does not have a line of narration; the film carries itself completely, which is an incredible accomplishment. If I wanted to use a highly structured videotaped spot, I'd hire Hal Tulchin of New York to produce it.

Pierre Vacho and Art Fillmore, film editor and cameraman, respectively, are partners in Confluence Films, in St. Louis, the successor company to Shelby Storck & Co. They do excellent work.

One way to help candidates look and sound their best in uncontrolled television is to prepare a list of twenty-five to thirty questions they are asked most frequently, define crisp and coherent answers to these questions, and urge the candidates to become so familiar with both that they can snap off the answer whenever the question is posed. This has several advantages. For one thing, it makes the candidate look better if he delivers sharp, concise answers to tough questions. For another, it helps assure that he will give the same answer to the same question whenever it is asked. In most campaigns the nuances of an answer may not mean much, but in a major campaign that is well covered by the press, even a slightly different approach will be seized upon immediately and the candidate asked to explain the apparent contradiction in what he said on September 15 in Topeka and on October 15 in Tacoma. Candidates often fail to realize the usefulness of this technique, and while they are quick to accept it in theory when it is proposed, often they simply fail to follow through—to define and memorize standard answers to standard questions—and late in a campaign still bumble their way through the same questions they were asked at the press conference announcing their candidacy.

The time buyer plays a crucial role in ever major campaign. A time buyer is simply the person who negotiates for and purchases the television and radio time for your candidate (and often newspaper space as well). Sounds like a reasonably simple job—but it can make the difference between winning and losing an election.

I'd go so far as to say that if Ruth Jones of New York had been buying time for Hubert Humphrey instead of Richard Nixon in 1968, Humphrey would have been elected president, or at least the race would have gone into the House of Representatives.

In an earlier chapter I mentioned that the agency we used to buy Humphrey's time in 1968 returned several hundred thousand dollars to Democratic national treasurer Robert Short after the election. Someone like Ruth Jones would never have allowed this much money to remain unspent, and the judicious injection of fifty or a hundred thousand dollars in certain states might well have made the difference.

But let me not dwell on presidential elections, because for every election for President there are literally a thousand elections for senator, governor, congressman, and mayor of large cities. What constitutes a good political time buyer in these campaigns?

High on the list I would put an understanding of the FCC regulations that govern the requirements of stations to candidates and candidates to stations. A good time buyer learns how to use whatever muscle is at his command to force stations to fulfill their regulatory obligations. Hopefully, this won't often be necessary, because in politics as in fables, honey draws more flies than vinegar. But no matter how sweet and charming my time buyer may be, I need the reassurance that he or she is thoroughly familiar with the rules and will make damned certain they are enforced if need be.

A knowledge of the market is essential. Much of this information can come from the rate card and the published ratings and audience count, but sometimes good political sense is demanded. Take a program that draws 2 per cent of the audience in New York City in midafternoon. Doesn't sound like much of a buy, does it? But if that program happens to be a Spanish-language movie, and you just happen to have handy a couple of commercials in Spanish aimed at the Puerto Rican voter in New York, that 2 per cent of the audience represents one hell of a good political investment, because they're identifiable voters and you can shoot your message straight at them.

The ability to interpret demographics and relate these to the thrust of the campaign is important. This calls for the selection of spots and programs to be run in areas and at times when the voters they were produced to appeal to are most likely to be watching or listening. Sometimes this doesn't take much skill: for instance, running farmer appeals early in the morning on rural radio stations, or messages aimed at women around soap operas. But often a great deal more skill, which is a marriage of intelligence and experience, is required. And when you are spending up to five thousand dollars for a single spot on one station in one state, or sixty thousand dollars for a prime-time minute on network, the placement of these spots can be critical.

Tony Schwartz had an interesting comment about Ruth Jones:

"She's the only political time buyer I've worked with who ever took the time to come to my studio and listen to our spots before we put them on a reel to send out, so that she would get the feel of what we were trying to say and be able to most effectively place the right spots on the right stations at the right times."

Seems like an obvious step, but I suspect there are time buyers in advertising agencies who may never even bother to listen to or watch the radio and television spots they are placing on behalf of an agency's political client.

An independent time buyer can often save a political candidate a pretty good chunk of money. Ordinarily, advertising agencies receive a 15 per cent commission for placing time. In one campaign I was involved in in 1970, we paid an independent time buyer a flat fee of twenty thousand dollars to buy time. Had we gone through the agency with the amount of time buys allocated in our budget, the commissions would have been forty-five thousand dollars. That's a twenty-five-thousand-dollar savings for the campaign, with the money either pumped back into other areas of the campaign or used to buy additional television and radio time.

I suspect that more and more sophisticated candidates will use independent time buyers in order to improve the quality and decrease the net cost of their buys. Several independent time-buying agencies have been formed around the country in recent years, and many of them offer superior service at lower fees than a candidate is charged by an agency.

There are two other areas of electronic campaigning that deserve attention here: computers and telephones.

When computer technology was first introduced to politics a few years ago there were fears that it would be a sinister influence on the electoral process. Computers are about as sinister as electric typewriters, and with cost of usage dropping regularly, eventually will be used in campaigns as much as electric typewriters are.

Computers can do one thing: work fast. They can't really do anything that can't be done by hand, or through mechanical processes. But they do these things so much quicker, and with so much greater accuracy, that, properly used, their importance is incalculable.

As Bagdikian says, they are amoral. We only get out of them what we put into them, or, as the saying goes, GIGO: garbage in, garbage out.

But there are areas of politics where computers can be of tremendous assistance, especially in states where voter registration lists already are on computer tape or disc. Computers are superb instruments for selecting precoded names they have previously ingested. In direct-mail campaigns, computers can speed the process fantastically and churn out what appear to be individualized letters to voters, substituting and rearranging paragraphs according to their programmed instructions.

In the Alaska primary in 1970 Mike Rowan devised a series of six letters with different possible paragraphs for a direct-mail campaign to native villages that do not receive television. The six basic letters and variable paragraphs permitted a package of thirty-six different letters to be sent to natives—and in villages where voters are wont to exchange and compare letters, it was important that the letters be at least slightly different. This effort had measurable impact in the remote villages of Alaska.

Computers allow us to introduce nice, homey touches into your direct-mail campaign—such as repeating the name of the recipient in the third or fourth paragraph, to make it appear that the letter is personal and not mass-produced. They can print out walking lists for election-day workers, identifying, through a previous canvass, voters most likely to vote for a specific candidate. This can maximize an election-day operation by identifying likely support and making it easy for campaign workers to find the people whose votes they feel they have and making certain that they get to the polls.

Sometimes lists can be purchased already on computer tape or disc, or which can be transferred to tape or disc. For example, if a candidate has a position on no-fault automobile insurance, and he wants to get this message to all automobile owners, and he can obtain a list of vehicle registrations in his state, a computer letter can be directed to these voters, perhaps with a different paragraph or two for voters who own trucks or sports cars or who live in a high-risk section of the state.

Computers are used extensively for fund-raising appeals in political campaigns. Both the Democratic and the Republican national committees maintain full-time computerized fund-raising operations. The Republicans got the jump on the Democrats here, and still use computers more effectively.

As a matter of fact, Republican campaign consultants were a step ahead of Democratic consultants in introducing and utilizing computers, although I believe the gap is narrowing, if it hasn't disappeared entirely.

Computerized campaigns can be especially effective in areas where voters are not easily accessible through the mass electronic media—television and radio. A Congressional race in Manhattan, for example, is an excellent place to use computerized mailings, because television and radio are too dear for that kind of campaign.

Some consultants specialize in the use of computers for organization purposes, just as others are more inclined to specialize in television and radio. Matt Reese, out of West Virginia and now based in Washington, and by everyone's standards the biggest man in politics (physically, at least), is one of the good computer-oriented professionals.

In the fantasy world of future politics, much has been written and many fears voiced over the threats posed by computer simulation. In theory, what this means is that you establish a model on a computer supposedly representative of the voting attitudes and habits of the constituency, and by feeding into the computer various positions advocated by your candidate, you will be able to tell how voters will react. In theory, this is fine. But in actual practice there are some real drawbacks, two in particular: time and money. It takes months to establish a satisfactory model, and the cost of creating the model and using it effectively often is more than the entire proposed campaign budget.

Eventually, at least in national elections, both the major parties will try simulation, but it is too expensive to use on a state level for any but the most affluent candidates, and still in its developmental stage. And in computer usage, as in television or radio or any other form of politics, money may help but it is no guarantee of success. Most observers concede that the best computers operation ever established by a political candidate was Winthrop Rockefeller's in Arkansas, and it helped him get elected governor a couple of times. But it didn't save him from being trounced by Dale Bumpers in the 1970 election.

If we've got to the fourth or fifth grade in our knowledge of how to use television in politics, we're still in kindergarten, or possibly the first grade, when it comes to computers. And I wouldn't look for any great political upheaval as the result of computer technology in the foreseeable future.

Telephones have been used in political campaigns ever since they became an integral part of the American household. In recent years, some refinements have been added, notably the use of tape-recorded messages, either by the candidate or by someone speaking in the candidate's behalf. Through electronic devices, messages can be dialed quickly into selected homes throughout the district or the state, sometimes through the use of WATS (Wide Area Telecommunications Service) lines. A WATS line enables you, for a flat monthly fee, to make as many long-distance telephone calls as you wish within a certain area without paying toll charges.

The cost usually is somewhere between five or six cents a call—fairly high for reaching voters.

I have mixed feelings about these devices. In selected instances, I can see their value. A candidate who is not well known, for example, might benefit enormously if a well-known and highly respected political figure—a senator or the governor, perhaps—cut a tape endorsing the candidate and urging the person receiving the telephone message to vote for the candidate. Again, you have some flexibility, which is helpful. A Spanish-speaking candidate or endorser might have some impact in Puerto Rican or Mexican-American areas, a well-known black some influence delivering tape-recorded messages to black voters. Or the candidate himself may have some influence via a tape-recorded telephone call.

Ordinarily, what you must do is balance the cost of the telephone operation against all the other ways you can spend money in a political campaign, and determine if the return is likely to be equal to or greater than the impact you can obtain through spending the money some other way. Occasionally the answer is yes; more often it is no.

There is a great deal of fear about the use of electronics in politics. I believe this fear is founded on fiction rather than fact.

The dirtiest politics practiced in America is not to be found in major campaigns where candidates are exposed and revealed to the public through television and radio, but in small-town and small-city elections where the voters never have an opportunity to see or hear the candidates, where cigar-smoking, big-bellied pols in the back room still literally name the candidates and get them elected to office through often-corrupt political machinery.

This kind of stuff won't work in major campaigns any more. Television is making it possible for candidates to speak directly to the people, and maybe, eventually, through the use of cable television, the people will be able to speak back.

Before television, candidates often found that the only way they could communicate what they had to say to voters was through the party organization. My preference is for candidates to talk directly to the people who are going to vote for them, without any filter between them and the voter.

It's no coincidence that party organization and machine politics entered their death stage with the advent of electronic campaigning, and I for one think this is good, not bad.

4

POLLS AND POLITICAL POWER

———

THERE IS ONLY ONE good reason to take a political poll: to help win an election. If a poll won't do that, it's not worth taking.

Political polls—particularly private political polls, as distinguished from published polls—are much misunderstood, even by politicians.

The published polls—Gallup and Harris nationally, Field and others within specific states—fulfill a useful function: they provide the electorate with some idea of who is ahead at a specific point in time, they provide some basis on which to gauge the popularity of a President and his potential challengers, they give some general information on attitudes toward major problems.

As tools in winning elections, they are useless.

Whatever value they may have is negative. (Of course, the person running against the candidate suffering from negative reaction to a published poll may benefit, but this is accidental.)

Former Senator Charles Goodell of New York no doubt disagrees with me, because he feels that the published polls, particularly that of the New York *Daily News*, which showed him running a poor third in a three-man Senate race, caused his defeat. I don't buy it. Polls measure how people intend to vote, or say they intend to vote, at a particular point in time. For every campaign in which the front-runner supposedly benefited from a published poll showing him ahead, I can cite an example of a candidate who failed to benefit from this so-called bandwagon effect. At the same time that Goodell was running third in published polls, he also was running third in private polls. His problem was that he was one of two liberals running against a conservative in a state where considerably more than half the voters called themselves moderates or conservatives.

As a matter of fact, I know that James Buckley decided to run in New York in 1970 because a private poll showed that two thirds of the voters who put a liberal/moderate/conservative label on themselves considered themselves to be either moderate or conservative in their political beliefs.

This kind of reservoir was a rich fishing ground for a good candidate, who was beautifully managed by F. Clifton White, a skilled professional.

A poll put Buckley into that race—a private poll. And no matter how much Goodell protests, I seriously doubt that the published polls drastically affected the outcome of that election, certainly not by enough to change the outcome.

Nevertheless, published polls can hurt a candidate. In the 1968 presidential election, the published polls hit Hubert Humphrey where it really hurts: in the pocketbook. The September and early October polls that showed Nixon ten to fifteen points ahead dried up Humphrey's money.

But when Humphrey was able to borrow enough money to launch his media campaign, his showing in the polls improved, money came in, and he was able to run a respectable media campaign for the final three weeks of the campaign.

Again, the polls only reflected what people thought; they didn't influence anyone. If they had, Nixon would have won in a landslide. Some of the early polls and prognostications based on those polls showed Humphrey might not even beat George Wallace— either in the popular vote or in the electoral college. As it turned out, the switch of thirty-six thousand votes in three small states, or the switch of one large state, would have thrown the race into the House and probably pushed Humphrey into the presidency.

Some people say this is merely because as Election Day drew near, voters reverted to traditional voting patterns: Democrats returned to the fold. Not true.

If it were, then why didn't Republicans return to the fold in

1964, when Lyndon Johnson's lead over Barry Goldwater held up from April through November? Because Johnson ran a tough, aggressive campaign and Goldwater never recovered from the early mistakes that had caused him to fall so low in the first place. (Agreed, a simplification: Considering the environment of the 1964 election, on the heels of the Kennedy assassination, I see no way that Goldwater could have won—but he could have made it a lot closer than he did.)

The kinds of polls that are of most concern to the professionals in this business are the private, unpublished polls. Some candidates and managers use these better than others; some don't even know how to use them.

I have always felt that opposing candidates could save a lot of money by using the same pollster, provided he is competent and honest (and most of the good ones are). What's in the poll doesn't mean much; what you do with what is in the poll means a hell of a lot.

In 1962, I was handling Endicott Peabody's campaign for governor of Massachusetts against the incumbent, Republican John Volpe.

A poll we took three weeks before the election revealed these two bits of useful information:

–Voters over sixty years of age, regardless of their political affiliation, strongly favored the Medicare plan that had been proposed by President Kennedy. Peabody was in favor of Medicare, Volpe had—gratuitously, and one might say stupidly—spoken out against it. (Volpe made his anti-Medicare remarks in a speech in Oregon, apparently unaware of communications facilities that allowed it to filter back to Massachusetts.)

–The Democratic candidate, Peabody, was getting a much smaller percentage of the labor-affiliated vote than a Democrat in Massachusetts could expect, particularly since Peabody favored most of the things labor was going after in that election and Volpe was opposed to most of them.

Using this information, we did two things:

First, we prepared a simple fold-over brochure with a cover photograph of a sweet little old lady who looked like anybody's idealized grandmother. The brochure message was simple: Endicott Peabody is in favor of President Kennedy's Medicare program;

Governor Volpe is opposed to President Kennedy's Medicare program. Nothing could be simpler—or more effective. We mailed this brochure to every voter in Massachusetts over sixty years of age. (Fortunately for us, Massachusetts has something it calls a police census, which lists each year every resident's name, address, and age.)

Second, we called labor leaders to a meeting, showed them the results of the poll, and asked them if they would distribute a brochure to their members explaining why they were supporting Peabody over Volpe. They agreed. We prepared the brochure, a big thing with a white-on-blue cover that proclaimed, "Labor Supports Peabody Because Peabody Supports Labor."

Inside, we listed eleven positions labor had taken in the campaign, and the positions Peabody and Volpe had taken on each. Peabody agreed with labor on ten and disagreed on one; Volpe agreed with labor on one and disagreed on ten. (The one in each case was different.) We printed a quarter of a million of these brochures and turned them over to various unions, whose members distributed them to workers at factory gates in the week preceding the election.

The result? Peabody upset Volpe by 5431 votes out of more than 2.1 million votes cast—the only time in the past twelve years that a Democrat won the gubernatorial election in Massachusetts.

With such a slender margin, it appears certain (at least to me) that these two pieces, which came straight from the poll, had enough impact to make the difference.

In 1968 I was retained by Lennen & Newell/Pacific to help them in their campaign to re-elect John Burns governor of Hawaii. This was no easy task, because Burns was seeking his fourth term, and the mortality rate of fourth-term governors is roughly equivalent to the life expectancy of an ice-cream cone in the Sahara at high noon.

Burns was older, less attractive, and less articulate than his opponent, Lieutenant Governor Thomas Gill. And besides all that, the first poll taken for him by Lennen & Newell showed him sixteen points down.

Fortunately, the poll was taken early—in December 1969 for a primary that took place on October 5, 1970—so we had time to act.

What the poll showed to us, basically, was that voters in Hawaii weren't really aware of John Burns's accomplishments as governor. There's a reason for this: Hawaii has a highly mobile population, and many of the people who were voting there in 1970 had been attending grammar school in Michigan or Minnesota or South Dakota when John Burns was first elected governor.

Armed with this knowledge, we plotted a media campaign designed to acquaint voters with Burns's accomplishments. We knew that Burns was personally not very popular at this time, so in our first wave of television and radio spots we concentrated on selling his accomplishments and pretty much ignored him. (This technique was not original; it has been used by candidates before, perhaps most successfully by Nelson Rockefeller in his 1966 re-election campaign in New York.)

Lennen & Newell, which did a superb job with Burns's media, devised a three-phase media program that was labeled in house "the Plan, the Man and the Plan, and the Man."

Our first wave of television/radio spots, shown in two spurts, hit early—they went on the air in March. We concentrated on half a dozen accomplishments of the Burns administration: schools, environmental protection, parks, housing, etc.

None of the spots asked voters to vote for Burns, nor did the governor appear in any of the spots. They were strictly issues-oriented, factual, and unemotional. All carried the tag line "Think about it."

Burns began appearing in the second wave of spots—sometimes in still photographs, sometimes in film clips. I don't believe he said a word in any of these spots, but they showed him in a variety of lifelike situations—with his grandchildren, on a construction site, at a housing fair.

Both these waves were produced in Hawaii by Lennen & Newell. While the second wave was hitting the air, the final spurt was being prepared by a different producer, Medion, of San Francisco. Medion's job was to sell John Burns the man.

We were getting some static by then from the opposition about how we were "hiding" the governor and not letting him speak or appear for more than a few seconds in any of our spots. It is the kind of criticism that can be damaging if nothing is done about it. We weren't concerned, though, because we knew that our final burst of television material would be *all* on John Burns the individual. Medion produced a package of spots and an excellent thirty-minute documentary film.

In the meantime we were polling steadily: a second depth poll, plus a series of weekly polls in Oahu, which contains approximately 80 per cent of Hawaii's population, and the neighbor islands as well. These weekly polls were by telephone, conducted by volunteers under the direction of a talented eighteen-year-old staff member, Rick Egged. By the closing weeks of the campaign we were interviewing something like two thousand voters every weekend.

These weekly polls allowed us to measure the impact of our media, and other events in the campaign over which we had no control—such as Gill's media, and various acts of government. One example: Burns, a devout Catholic, allowed a liberal abortion bill to become law in Hawaii even though expressing personal opposition to it.

Thus we were able to tell exactly what was and what was not having an impact. By September Burns had closed the gap to three or four points. When the documentary hit, along with our final wave of Burns-the-man spots, he pushed ahead in the polls, and actually got about 54 per cent of the vote—some of it through an excellent organization that complemented the media splendidly and pulled out all of the potential Burns vote.

Media structure and organization in the Burns campaign in Hawaii in 1970 was skillfully plotted and planned, the lessons of the polls were absorbed and utilized, and the quality of production was superb. Four weeks after the primary Burns ran over his Republican opponent, Sam King, and was re-elected for a fourth four-year term.

In another campaign in 1970, the first poll was so bad the candidate didn't even show it to his campaign staff, which, I think, is a debatable decision. He showed them the issues material but not the vote. Maybe his reasoning wasn't all that bad; the candidate was Frank Licht, governor of Rhode Island, and our first poll showed him trailing the Republican candidate, Attorney General Herbert DeSimone, by a horrendous twenty-nine points: 48 per cent for DeSimone to 19 per cent for Licht.

Not only that, but this was the first time we had ever taken a poll for an incumbent governor in which the candidate received a net negative rating. Make no mistake: Frank Licht was not a popular man in Rhode Island in the spring of 1970.

If we had been taking the poll only to find out who was ahead, or to attempt to predict the outcome of the election, the only sensible decision would have been to withdraw or concede. But Frank Licht, one of the most intelligent candidates I have ever worked for, wasn't about to give up.

And one thing the poll isolated was the fact that there was only one major issue in Rhode Island in 1970: taxes.

Licht (pronounced Leech—and if you don't think that's not an obstacle in a campaign, try it sometime) had scored a stunning upset in the 1968 gubernatorial election over Republican incumbent John H. Chafee. He had been the Democratic nominee primarily because most people in the party had felt that Chafee was unbeatable, and they hadn't wanted to serve as the sacrificial lamb. Well, Licht is no lamb, and he became a lion who bit Chafee's head off.

Chafee had got into trouble because he'd proposed a state income tax, something the state really needed, but campaigning *for* a tax usually is a form of political hara-kiri, and Chafee had greatly assisted in his own demise. Licht had capitalized on the opposition to the income tax and promised that if he were elected there would be no state income tax.

He'd won, and he'd imposed no income tax—but he *had* created something called an investment tax, which had the twin failings of not producing enough revenue to meet state needs and getting everybody in the state upset, even people who didn't have to pay the tax. Basically, this was a tax on interest from savings, and while a lot of people didn't have to pay it, almost everyone had to fill out some onerous forms several times a year.

By isolating the resentment against the tax as THE issue in the campaign, Licht could zero in, run a one-issue campaign, and barely squeak by. I don't know if DeSimone was polling or not, but if he was, he certainly didn't make as effective use of his poll information as Licht did. It's pretty hard to blow a twenty-nine-point lead, but DeSimone managed it.

DeSimone tried to tread so lightly with his own proposals that he was subject to a strong counterattack by Licht, who raised doubts in the minds of voters about what DeSimone would do if he were elected, where his tax revenue would come from.

The election wasn't decided until the absentee ballots were counted, and then Licht emerged the winner by fewer than fifteen hundred votes.

Early in 1971, however, Licht succumbed to the inevitable and introduced a state income tax. If Licht had had to run on February 5, 1971, instead of November 5, 1970, he would have been buried. But he did what needed doing for the state, even though it may well put him out of office in 1972.

Defining the message the candidate should communicate to voters is critical to the success of the campaign. This is where a poll is invaluable.

I personally would no more try to run a campaign without adequate polls than I would try to sail the Atlantic without a compass. And this is not to say that a candidate should examine the results of the poll, see what the voters want, and then go out and promise them that. It's not so simple.

Ordinarily a candidate will have ten or fifteen ideas for programs. This is too many to effectively utilize in a campaign. To use so many dilutes the message of the candidate and causes some confusion in the minds of voters.

It is much better to narrow the issues on which you wish to campaign to a manageable number, say four or five, and concentrate on those. A poll can help a candidate establish a list of priorities. If he is contemplating fifteen issues, and the poll shows that voters strongly favor five, accept another five, and are cool toward the remaining five, then it takes no special genius to recognize that the five the voters favor are the ones the candidate should emphasize.

Sometimes a candidate learns that an issue he favors is opposed by the voters. We never tell a candidate to change his principles as the result of a poll—but we often suggest that he de-emphasize one position and put greater emphasis on another.

For example, in the fall of 1966 we did a poll for a freshman congressman who had gone into office during the Johnson landslide in 1964. Two years later his position on bombing North Vietnam was considerably at odds with the President's—and, as it turned out, with that of his constituents. He favored an immediate cessation of bombing; the voters in his district did not. We didn't tell him to change his position on the theory of there-go-the-people-and-I-must-follow-them-because-I-am-their-leader, but suggested he concentrate on other issues in the campaign, which the poll also has revealed. We told him that if anyone asked him a direct question on his position on bombing, he should tell the questioner the truth, that he was in favor of an immediate bombing halt.

That's different from unilaterally making a bombing halt the big issue. If he had made bombing a big issue, he probably would have lost; as it was, he squeezed by while forty-odd of his colleagues elected in 1964 were going down the drain.

And there's an old saying in politics that you can't be a good congressman unless you *are* a congressman. He played the bombing issue effectively, survived to fight another day, and has been a consistent supporter of peace movements in the Congress since then. Had he not pulled in his wings early in the campaign, the chances are he would have lost, and his Republican opponent that year took a much harder line on the war than he did.

In Pennsylvania in 1966 Milton Shapp was in favor of increasing the minimum age to get a driver's license from 16 to 18, and also was in favor of lowering the voting age from 21 to 18. We polled, and found that a high percentage of voters agreed with his idea of increasing the minimum age for drivers, but disagreed with lowering the voting age. (This is another case of an idea whose time had not arrived.) So in our campaign materials that year we emphasized his position on driving licenses, ignored his feeling about lowering the voting age.

Whenever he was asked a direct question on lowering the voting age, he always replied that he was in favor of giving eighteen-year-olds the vote, but we didn't publicize this in the material we were turning out.

Sometimes polls can be used to keep candidates out of a race. In Maryland in the spring of 1970 there was a lot of talk about former ambassador and ex-Peace Corps head Sargent Shriver running for governor against incumbent Marvin Mandel.

Interestingly, our earliest poll showed Mandel running ahead of Shriver by a substantial margin—but we realized how misleading this could be. Shriver is an attractive and articulate person. The brother-in-law of President Kennedy, he had access to large sums of campaign funds. Physically he is much handsomer than Mandel.

But Shriver had two immediate disadvantages: he wasn't very well known in Maryland, although he had maintained a home there for years, and he had no political power base. Few political figures in Maryland leaned his way, and, for some reason inexplicable to me, Shriver appeared determined to court their favor instead of plunging headlong into the race and defiantly crying that he would let the people decide.

My feeling, as a consultant to Mandel as well as his pollster, was that we probably could take Shriver if he decided to run, but that it would cost a lot more money than Mandel had planned to spend in his campaign to do so.

Utilizing these facts and intuitions, we did a few useful things:

First, we leaked pertinent sections of the poll to political figures in Maryland (including Shriver). The poll was accurate; we didn't juggle any figures around. Nor did we bother explaining that we felt that Shriver would inevitably improve as he became better known.

Political leaders who might have had some doubts about Mandel's ability to win a primary or general election were impressed. (Mandel had become governor through his selection by the Maryland legislature. He had been speaker of the Maryland House when Spiro Agnew became Vice-President. At that time, Maryland had no lieutenant governor, and the constitution provided that the legislature would select a governor. Mandel, a veteran legislator, won this contest easily, but he had never been in a statewide election.) Mandel's contacts with political figures in Maryland were much better than Shriver's, and, armed with a poll showing him running well ahead of Shriver, he had little difficulty persuading them to pledge to him.

Wherever Shriver turned, he found his way blocked by politicians who promised him all kinds of support if he would run for congressman or senator or something else—but not for governor.

Another thing we did was go on the air with a very early media campaign—a campaign aimed not at the million-plus voters in Maryland, but at one man, Sargent Shriver. The whole thrust of the campaign was to convince Shriver that Mandel had popular as well as political support.

The spots, created by Bob Squier on television and Tony Schwartz on radio, emphasized the endorsement of ordinary voters around the state who spoke in glowing terms about Mandel. These were real, not faked, and did reflect Mandel's support.

Shriver eventually decided not to run, and, for all practical purposes, the Maryland election was over on the day that filing closed. Mandel's fifty thousand dollar investment in an early media campaign probably saved him a quarter of a million or more that he would have had to spend if Shriver had decided to run, and also got him some favorable early statewide exposure.

As it was, Mandel coasted through the primary with token opposition, and in the general election received a higher percentage of votes than any other candidate for governor in 1970 except George Wallace, who was virtually unopposed in the general election in Alabama. Much of the credit for Mandel's victory must go to his staff, particularly his campaign manager, Joe Anastasi, and his press secretary, Frank DeFilippo, a former prize-winning political reporter.

In that same election in Maryland, Senator Joseph Tydings and his staff apparently misread or misinterpreted his polls, because some of his moves late in the campaign were contrary to what we had expected, based on the information contained in our polls.

We measured Tydings' strength in our polls for Mandel, and although he consistently ran ahead, by much smaller margins than Mandel, the warning flags were up. Up but not heeded, because Tydings, after a mid-campaign period of concern, apparently thought he had the election won, and wound up losing by nineteen thousand votes.

Tydings was hit hard at the end by his opponent on his gun-control proposals—proposals I happen to agree with entirely—and for a *Life* magazine article that cast doubt on his ethics, but these were eminently predictable issues that should have been anticipated and headed off.

Running a campaign without a poll is like trying to find your way through a strange country without a road map. Very often what politicians think people are thinking is quite different than what the people actually are thinking. Politicians—and here I am including almost everyone in this business—have a bad habit of talking to the same people all the time. They may have one hundred conversations in a week, probably five conversations each with twenty different people, or maybe twenty conversations each with five different people. I remember sitting in a campaign office in Philadelphia one day discussing the reaction of the black community to a proposal we were planning to make. We discussed it for an hour, with as many different views as there were people present.

Suddenly I looked around the room and realized that everyone was white, and more than half of them didn't even live in Philadelphia.

"Hey," I said, "what the hell are we doing? In three days we can take a poll in the black wards and find out exactly what the reaction is, with a pretty good idea that we'll be right."

We did—and the results were different from what most of the experts present thought they would be.

While sometimes polls serve a useful purpose if they no more than substantiate views already held, sometimes the views uncovered are quite different from what campaign directors and candidates think they will be. Sometimes when this happens the polls are disbelieved, or the pollster is accused of taking a bad poll.

In 1970 we took an attitudes survey in a northeastern city for an election not to take place until 1971. But in the course of taking the poll we measured a state-senate race currently being waged. Our poll showed the Republican running pretty close to the Democrat in a couple of heavily Democratic wards.

"There's something wrong with that," said the Democratic city chairman. "We can't be doing that badly in those wards. There must be something wrong with the poll." Three weeks later the Republican candidate scored a major upset in the state-senate contest.

If a poll shows a result completely at variance with what a campaign manager believes the situation should be, the best thing to do is go right back into the area with the same or a different pollster, probably with a broad rather than a deep survey, and check the initial results.

This happened to us once in North Carolina, when we were commissioned by one of the South's astute political minds, Bert Bennett, to take a poll for Richardson Preyer, then a candidate for the Democratic nomination for governor. The Preyer people were in a hurry for the results, and I spent a Saturday afternoon putting together figures and, finally, getting on the phone to Bennett.

"Bert," I said, "I'm afraid you've got some troubles. Our figures show that Preyer is going to lose."

"Joe, that just can't be," Bennett said. He was particularly surprised because in a three-man race our figures showed the man considered to be running a poor third to be neck and neck with Preyer, with the man supposed to be second far down the scale.

"I'll tell you what, Bert," I said, "I'm willing to admit that you know a lot more about North Carolina politics than I'll ever know, but I've checked our polling people and they tell me that these are the results they found. Here's what I'll do: You pick out two or three counties and write down on a piece of paper what you think the vote ought to be in those counties. I'll go in at my own expense and repoll the counties, just asking the vote and demographic questions. If the results are different from what we show statewide, I'll do the whole damned thing over again and won't charge you a penny."

He made out his list, we did our interviews, and his list was wrong. Preyer, really a sweet guy, was not pulling the way his supporters had thought he would.

One reason, perhaps, is that his opponent acted like one of "us folks," while Preyer, a graduate of Princeton and Harvard Law, and a former federal judge, seemed a little distant to the voters. And, needless to say, there are more of "us folks" in North Carolina than there are Harvard-Princeton graduates, so Preyer lost.

Fortunately for North Carolina, and the country if I may say so, Preyer subsequently was elected to Congress from the Greensboro district, where he is an eloquent spokesman for his area. (He also has one of the finest collections of jazz records of anyone I know, but that's revealing a side of the congressman/judge/Harvard-Princeton man that few voters ever get to see.)

We're learning how to use polls better every year. We've come a long way from when polls were a head count indicating who was ahead in an election. But there's a balance to be drawn: It's possible to make polls so complex, so involved, so detailed, so cumbersome that they can't be used effectively by the people who have to use them. I don't have a lot of sympathy for academic pollsters who do the survey, turn over a voluminous report, and disappear. As I've noted, the poll doesn't mean a damned thing; what means something is how you are able to make use of the information in the poll report. And if the report is so fat, and the key facts hidden or unnoticed, or not called to the attention of the reader, then there has been a communications breakdown that could negate the value of the whole poll.

In most of the campaigns in which I serve as consultant, my firm also does the polling. This is not true all the time, and I never make it a condition of my being hired; on the contrary, I tell prospective clients that I don't really care who takes the poll, so long as it is a competent pollster, but it is essential that someone take a poll before I'll agree to get involved. And, of course, we take polls in many campaigns in which we have no other involvement. There are ten or twelve good polling firms around that I know of (there may well be more that I don't know of) and in whose ability to take a proper political poll I would have confidence. And there are a couple, including some of the well-publicized ones, that I have doubts about—not because the principals aren't competent, but because they have taken on so much business that the questionnaire and interpretations are done by people of little experience.

A political poll is a living, pulsing document—if it is used right. My pet irritation is the candidate or campaign manager who commissions a poll, get the results, and locks the report in the bottom left-hand drawer of his desk, pulling it out occasionally to surreptitiously show a cigar-chomping crony—but never giving the results to his radio and television producers or his advertising agency or his field men. Sheer stupidity may be a cliché, but that's the description that fits this kind of behavior.

Dr. Walter DeVries, of the University of Michigan, who unfortunately works only for Republicans, is the best academic pollster I know. He long served as a consultant to Market Opinion Research, of Detroit, a competent firm. Walter, perhaps befitting his academic background, always comes up with interesting reasons for what affects voter behavior, but that makes a whole new book and it's his, so I'd better let him tell it.

But I don't give away any secrets when I report that DeVries believes he has isolated the variables, at least in a specific Michigan campaign, that influence voters.

In his postelection survey following the 1970 gubernatorial election in Michigan, DeVries prepared this chart of factors that influence undecided voters:

RELATIVE IMPORTANCE OF FACTORS THAT INFLUENCE THE VOTING DECISIONS OF 1970 GUBERNATORIAL UNDECIDEDS. (May 1970: n=809)

Very Important (5.0 & over)	Important (3.0–4.9)	Not Important (1.0–2.9)
Television newscasts	Talks with friends	* Magazine advertisements
Television documentaries and specials	Radio talk shows	Television entertainers
Newspaper editorials	Magazine editorials	* Billboards
Newspaper stories	* Talks with political-party workers	* Telephone campaign messages
Television editorials	Talks with work associates	Movies
Television talk shows	Radio editorials	Stage plays
Television educational programs	* Political brochures	Phonograph records
Talks with family	Talks with neighbors	
Radio educational programs	Magazine stories	
Radio newscasts	* Newspaper advertisements	
The Democratic party	The Republican party	
* Contacts with candidates	* Television advertisements	
	Books	
	* Political mailings	
	Membership in religious organizations	
	Membership in professional or business organizations	
	* Radio advertisements	

* Can be controlled by candidate.

Notice that only one of the factors that undecided voters listed as "very important" in helping them make their decision, can be controlled by the candidate, and most of the other factors they listed as "important" or "not important" are not under the candidate's control.

We must remember that these are what undecided voters *say* influence their thinking. Voters may well not be able to distinguish precisely what causes them to settle on one candidate or another because of the media mix and total surround of the environment late in a campaign, but it is nevertheless interesting to have their views, and their views are certainly as accurate a measurement as we now have. I do disagree with DeVries' contention that all these factors are beyond the candidate's control. A candidate can control, or at least influence, his appearances on the news, for example: He can influence news stories, talk shows, attitude of the party, word of mouth, editorials, and stories. He may not have *absolute* control over these media, but he certainly can have some influence on their effect.

We've been experimenting with various questions to try to find out what we can about the effects of media in a campaign. Some things we already know: poor people, and those with little education, tend to watch television a lot more than wealthier, professional, or better-educated voters. So messages aimed at the poor and under-educated are best conveyed through television; weighty messages are better transmitted through newspaper ads and other printed materials.

In almost all our polls we take a measurement to try to determine where people *think* they get most of their information about politics and government. Usually, but, interestingly, not always, television leads. In some states, or some sections of states, newspapers run ahead of television, and in these areas the poll information can serve as a time-and-space placement guide for our advertising agency.

We also fool around once in a while with questions like this, the brainchild of Michael Rowan: "After you have seen a thirty-minute film about a political candidate, what would you like to *feel* about that candidate?"

Maybe it's a clumsy and awkward question—but the results are astounding: almost without exception, what people want to *feel* about a candidate is that he is *honest and cares about their problems.*

Not that he has the same opinion about issues that they do, or the same stands on controversial positions, but that he is honest and he cares. Issues, as a matter of fact, score very low on polls, even when the question is asked differently. For example, we'll often ask a question something like this:

"Which do you think is the more important quality for a candidate to have—that his position on the major issues is similar to yours, or that he is an honest man who can cope with situations as they arise?"

The results here are overwhelming: invariably voters prefer an honest man who can cope with situations to a candidate whose position on the issues is the same as theirs, and usually by a margin of four or five to one. This kind of information can be dynamite in the hands of a campaign director or media chief, because then he knows that he doesn't have to worry so much about emphasizing his candidate's position, and can concentrate on emphasizing his character.

Mayor Kevin White of Boston said it well in a televised interview utilized as a spot in his 1970 campaign for governor of Massachusetts: "It would be great if they handed you a check list of problems, and after you were elected you could go down the list bing-bing-bing and take care of all the problems. But that's not what happens. I had no way of knowing that two months after I took office as mayor of Boston, that the biggest problem I would face would be getting fuel oil into the city to keep the people warm. That's not the kind of thing you can anticipate. What you need in office is a man who can cope with situations as they arise, situations that no one even thought of."

People vote for people (or against people) and not for issues. (Perhaps the best example of this was the New Hampshire presidential primary of 1968, when a postprimary survey revealed that half the voters who voted for Senator Eugene McCarthy had no idea of his position on the war in Vietnam, and many people thought he was a hawk. This is a clear case of people voting for a man, not his ideas, although his ideas were what attracted national publicity and attention.) In Marvin Mandel's gubernatorial campaign in Maryland in 1970, we tested voter reaction to his stand on a controversial abortion bill. An earlier poll had showed that a majority of the voters favored the bill, but Mandel, for a variety of reasons, vetoed it anyway. Later in the campaign, in another poll, we asked voters if they agreed or disagreed with Mandel's veto of the bill. Most of them disagreed. But we followed up by asking those who disagreed, a question that went like this: "Despite the fact that you disagree with Governor Mandel's veto of the abortion bill, do you think you might vote for him anyway?"

About 70 per cent said yes, 15 per cent said no, and 15 per cent were undecided. By cross-checking we found that most of the 15 per cent who said no, probably wouldn't have voted for Mandel under any circumstances.

With these results in hand, we relaxed about the abortion question and just ignored it the rest of the way.

The demographic and geographic breakdowns of poll responses can be invaluable to media strategists. If an issue can be isolated that has particular appeal to blacks, or to young people, or to old people, for example, then it is possible to zero in on the appropriate group.

Blacks can be reached through black radio stations and newspapers, or by circularizing black neighborhoods. Young people are accessible through spot adjacencies in rock-and-roll radio stations or programs. You can hit the elderly by mail or by buying television time next to the Lawrence Welk show or other television programs with a particular appeal to the elderly. You also can determine if a local announcer would be more effective than a national announcer in various states, or even regions within states.

Knowing what a specific demographic group is particularly interested in can be of tremendous value to a radio/television producer and time buyer. Not all candidates take full advantage of this yet; more of them will as time goes by.

Geographic breakdowns are equally important and useful. Issues that appeal to city dwellers may have no interest to voters in suburbia or upstate media markets. Clearly the fare rise in New York subways isn't of much concern to the voter in Fort Plain, New York. This may be too obvious an example to need substantiation in a poll, but there are others more subtle, and the geographic breakdowns in a poll, particularly when melded with the demographic constituency of a geographic area, are valuable inputs to media producers and time buyers.

Polls also can be utilized for negative campaigns. For example, if your candidate's opponent has come out with a handful of issues,

and testing reveals that two or three of these are decidedly un-
popular with voters, then a campaign can be directed against the
opponent on those issues.

But, let me repeat, information in the polls isn't any good unless
you put it to use. An example: In Massachusetts in 1970 one of
Mayor Kevin White's chief aides, Charles Ryan, urged from early
spring that White come out in favor of off-track betting as a revenue-
producing measure in Massachusetts. White opposed the idea, and
one of the reasons he opposed it was because he felt that Massachusetts' heavily Catholic constituency would be against legalized
betting.

We polled in the spring—and found that more than 70 per cent
of the voters favored off-track betting. White still didn't want to act.

We polled again in the fall, after White had won the primary.
Same results—and in both cases the percentage of Catholic voters
favoring off-track betting was *higher* than that of non-Catholic
voters.

White continued to resist the idea, while at the same time groping
for a "big issue" that would add some life to his campaign.

Finally, with less than a week left, White decided to go with the
off-track betting proposal. It received immediate favorable response, and virtually no criticism. But because we used it so late,
we weren't able to properly orchestrate the issue or obtain maximum
value from it. We could do a newspaper ad and a radio spot, but
it was too late to use it effectively on television, or to effectively
use supporting statements from district attorneys and other law-
enforcement officials who had expressed a willingness to speak out
favorably on the issue.

The idea was good but the timing was bad. I'm not saying that
White would have won the election if he had come out sooner for
off-track betting, but this kind of procrastination was typical of a
campaign that was lost, and conceivably could have been won.

Polls also can be of great help in structuring a media budget.
In the Ohio Senate primary in 1970, for example, we found that John
Glenn was known by virtually everyone in the state, whereas his
opponent, and our client, Howard Metzenbaum, was known by very
few. This meant that Metzenbaum's first job was getting people
to know who he was. Glenn didn't have this problem, yet spent a
barrel of money on billboards, whose primary purpose is name

identification—and than ran short of money for television late in the campaign.

Polls, incidentally, can be used effectively outside the United States as well as within the country. In our efforts to re-elect President Ferdinand Marcos in the Philippines in 1969, we polled extensively. I would write the questionnaires, they would be translated into Tagalog and other dialects, field work would be done by a Filipino market-research firm and the results processed in Manila, and then I would help interpret the results and make political recommendations on the findings. We employed the same procedure in a European election.

In some countries, England, for example, political polling is in an advanced stage, although I would have to disagree decisively with Humphrey Taylor, managing director of Opinion Research Centre, London, who at the 1970 conference of the International Association of Political Consultants said he felt that political polls in Great Britain were far advanced over those in the United States. There are good polling firms in Great Britain, but my observations lead me to believe that political polling in the United States is more advanced and more widely used than in England. The Conservative party did use polls effectively in 1970, and the Labour party did not, and this was one of the reasons for the Conservatives' great upset victory.

Curiously, the British publicly resist advances in political techniques, such as polling, and then quietly use them. When I first began talking with representatives of British political parties about polls, for example, in the spring of 1963, I was told by a representative of the Conservative party that they considered private polls "unethical" and would not use them. Apparently they have changed their minds.

It may be of some interest to some readers to know how most political polls are taken in the United States. First of all, virtually all private polling firms that work nationally use the same interviewers. None of us can afford to keep a national staff of interviewers on the payroll, just waiting for someone to hire us. The *public* pollsters, Gallup and Harris for instance, can and do maintain permanent staffs, because they know they will be polling regularly on a national basis.

But it would be senseless for me, or any other pollster, to maintain a staff of interviewers in, say, Wyoming, in the hopes that someday someone would retain us to do a poll there. What all of us do is work through interviewing-supervisors in the various states, who provide the bodies to do the physical interviews. Nor is it practical to fly a stable of interviewers around the country, because this would add considerably to the cost of the poll.

These interviewers are mostly housewives, many with college educations, who don't want or need a full-time job, but who like to work occasionally and find poll-interviewing interesting; for some reason, a high percentage of interviewers, particularly in the Northeast, are Jewish. Most pollsters structure their questionnaires so that very little subjective interpretation of response is required by the interviewer, even on open-ended questions, and all provide interviewers with detailed instructions on how questions should be asked.

Coding and data processing usually are done at the headquarters of the firm. Some pollsters send their results to a computer service center for tabulating; others, myself included, prefer to use our own in-house data-processing equipment, because this allows us complete control and tighter security over poll results, and also permits us to make special runs quickly if we need a cross tabulation or a quick count on a specific question.

The real keys to useful political polls are the questionnaire and interpretation of the results. A faulty questionnaire is going to produce a faulty poll. Misinterpretation of the poll data can send the candidate's campaign off in the wrong direction, or ignore potential gold mines of votes because the pollster fails to recognize the significance of certain data. This is why, on campaigns in which we are involved but not retained as pollsters, we insist upon seeing the questionnaire before it goes into the field, having some input into the questionnaire, and then analyzing the poll data after they have been tabulated. All pollsters have slightly differing styles or ways of asking questions, and this is not to criticize those whose methods are different from mine. But most pollsters don't have to do anything with the results after they are obtained, whereas people like me, who are in the business of running campaigns or counseling candidates as well as taking polls, must put the poll results to work, and consequently have a deeper interest in the form of the questions and responses.

A Congressional-district poll should cost $3000 to $4500; a statewide poll $7500 to $12,500, depending upon the state. There really are three factors that affect the cost of a poll: the length and complexity of the questionnaire, the number of interviews, and the geographic area under consideration. Sometimes the geographic area is a problem because it is so spread out, such as in some of our western states, and sometimes because it is so compact: Manhattan, for example, is one of the most difficult areas for a pollster to take a good reading of, because almost everyone lives in an apartment building and is rightfully hesitant about letting strangers prowl the halls knocking on doors. This often means standing in front of the apartment building trying to corral residents as they leave or enter, or, as an alternative, trying to do depth interviewing by telephone.

Black and Puerto Rican enclaves also are difficult to poll. White interviewers resist going into black neighborhoods—and black voters resist speaking freely to white interviewers. So, obviously, you try to use black interviewers in black neighborhoods and Spanish-speaking interviewers in Puerto Rican neighborhoods.

For years I have been attempting to get the Democratic National Committee to encourage independent pollsters and Democratic committees and candidates throughout the country to standardize certain questions and demographic breakdowns on all polls, and to provide the answers to these questions, with breakdowns, to the National Committee for analysis. This would give the National Committee a constant reading on voter attitudes toward national issues and presidential candidates, at little or no cost, and if the questions and breakdowns were standardized, the committee would be comparing apples with apples instead of apples with oranges.

We made some progress toward this goal in the Humphrey campaign in 1968, and I would hope that further strides will be made in the 1972 campaign.

Incidentally, the *private* polls taken for Humphrey in 1968 were a great deal more accurate than the public polls. My firm, for example, polled six states for Humphrey—Massachusetts, Pennsylvania, New York, New Jersey, Ohio, and Connecticut. Our polls showed we would win Massachusetts, Pennsylvania, New York, Connecticut, and New Jersey, and lose Ohio.

We won Massachusetts, New York, Pennsylvania and Connecticut, and lost New Jersey and Ohio, which means we were right on five out of six.

But while we were showing Humphrey, accurately, winning three big states and a small one, the only one the national press was awarding to Humphrey was Massachusetts, and we were accused, among other things, of faking polls, something I have never done and which I don't believe any other good pollster does either.

Private polls taken for Humphrey by other polling firms also showed him much stronger than the public polls or media commentators made him. It came as no great surprise to us that Humphrey did as well as he did, even if the results were astounding to some who were using the public polls and national press as a guide.

One reason for this, of course, is that when you poll an individual state for a presidential candidate, you take almost as many interviews within that state as the national public pollsters do in the nation, so consequently the margin of error is significantly reduced.

Most political polls are face to face, and we have found this to be the best method, by far, in depth polling, although some pollsters concentrate effectively on telephone polls and claim that their results are equally satisfactory. I personally have found telephone polls to be most effective for quick reactions. Perhaps the best example, in my own experience, of how telephone polls can be used for quick reaction occurred in Massachusetts in 1962. Edward M. Kennedy was contesting Edward McCormack for the Democratic nomination for United States Senate. Kennedy was barely old enough to be elected to the Senate, and there was a fair amount of resistance to his candidacy.

He and McCormack engaged in a televised statewide debate late in the campaign. A few minutes after the debate ended, my telephone rang, and Larry O'Brien, then Director of Congressional Relations for President Kennedy, was on the other end.

"The President wants a reading on what people thought of the debate," O'Brien said.

"Fine," I replied. "When does he need it?"

"By five o'clock tomorrow afternoon."

Using a brief questionnaire and a lot of long-distance telephone calls, we obtained the reaction (which showed that most people thought Kennedy had won the debate) and delivered the results to the President by phone on schedule. This would have been impossible to do with personal interviews on that short notice.

While we don't like to use volunteers for depth studies—a frequent suggestion by campaign managers who want to cut costs—we find that volunteers can be used effectively for quick interviews to determine trends. Often we will establish a procedure for volunteers to poll either house to house, at shopping centers, or by telephone, on a periodic basis: biweekly, weekly, even daily late in a campaign.

These polls are useful in determining movement among the candidates, and to measure how different variables in a campaign are affecting the vote—things such as the start of a media campaign, or a major non-controlled issue such as a scandal, or news of a major increase in unemployment rates, something of similar import.

No one would base his campaign strategy on polls like these, but they are helpful in determining trends that can be acted upon.

Polls are here to stay in political campaigns, and they will continue to improve, but I don't think there is any danger of pollsters controlling campaigns or having any nefarious influence on our process of elections.

Polls merely measure voter attitudes. The use campaign directors and candidates make of that information is what is important. A library full of scholarly books doesn't make an educated man if he doesn't read them and act on what he has learned. And that's true of polls, too.

5

HOW I APPROACH A CAMPAIGN

EVERY POLITICAL MANAGER or consultant approaches a campaign differently. There is no right or wrong way to run campaigns, although most of the better managers and consultants I know tend to follow some basic guidelines determined by their experience and their tendencies: media or organization.

You start with the candidate (unless you are involved in a non-candidate election, such as a referendum or a bond issue; but let's stick to electing candidates, because these elections are more fun).

How do I get candidates? Mostly by waiting for the telephone to ring. We don't solicit business, for some pretty good reasons:

- –When you start seeking candidates you relegate yourself to the same level as ambulance-chasing lawyers and hucksters.
- –If a candidate comes to you, he usually has done some prior investigation and at least *he* feels you can work together.
- –When the candidate makes the approach, he is more likely to listen to what you have to say. And this is really the important part.

While I have managed a lot of campaigns, I now confine myself to political counseling and polling. You can manage effectively only one campaign at a time; you can consult in several simultaneously. The biggest mistake most consultants make, particularly those starting in business, is that they try to work on too many campaigns at the same time, thus spreading themselves too thin, doing a poorer job for their candidates and thus diminishing their reputation.

About the only thing that would induce me to go back to managing campaigns is a clear shot at running a campaign for President, and even then I would be hesitant. To manage a campaign in a major election means giving up a year of your life for a candidate, and I don't have that many years left. (And in the long run I really don't care an awful lot who is elected governor of Arkansas or senator from South Carolina—at least not enough to give up a year of my life in his behalf.) Managing a campaign is a full-time, twenty-four-hours-a-day, seven-days-a-week job. Counseling takes considerably less time, although it does involve an extraordinary amount of travel.

As I noted in the chapter on political consultants, I work only for Democrats I like. Contrary to the thinking of many people, the fee involved is secondary, and sometimes irrelevant. I charge reasonably high fees, but, I think, deliver value for what I charge, and so do other consultants who are any good at all. Often I hire other consultants, in specialized areas, whose fees are higher than mine, but I don't quarrel with this.

The first meeting with the candidate can be very revealing. Usually some of his advisers, friends, or members of his family also are present. Sometimes there is a great deal of skepticism about the value of the kind of work we do, and if we encounter this attitude we usually have a short, polite, and final meeting. There is no point in my getting involved in a campaign if the candidate or his close advisers have doubts about what contribution I can make to the campaign. Life is too short, and there are too many candidates around who will be easier to work with.

Sometimes you run into situations in which the candidate and his people may be lovely individuals, but simply don't follow your advice. The thing to do then is to leave, and I do. In 1970, for example, I was retained by Howard Samuels to help him in his quest for the Democratic nomination for governor of New York. I like Howard Samuels; I consider him a good friend. But I was supposed to be directing his media, and he simply wasn't following my advice. So I explained to his campaign manager, an intelligent and likable young man named Ken Auletta, that it was senseless for me to remain with the campaign: they were paying me a fee for advice that they weren't taking, and my name was linked with a campaign in which I really was having no influence. There was no point in their continuing to pay me for advice they weren't using, and I didn't want my name used in a campaign in which I really didn't have the authority to do what I wanted to do. So we parted, amicably, and maintained our friendship. Ironically, soon after I left the campaign, Samuels began implementing some of the suggestions I had made, and in the end ran an extremely effective campaign that permitted him to come within forty-four thousand votes of defeating the heavily favored Arthur Goldberg in the primary.

Goldberg has to be one of the poorest candidates who ever came down the pike. I don't know if Samuels could have beaten Rockefeller in 1970, but I do know that he would have given him a much tougher race than Goldberg did. Goldberg's selection as "the" candidate by political leaders in New York maintained the Democratic party's tradition there of putting up some extraordinarily inept candidates for governor and senator, which is one reason why the Democratic party hasn't won an election for senator or governor in New York in twenty years, with the single exception of Robert F. Kennedy, and I guess we all agree his was a special case—and he wasn't exactly the darling of the party leaders in New York when he announced his intention of seeking the nomination for senator in 1964.

After I have had a meeting or two with the candidate, and believe I can help him, and like him and his ideas well enough to get involved, I send him a letter outlining what I think I can do for him and how much it will cost. We don't quibble over fees; we set a fee, and the candidate accepts it or rejects it. And we seldom have written contracts. I am willing to trust my own judgment in making an agreement with a candidate, and if I don't think I can trust the candidate I can't imagine how I can get the voters to believe that they should trust him.

Sometimes you have good candidates shot out from under you through no fault of their own. In 1970 I was involved with two different candidates for governor of California, neither of whom eventually made the run. The first was Martin Stone, young and energetic chairman of Monogram Industries, who early in 1969 was seriously considering a bid for the Democratic nomination. Stone is the kind of candidate I prefer to work with: bright, innovative, knowledgeable about modern campaign techniques, willing to try new methods, surrounded by good staff people, attractive, articulate.

The fact that he wasn't well known statewide didn't bother me a bit. He, fortunately, had the resources to become well known, and with today's mass-communications techniques it's possible to make an unknown a household word, to use the Vice-President's phrase, in something like seventy-two hours if you really want to. Stone had a lot of things going for him. One of the agreeable facts of his life (to me, anyway) was that he used to spend his free afternoons during the spring and summer pitching batting practice for the Los Angeles Dodgers. What does this have to do with a man's ability to be governor? Absolutely nothing; I just liked the idea.

But the third-quarter earnings report of Monogram Industries in 1969 was substantially poorer than the third-quarter earnings report in 1968, and Stone felt that his first obligation was to the stockholders in his company, and he decided to postpone, at least temporarily, his desire to seek high public office.

Within a week or ten days I was contacted by a representative of Mayor Joseph Alioto of San Francisco, another contender for the Democratic nomination for governor, and one with immediate visibility and identifiable posture. Alioto presented a special and interesting challenge: *Look* magazine had published an article about him implying he was linked to the Mafia, a charge Alioto vociferously denies, and which caused him to bring a lawsuit against *Look,* which has not been resolved at the time of this writing. Alioto is a formidable candidate: extremely intelligent, articulate, with a natural power base. I believe we could have overcome the liabilities of the *Look* article, but early in 1970 a newspaper story broke accusing him of kicking back part of his fee on a law case in the state of Washington to the attorney general of the state, John O'Connell. Legally, I am convinced there was nothing wrong or unethical in what Alioto did; he says he'd have no difficulty explaining the transaction to a group of lawyers or judges. But to the public it looked bad—especially coming on top of the *Look* charges. Alioto might have been able to survive one of the charges or the other; the two together was too much, and our poll showed he had lost credibility with the voters. Reluctantly but wisely, I think, Alioto withdrew, leaving the field to Jesse Unruh, who became the

Democratic nominee against incumbent Ronald Reagan. (Fortunately, I had an opportunity to help Alioto in his campaign for reelection as mayor of San Francisco in 1971. His campaign manager was Sanford Weiner of San Francisco, a top-flight pro, and I assisted by taking a poll and providing some counseling, especially on media. Our first poll showed Alioto ahead by only two percentage points, but an effective campaign helped him win easily.)

I was disappointed in Unruh's campaign. He deserved a better fate, and I really think there was a possibility of defeating Reagan in California in 1970. Later, after the election, at a seminar sponsored by the American Association of Political Consultants, I heard Unruh's campaign manager explain their strategy, and I was astounded; I just couldn't believe that they believed the kind of campaign he was outlining would have upset Reagan. Again, I have no way of knowing if I or anyone else could have helped Unruh win, and hindsight is beautiful, but let's just say that if I had been doing Unruh's campaign in 1970 we certainly would have done a lot of things differently, and I'm willing to stake my life (or at least my reputation) that we'd have made a better showing.

We try to get to know our candidates as well as possible. This means spending time with them in social as well as political situations. Sometimes a lot of this time seems like wasted effort, but what it really accomplishes is to establish a feeling of mutual liking, respect, and trust. The better a candidate knows me, the more likely he is to accept my ideas without reservation. I'm getting too old to fight candidates who resist ideas. I don't mind their questioning or even rejecting them with good reason, but if a candidate consistently resists the advice he is paying to receive, I'll either leave the campaign, if I consider it serious enough, or else shrug my shoulders and let him go his own way.

Times are changing, though. In my early days as a consultant I was invariably told when I went into a new state:

—"You might get away with that in New York, but it won't work here." (Unless of course, you were in New York, where they would say, "You might get away with that in California, but it won't work here.")

—"But we've *always* done it this way." (A pretty good reason for trying something new.)

Usually, the closer I become to the candidate the more I can help him. One of the best campaigns I've ever handled, very early in my career, was for district attorney in the western district of Massachusetts. My candidate, who is one of my closest friends, was Matthew Ryan, and we were faced with a nine-man primary. One of the jobs of a manager or a consultant is to innovate, to capitalize, to turn apparent liabilities into assets. During that primary, in the early fall of 1958, the Springfield newspapers had a blackout on political news. They apparently wanted some outrageous change in a tax bill that would have brought them enormous benefits, and when neither Senator Leverett Saltonstall nor Senator John F. Kennedy nor Congressman Edward P. Boland would intervene, they reacted childishly and declared that henceforth there would be no political statements carried in either the morning or the evening newspaper, which were the only papers in town. Hardly a realistic or mature approach, but that's what they did and it's on the record.

You don't have a lot of money to spend in a primary for DA in the western part of Massachusetts, so you try to use a little ingenuity. A thought struck me one night at home; I called Ryan and he agreed to try it.

The next morning I telephoned the advertising department of the newspapers and asked if there were any restriction on the style of type we could use in an ad. There was a puzzled silence, and I was told no, none at all.

"Fine," I replied. "I want to reserve a full page for next Sunday." (Two days before the primary.)

"Okay."

"Now tell me the deadline for getting the copy in for the Sunday ad."

"Noon on Friday."

"Right."

Having been a reporter and makeup editor on those newspapers, I was familar with the type and headline styles of the *Sunday Republican*. So I promptly proceeded to write and asemble a full page of copy, photographs, even a cartoon. The package was delivered to the newspaper at ten minutes to twelve on Friday. The page looked just like any other page in the *Republican* that Sunday— except that every item was about Matthew Ryan, including a lead article with the headline RYAN RATED BEST-QUALIFIED CANDIDATE FOR DISTRICT ATTORNEY.

We had the legal disclaimer, of course—in small type at the top of the page—and a legal signature in the lower right-hand corner. You might have to look hard to find them, but they were there.

This might have worked all right even if the papers were carrying political news, but with the political blackout that had been in force, the full page about Matty Ryan struck like a bombshell. A harassed advertising executive called me at my home on Sunday noon to tell me that by eleven o'clock Sunday morning he had received calls from every one of the other eight candidates or their managers, and from most of the executives on the newspaper. The next day the paper passed a rule banning type styles in advertisements similar to those used in their news columns.

On Tuesday Ryan won the primary by sixteen hundred votes, was elected district attorney two months later, and has served ever since without opposition in either primary or general elections.

Here, again, every candidate had the same opportunity to utilize an existing situation, and most of them did run full-page ads that Sunday, but none had the impact ours did. (I don't always get the bright ideas; I've had people on the other side in other elections come up with equally effective concepts that have helped torpedo or seriously bruise my candidate.)

I'm not suggesting that candidates should always blindly follow my suggestions, or those of any consultant. But if a candidate consistently resists trying something new, or utilizing recently developed techniques, then this probably is reflective of his whole campaign and his attitude toward the election.

When anyone in my business comes up with a new idea, it's usually good for one go-around before it is picked up and absorbed by other astute candidates and consultants. That's why we always are looking for something new, something that will give us a competitive edge.

In 1970 we experimented with something I call the "spurt technique." Political time buying on television and radio follows a traditional curve; you usually start about three weeks before the election and build up to a heavy concentration the final week. We've even evolved a reasonable formula: spend one sixth of your money the third week before the election, two sixths the second week, three sixths the final week. It works okay, and we still use it where appropriate.

The problem with this is that you are on the air at the same time everyone else is, and if you are involved on behalf of a gubernatorial candidate in a state that also has a Senate election that year, then you have at least four statewide candidates competing for prime time. If it's a presidential year as well, add two more. Plus an occasional candidate for congressman or for another statewide office such as lieutenant governor or attorney general or state treasurer, and the airways get pretty cluttered.

So we played around in 1970, and with some success, with going on much earlier in the campaign than we might otherwise have done, at a time when we had the airwaves to ourselves. Usually we'd go on for a week of television followed by a week of radio, or maybe leave a gap of a week between the television and the radio spurts. In some cases we kept this up through the summer, in others we went on with a heavy spurt and stayed off until the full-blown media campaign was about to begin.

This technique worked particularly well for Governor John Burns in Hawaii and Governor Marvin Mandel in Maryland, who had differing but equally serious problems early in the year. Burns's problem was that people had forgotten his accomplishments as governor and consequently his polls showed him running sixteen points behind the challenger, his own lieutenant governor, in the primary. In Mandel's case he needed to show popular support to keep a potentially tough opponent, Sargent Shriver, out of the race. In both cases the early spurts did what they were supposed to do, and the candidates won.

We also used early spurts for Larry Carr in Alaska and Kevin White in Massachusetts, with less effect. The spurts, I'm sure, weren't the causes of their defeats, but neither were they able to prevent them.

Tony Schwartz has suggested an idea that makes good sense and which we use when we can persuade the candidate to go along: the one-minute speech.

Schwartz's theory is that if a candidate is giving a speech that will be covered by television, and he speaks only for one minute, that's the minute television will have to use. If a candidate speaks for fifteen minutes or half an hour, the stations still may use one minute of his speech—but it will be one minute that *they* select, and it may not be the same minute that we'd like to have broadcast. In fact, it might show him in an uncomplimentary pose, or saying something reasonably controversial that could be yanked out of context or was on a subject unrelated to the main thrust of his talk that day or came at a moment when he was being heckled.

Candidates often resist the idea of the one-minute speech, possibly because they like to hear themselves talk more than the audience does. Some quickly grasp the idea, however, and use it for maximum effectiveness. In April 1971 a black candidate we were helping, George Russell, announced his candidacy for mayor of Baltimore. We had impressed on Russell the fact that the news at his announcement *was* the announcement—that's what we wanted to get out of the press conference, the fact that City Solicitor George Russell was announcing his candidacy for mayor. Mike Rowan prepared a speech that took Russell exactly two minutes and fourteen seconds to deliver.

Then he called for questions. The press, surprised and a little off guard, asked only three. There was a brief pause, and Russell's campaign co-ordinator, Francis Knott, promptly and astutely declared the press conference over.

Television, radio, and newspapers gave Russell excellent coverage —and on our terms. The stations used almost all of his announcement, and we succeeded in delivering precisely the message we wanted to get across.

There's no reason why this technique must be limited to announcements. It can work whenever a candidate makes a statement or delivers a speech before an audience—and how many participants at political dinners wouldn't be tickled to death to have a candidate speak for a minute instead of an hour? He might win the election just out of gratitude.

The candidate can be surrounded by other people who can say nice things about him and talk about his positions. But the candidate's statement should be short, so that, when it is reported, only what he wants conveyed will be in the message he delivers. In effect, this is pre-editing. Pierre LaPorte, later the victim of a kidnap-murder by Quebec separatists, used this technique with extraordinary effectiveness in announcing his candidacy for premier of the province in 1969.

We prefer that a candidate never face a press conference or an open meeting unless he has had a tough dry run ahead of time. He should know the issues and his positions cold, and seldom if ever get caught unawares. If he has difficulty with an unanticipated question at one meeting, there's no excuse for his being unprepared to answer the same or a similar question crisply and authoritatively at the next meeting. Being a candidate involves a lot of homework, and the good ones do it.

Another thing we try to do in a campaign is find the candidate's natural base of power, if he has one. Many candidates don't, but most of them do: he might be a congressman seeking statewide office who can count on heavy support from his home district, or an educator who can look to teachers and other academics for help, or a black who wants to get the most possible votes out of the black community, or a liberal or a conservative who can (hopefully) count on voters of similar persuasion to help him along.

What candidates and their staffs sometimes ignore, however, is the fact that voters may not be aware of the particular affinity the candidate has with them. They may not know that he is a liberal or a conservative, or a teacher, or even a black. In the Baltimore mayoral election in 1971 our first poll revealed that more than a quarter of the black voters in Baltimore didn't even know that George Russell was black. The blacks who did know he was black gave him massive early support: he fared much less well among blacks who didn't know if he was black or white, or thought he was white. This caused us to make some minor changes in our campaign plan in order to insure that every black voter in Baltimore knew that George Russell was black.

I once worked on a newspaper with a reporter who was particularly skillful at interviewing prominent public figures who came to our city. The reporter, Franklyn Buell, made it a practice when he had an assignment to conduct such an interview, to find out what the subject's hobby was, and then spent some time learning about it, whether it happened to be mountain climbing or collecting stamps or scuba diving. He'd always open his interview with some conversation about the person's hobby, get involved in a discussion about that, establish a rapport, and walk away with a much better interview than most other reporters got.

This is the same principle: finding out what people are interested in, and letting them know you share that interest.

Most candidates are joiners, and often membership in various civic, fraternal, professional, and veterans' organizations can be useful to a candidate, because then he can send mailings to other members of these organizations addressed "Fellow Member," or, even better, someone else in the organization can write to the other members to remind them that the candidate is one of them and what a fine fellow he is.

This belief that membership in associations can win elections leads to some strange suggestions. In the 1960 presidential election I was working out of Democratic National Committee headquarters in Washington as an assistant to Larry O'Brien. One day Larry was out of town and a harried receptionist found me in a back office.

"I hate to ask you to do this," she said, "but there's a man out there who has been here every day this week and he insists on seeing Senator Kennedy because he claims he has some information for him that will absolutely assure him the election. I don't know if he's a nut or what he is, but I'd hate to think he really did have something useful and nobody would listen to him."

I said sure, I'd talk with him. In a few minutes she led a well-dressed middle-aged man into my office. I closed the door and asked him what we could do for him.

He regarded me suspiciously. "Where's Mr. Kennedy?" he demanded.

"He's out campaigning," I explained, "and won't be back in Washington for a week. But if you have any information for him I'll be glad to take it and make sure he gets it."

"Do you talk with him often?"

"Several times a day," I lied.

"This is dynamite," he said. "It could blow the whole election wide open. If he does what I tell him to do, he'll win in a landslide."

"Well," I said, "why don't you tell me and I'll pass it along to him."

"Can I talk here?"

I assured him he could.

"All right," he said. "I'll tell you."

He peered around the room, settled himself snugly in a chair, and in a voice barely above a whisper, said: "You know about the Catholic problem in this campaign?"

I conceded that I had heard of it.

"Well," he said, leaning close, "here's my plan: have Kennedy join the Masons!"

"Join the Masons?"

"Sure. Everybody thinks the Catholics and the Masons hate each other, so if Kennedy joins the Masons, he'd have both groups in his corner and he couldn't lose."

But getting back to reality: The most important person in any campaign is the candidate. What are the qualities I look for in any candidate for high political office? I have organized two lists, one of characteristics I believe are important for a candidate to have, and another of characteristics that are not terribly important:

Important	*Not Important*
Intelligence	Age
Honesty, integrity	Physical appearance
Ability to make decisions	Experience in office
Grasp of issues in campaign	Net worth
Understanding of media	Family situation
Ability to raise funds and ask	Race
for money	Religion
Willingness to work hard	Ethnic background
Ability to inspire confidence	Political contacts
Flexibility	
Ability to absorb ideas	
Understanding of political research	
Ability to delegate responsibility	
Sense of humor	

Let's look first at the list of characteristics I consider not important in a campaign, and perhaps consider some of the candidates I have worked with and apply their personal qualities to the list.

Because I work chiefly in statewide elections for governor and senator, we seldom get candidates who are under thirty, although we have helped a few younger than that in Congressional contests.

But by the time a man is ready to go for senator or governor he usually is in his mid-thirties or older. We've also worked for candidates in their sixties, although I personally have never worked for anyone in his seventies and it would take an exceptional person of that age to convince me that he deserved election or re-election. But aside from the clear detriment of approaching senility, the age of the candidate appears to me to have very little to do with his ability. You may structure your campaign variously, of course, whether you have a young candidate or a mature one, depending not only on the age of your tiger but on that of his opponent as well.

So far as physical appearance is concerned, no one wants to work for a slob, and most candidates I've known have been presentable. There was one exception: ten years or so ago I was asked to help in the re-election campaign of an elderly congressman from West Virginia. I had never met him, and went to his office for a chat. He was a mess. As we talked, he smoked a cheap cigar and the ashes kept tumbling on his shirt and vest and trousers and desk. Being young and hungry at the time, I might have put up with that, but when he kept turning around and whanging away into a brass spittoon by his desk, I decided that that was a campaign I really didn't want to get involved in. The people of West Virginia retired him from office a few months later.

Candidates, even the most liberal-thinking ones, tend to be conservative in their dress, and some are fastidious. The Kennedys may be the cleanest candidates ever; Jack, Bobby, and now Teddy all bathed and changed frequently while campaigning, often several times a day. Mike Gravel, the senator from Alaska, has a toga-like robe he bought in Mexico that he claims he is going to wear on the floor of the Senate some day, and if he does, that will cause me to make my first visit to the Senate gallery. Candidates are conscious of their dress, and it's a matter they can do something about.

Physical appearance—height, weight, attractiveness—are more difficult to change. I don't really care if a candidate is handsome or not; I guess I'd rather have one who was than wasn't, but not many of the candidates I've worked for have been sought after by Hollywood scouts; although a few—Gravel, Kevin White, Endicott Peabody, Harold Hughes—certainly are handsome men in anyone's evaluation.

You seldom have a roly-poly candidate (some politicians get that way after they've been elected). In our weight-conscious American society, candidates tend to stay reasonably lean, and part of it may be the job: being a candidate is tough work, and I think some enterprising graduate student could do an interesting study some day on the metabolism rates of successful candidates versus the general public. But a candidate's height and weight are insignificant factors in his ability. So far as I can remember, I've suggested to only two candidates that they do so much as change an item of their dress, and both involved socks. Milton Shapp in Pennsylvania used to wear horrible maroon socks that barely covered the tops of his ankles and exposed about a foot of shinbone when he sat on a platform. Not only did Shapp refuse to change his sock style, but he used to make jokes about it, which was okay. (After Shapp lost in November 1966, I sent him for Christmas half a dozen of the brightest pairs of red and maroon socks I could find, with a note: "What the hell, now you can wear anything you want!" I don't know what Milt wore on his feet in his successful 1970 campaign, but I suspect it was his same short maroon socks.) The other candidate was Charles Ryan, former mayor of Springfield, Massachusetts, who in his first campaign wore white woolen tennis socks. I suggested he switch to something more conservative, and he did.

Experience in public office never seemed to me to be particularly important, and I certainly never would reject a candidate on the basis that he had not come up through the ranks and served in lesser offices before going for governor or senator. In many cases, I think the fact that a candidate has not held office before is an advantage, although it is useful if he has attained a degree of achievement in his field of work. Sometimes the citizen candidate goes into a campaign with real advantages over an officeholder, even a non-incumbent officeholder. For one thing, he has no voting record that can be exhumed and examined under a microscope. For another, it gives you the opportunity to set him off from the "politicians"—a negative word in the American lexicon.

And despite the alleged crassness of political consultants, I couldn't care less what a candidate is worth financially (provided that he is willing to make the effort to raise the money he'll need to conduct his campaign). As a matter of fact, aside from some polls, I can think of only two candidates I've ever worked for who have been really wealthy men: Milton Shapp, and Smith Bagley of North Carolina, and both of them lost their general-election contests the years I worked for them.

Nor does it disturb me if the candidate has been divorced or separated or never married. In some states, I concede, there remains some prejudice against the divorced man, but this is fading and I can't think of a single instance in which a man's divorce was the cause of his defeat, and I can name a dozen cases of divorced candidates who were successful.

I've worked for white men, brown men, and black men, and some day I hope to work for a yellow man. I've never found that the color of a man's skin had anything to do with his ability to cope, although I recognize that there remains some prejudice against black candidates (or white candidates running in black areas). This is a factor to consider, and it may be that in some states the best advice you could give a black man would be not to run, but I certainly never would turn down a candidate just because he is black. I gave a speech to the Institute of Politics at Millsaps College, Jackson, Mississippi, in the spring of 1971, shortly after Charles Evers had announced his candidacy for governor of Mississippi, and I was asked what advice I would give Evers in his campaign. I explained that what Evers had to decide was his real objective in the campaign: If it was to provide a black forum in Mississippi, or help black candidates for lesser office, or set the base for a future campaign, then by all means he should run. But if his real objective was to elect the best candidate for the black people of Mississippi, I suggested his cause was self-defeating and might well insure the election of an ultraconservative governor instead of a more moderate one. Actually, this did not happen: while Evers was badly beaten, the winner was a moderate white.

Religion and national background hardly seem worth mentioning. Half the time, I never know my candidate's religion, at least not at the start of the campaign, and I couldn't care less. I've worked for Jews, Catholics, Baptists, atheists, agnostics, Methodists, Episcopalians. (I think I may be the only political consultant in the United States who, at one time or another, has worked for all three Jewish governors in America today—Shapp of Pennsylvania, Licht of Rhode Island, Mandel of Maryland.)

Nor do I care if a candidate has any political contacts or links. Again, in many cases it may be a real advantage for the candidate to have no political ties whatsoever, and to run completely independently of any political organization.

So much for the qualities I think are not important; now let's look at some I feel are important:

At the top of the list I would place intelligence. From time to time I've worked with and for candidates whose intellectual ability was not high, and the experiences were disappointing. With campaigning so complex and sophisticated today, I don't see how it would be satisfying, or even possible, to work for a candidate who was not bright. (Notice I'm not saying anything here about the demands of office; my interest in candidates extend only to election day. But clearly it takes an intelligent candidate to make an intelligent governor or senator.)

Honesty and integrity I place close to intelligence as essential prerequisites. I joke in speeches and seminars sometimes about how I think I'd rather see a smart crook rather than an honest dope get elected, but I wouldn't work for a man I didn't consider honorable.

The voters place an increasingly high premium on honesty. In our open-ended poll questions, when we ask voters the qualities they most want to see in a candidate for high public office, honesty invariably comes first, and by a wide margin. Here's one small example to show you how much voters value honesty, and how their vote is affected by their belief in a candidate's honesty: In the spring of 1971 we did a poll for Bert T. Combs, former governor of Kentucky who was seeking the Democratic nomination for governor against the incumbent lieutenant governor of Kentucky, Wendell Ford. We asked voters whom they considered to be the more honest man, Combs or Ford. Then we broke down the responses of those who thought each was the more honest to see how voters intended to cast their ballots, with these results:

Planned to Vote for . . .	Thought Combs More Honest	Thought Ford More Honest
Combs	94.5	5.5
Ford	——	90.2
Undecided	5.5	4.3

Sure, there may have been other factors that influenced these voters' decisions to vote for Combs or Ford; maybe they felt each was more honest because they had previously decided to vote for him. But when you pull out the figures for those who thought both candidates were equally honest, and those who didn't know which was more honest, they looked like this:

Planned to Vote for . . .	Thought Both Equally Honest	Didn't Know
Combs	60.0	45.5
Ford	30.3	31.5
Undecided	9.7	23.0

There's a rather overwhelming difference here. Another example, cited in a later chapter, was the Alaska gubernatorial primary in 1970, when our postprimary poll revealed something like this:

"Who would you say raised the best issues in the campaign?"

"Larry Carr."

"Who had the best television?"

"Larry Carr."

"Who had the best newspaper advertising?"

"Larry Carr."

"Who did you vote for?"

"Bill Egan."

"Why?"

"He's honest."

I don't understand how a consultant could or would knowingly work for a candidate who wasn't honest. It's possible, of course, that what one man considers honesty, another man considers to be a lie, but that's a matter for individual subjective interpretation. And I, for one, believe that most candidates are honest men of integrity—even those on the other side.

The ability to make decisions I consider an absolutely essential quality not only for a candidate but for campaign managers as well. So many campaigns are stalled simply because the candidate won't make a firm decision one way or another; a flat "no" is better than a "let's think about it for a while," a phrase that leads inevitably to inaction.

I like candidates who listen to all sides and then, with reasonable swiftness, make up their minds and stick to their decision unless it is proved wrong.

While I consider the personality and personal characteristics of the candidate much more important than his stand on specific issues, it is essential that the candidate clearly understand and be able to articulate the issues in the campaign and his position on those issues. Perhaps this is part of the over-all personality package; whatever it is, it's important, and I couldn't work for a candidate unless he made it his business to learn the issues and define his position on them. That's also why the ability to absorb ideas and information is critical to a candidate. No one can be expected to be familiar with all the nuances of all the issues in a campaign—and the candidate who is a slow learner is at a real disadvantage. While Larry Carr lost the only campaign he ever entered, for the Democratic nomination for governor of Alaska in 1970, he had an uncanny ability to drill himself full of the information available about every issue in the campaign, digest it, formulate a position, and articulate it. By the time of the primary in 1970 I am certain that Larry knew more about the problems of Alaska and what to do about them than anyone in the state, and I don't think that the man who beat him, Bill Egan, would quarrel with that statement. Tom O'Connor of Massachusetts was another with great ability to absorb, store, and disgorge information. O'Connor's depth of knowledge might not have been as great as some others, but he could zip over the highlights faster than anyone I've known and think quickly on his feet.

There is no way for a candidate to win consistently in state-level or national elections unless he has some understanding of the media. The candidate may have the best message in the world—but unless he can communicate it to the voters he's lost, and media is the means for political communication. Candidates who don't understand television and radio—and won't take the trouble to learn—are in real trouble, and cause severe problems to the campaign. Senator Gravel has made an intensive study into media penetration; he probably understands the use and power of electronic media better than anyone else in Congress. Hubert Humphrey came to appreciate the potential power of television only in the closing week or two of the 1968 presidential election; if he runs for President again, he'll be a much better candidate.

You'd think that candidates whose careers often are inextricably linked with their political communications programs would make a real effort to learn about how political communications are used these days, but, sadly, most of them don't. The American Association of Political Consultants regularly invites members of Congress to its periodic seminars on political communications and campaign techniques; the only senator ever to attend was Gravel, who has attended several sessions, including an International Association of Political Consultants conference in Paris, and the only congressman was Nick Begich, coincidentally also from Alaska. Howard Metzenbaum turned up at one before he became a candidate for senator in Ohio, but it never ceases to amaze me that senators, congressmen, governors, and aspirants to these offices fail to take advantage of the opportunities to learn about advances in various forms of political communications techniques. Their argument is that they're too busy with other matters, but I've always felt that an officeholder's chief obligation is to be re-elected, on the theory that you can't be a good congressman unless you *are* a congressman.

Anyway, if a candidate for high office doesn't have any idea about the complexities of the media, he probably will be impossible to work with and is to be avoided.

While few of my candidates are personally very wealthy, all the good ones had the ability to raise enough money to run an adequate campaign, and for "ability to raise" you can substitute "willingness to ask" without distorting the sense of the sentence at all. I noted earlier how LeRoy Collins, of Florida, was psychologically unable to tap the resources at his command, and occasionally you do run into a candidate who simply won't, or maybe can't, ask for money. It's a tough position to be in, I concede, but, hell, the cheapest way to run a campaign is not to run, and if the candidate isn't willing to make the effort to find a top-flight finance chairman, organize a high-level, aggressive finance committee, and make calls and have personal meetings with potential contributors himself, he probably won't get very far in his campaign.

Of all the candidates I've ever worked for, I'd have to say the best fund raiser was Endicott (Chub) Peabody, the former governor of Massachusetts. Peabody ran for statewide office five times in twelve years—three times for governor, once each for senator and attorney general—and in several of those races had tough primaries as well as difficult elections. The son of an Episcopal bishop, Peabody could in no way be considered a wealthy man (even though some thought he was), but he worked harder at raising money to run his campaigns than anyone I've ever met. In the course of his various campaigns he probably raised seven or eight million dollars on sheer perseverance. The only way to raise money in a campaign is to ask for it, and the candidate too shy or too reluctant to do this is going to wind up with inadequate financing.

The willingness to work hard to raise funds goes hand in hand with the willingness to work hard in all other phases of the campaign. Most good candidates, perhaps all of them, are hard workers: they work late, get up early, go hard all day long. In fact, they're about the hardest-working breed of cat I know. The laziest candidate I've ever run across, and fortunately he happened to be on the other side, was Henry Cabot Lodge. His candidacy for Vice-President in 1960 was a debacle, and the stories of his unwillingness to maintain a rigorous schedule are unbelievable. I imagine his running mate in 1960, Richard Nixon, climbed the walls more than once over Lodge's non-efforts, and with the election as close as it was, it is not inconceivable that a more aggressive effort on Lodge's part might have made the difference in that election.

If a candidate isn't willing to make the sacrifices a major campaign requires, there's an easy solution: don't run. If he is going to run, he should be prepared to work his tail off.

And this goes with another of my prerequisites for candidates: the ability to inspire confidence, not only among the voters but among his staff as well; maybe particularly among his staff, because if he can't get his staff enthused over his candidacy, I don't see how he can possibly get the voters very excited. I've seen the occasional campaign in which the candidate's own staff were lukewarm about his efforts, mostly because they felt they were working harder than he was, and these campaigns usually end in disaster. Maybe this is a good thing so far as the country is concerned, because if a man won't work hard to get elected, I see little incentive for him to work hard *after* he is elected.

A candidate must be flexible, and ready and able to adapt to situations as they arise in a campaign. While we always like to work from a plan, and to act rather than react, circumstances change in a campaign, and the candidate who does not have the ability to adjust to changes finds himself at a distinct disadvantage, maybe a hopeless disadvantage.

In addition to understanding media, a candidate also must have some grasp of the research techniques that go into the production of the media he will be using in his campaign—particularly polls. Any candidate who sneers at polls deserves to be sneered at himself, because polls and other forms of political research are an indispensable ingredient in complex campaigns, and if a candidate doesn't believe in them or doesn't understand how to use them, he's in trouble before he starts, and his opponent can take the edge. And with so many campaigns decided by a couple of percentage points, that edge may make the difference.

A candidate has got to be able to delegate responsibility. He can't be the candidate and the campaign manager; that is slow suicide, but fatal nevertheless. He must be able to trust his campaign manager, and give him the authority as well as the responsibility that go with the position. He must be able to accept the fact that others will make decisions that he may be held accountable for—not major policy decisions, of course, but the day-to-day decisions that are the oil of any campaign's machinery. If he insists on calling all the shots, dotting all the i's and crossing all the t's, there is a beautiful opportunity for him: managing someone else's campaign. I go for weeks sometimes without ever seeing the candidate I may be working for; he has his job and I have mine, and if we both do our jobs well he'll probably win.

Last on my list of candidate prerequisites is a sense of humor. If a campaign can't be fun, there are lots of better ways to spend your time. I'd have had a dull time working for Calvin Coolidge. Most candidates I know have sharp, quick wit, and are willing to tell jokes on themselves as well as on anyone else. I once did some work for a congressman who had been arrested for beating his wife. In subsequent campaign appearances he never failed to mention, "Well, at least you know I'm a fighter." It always brought the house down, and he was re-elected. The Kennedys, particularly Robert and now Ted, have always had the ability to poke fun at themselves.

And it's not only a public sense of humor that is important, but also the ability to relax in private and see the humor of the situation. Let's face it: there are few candidates running on either side who could cause the collapse of civilization as we know it; the republic likely will survive no matter who wins. You just can't take this business too seriously, either as a candidate or as a campaign manager, or you're in trouble. If you're going to spend as much time as a campaign takes, as candidate or spear carrier, you might as well enjoy yourself in the process.

So much for the candidate.

After the candidate come the campaign staff, and, as important as the candidate is, the staff can make or break him, particularly in a tight election between evenly matched candidates.

Behind the candidate is the campaign manager, whose chief qualifications I would define thus:

1. Basic intelligence.
2. Understanding of media.
3. Ability to make decisions.
4. Complete loyalty to the candidate.
5. Complete trust of the candidate.
6. A good administrator.
7. Available full time.

If he also happens to know something about politics, that is helpful, but I wouldn't sacrifice any of my seven qualifications for that one.

I believe a campaign should be run by one person—call him manager, director, chairman, anything else. But he's the one who should call the shots and be responsible for spending the money.

The campaign manager should know where he can lay his hands on the best consultants in specialized areas. He may retain a generalist like me to help him do these things, or he may well have the ability to do it himself.

For a major campaign, his first job will be to find the one best television producer for his needs. In 1971, for example, we retained Medion, the San Francisco-based film producers, to make the spots for George Russell in his campaign for mayor of Baltimore. There are a lot of good firms in the New York-Washington area, but we went to Medion on the strength of the material they had produced for Wilson Riles in his successful campaign to unseat Max Rafferty as Superintendent of Public Instruction in California in 1970. Riles, like Russell, is black, and Medion demonstrated a rapport and sympathetic approach with Riles that we felt would be useful for Russell.

I'd look next for a radio producer, and admittedly am prejudiced in favor of Tony Schwartz, although even Tony will concede there are other good radio producers around. Not only is the producer important, but also the announcer; Bob Landers, for example, can take routine copy and make it sparkle.

You need someone to handle the graphics in the campaign—everything from letterheads and billboards to brochures and newspaper ads.

And, of course, a time buyer. Now you may be able to find all these specialists in one advertising agency, but my personal preference leans toward independent producers, especially in television and radio.

Most candidates can benefit from a television coach, and a director of special television programs such as Q-and-A sessions, telethons, and debates.

A polling firm should be retained early, and ample funds should be provided for at least two polls, preferably three, and some late quick-reaction probes.

An issues group or team is helpful: people, often academics or young lawyers, who will study and develop issues and prepare position papers for the candidate and the media producers.

The press staff calls for an over-all director, a press aide to travel with the candidate, and at least one member of the staff who has a background in electronic media. Too often in the past, the press secretary has come from a newspaper or a wire service, with little real knowledge or appreciation of television and radio. Someone on the staff should know his way around in these fields.

I'd organize an advance team, both media and political, to insure the candidate's obtaining maximum possible coverage and exposure on all his trips.

The person in charge of the candidate's schedule is an important cog in the campaign organization. This should be someone with a thorough knowledge of the state, and the ability to handle the logistics involved with moving a candidate and his staff from place to place during the campaign.

An office manager who will make certain the mail goes out on time, the press releases are duplicated when needed, the office is adequately supplied with typewriters and duplicating machines and telephones and all the other equipment and supplies required to run the campaign—he (or she) is the quartermaster of the campaign, and breakdowns here can be serious.

A competent finance chairman is indispensable. He should be prepared to devote a lot of time to the campaign, and to organize statewide and regional fund-raising committees and appoint sub-chairmen. The campaign may well rise or fall through their efforts. They should know whom to seek money from, how much to ask for, when to go back. They must organize fund-raising events—dinners, receptions, barbecues, etc.—and also explore other facets of political fund raising: direct mail to selected lists, arm twisting in its various forms. They must be prepared to beg and plead poverty to one potential contributor, and put on a show of confidence and self-assurance to another. All good fund raisers are amateur psychologists who can sense the amount of money they should seek from any prospective contributor.

Every campaign needs a person who pays the bills—call him a comptroller, auditor, what you will. No bill should be paid without his approval, and the approval either of the person who authorized the expenditure, or the campaign manager, or both. This person, or another, also may serve as the campaign purchasing agent, who will negotiate with printers, suppliers, real-estate agents, and all the others who provide goods or services to the campaign.

A director of organization who will put together a statewide team of local chairmen and committees is necessary, and he may well be assisted by a clutch of troubleshooters who will roam the state under his direction, patching and tacking, consoling and browbeating, talking sweet or talking tough, getting old enemies to work together. Not an easy job, but an important one.

Someone should be in charge of volunteer workers. Usually this turns out to be a woman, but there's no special reason why it should—or why a woman shouldn't fill any of the other slots in a campaign, from candidate down. Getting volunteer workers is the first task; making certain they have assignments to carry out is equally as important.

A good secretarial staff is essential. I think the candidate should have his own private secretary, who keeps track of his movements and personal communications. Campaigners sometimes have a tendency to try to economize by bringing in cheap (i.e., inexperienced or not very good) secretarial help, or by depending on volunteers. Sheer stupidity. One top-drawer secretary is worth three mediocre ones, and because secretaries in campaigns work a hell of a lot harder than secretaries in most offices, and much longer hours, they deserve correspondingly high pay. (Sometimes, of course, the secretaries, and other members of the staff, are gambling on the campaign, in the hopes of landing a job in the governor's office or the senate staff if the campaign is successful. It's okay to dangle these goodies, but only if you mean to follow through if the candidate actually wins.)

A position that bears an importance out of proportion to its cost is that of receptionist and/or switchboard operator. To most people who call a campaign headquarters, the person who answers the telephone is *the* spokesman for the candidate, and the impression left by a telephone operator, good or bad, can influence an unreasonable number of votes. The same holds true, perhaps more so, for people who visit the headquarters. The greeting and reception they receive influences their voting behavior—and what they say to their friends—a lot more than any speech the candidate will give, or any position he will adopt on a specific issue.

Liaison with special-interest groups is required. These groups vary from state to state, election to election. In most states the important ones include labor, blacks, young people, old people, teachers, lawyers and other professional groups, Spanish-speaking citizens in a few states. Ferreting out the right person to work with each of these groups and serve as a liaison with the headquarters organization and the candidate is a painstaking job, but a worth-while one.

A campaign is like an iceberg: the public sees only the tip. What goes on under the surface or behind the scenes often determines how effective—or ineffective—the campaign effort will be.

A superb candidate might survive a poor staff—but, then, if he really were a superb candidate he wouldn't have a poor staff.

While all these things are going on, the campaign manager and/or his team of assorted specialists are assembling a campaign plan. This includes basic over-all strategy (the message), the media plan, the budget, and scheduling.

It's always better to start off with a plan and change it than to wander around with no clear idea of where you are going and when you plan to get there. As noted several times earlier, timing is critical. The candidate has strong if not complete control over the peaking of his campaign. His manager knows whether the candidate needs early exposure or whether he should wait for a last-minute blitz, if he needs name-identification activities or can concentrate on persuading and motivating voters, whether the campaign will be basically media or basically organization, if it will be necessary to bring in a firm that specializes in computer delineation of voting patterns by precincts or one that will utilize computers and telephone banks to attract as many volunteer workers as possible to the candidate's camp.

Decisions must be made on a debate: Should we or shouldn't we? Should the candidate challenge or wait to be challenged? If the decision is not to debate, how do we avoid it? Or, conversely, how do we try to pressure our opponent into a debate if we want one and he doesn't?

The complexities of a modern major campaign require the presence of a full-time manager. Consultants can help, but they can't do the job, and they are deluding themselves and conning candidates if they pretend they can.

If you're going to spend half a million dollars, and that's about the minimum it costs to run a statewide campaign in all but the smallest states, it only makes sense to get the best people, compensate them adequately, and let them do the job.

The candidate's fate may be in their hands, and he gains little by making them work in handcuffs.

LESSONS LEARNED IN LOSING
The 1966 Election for Governor of Pennsylvania

MILTON JERROLD SHAPP was elected governor of Pennsylvania in 1970 without any help from me whatsoever.

Without any help, that is, in 1970, or at any time since Election Day in 1966.

All of us in this business admit to ourselves, if rarely to anyone else, that the number of campaigns that are won because we are involved but that would have been lost if we were not involved, is small. There are some reasons for this, which I'll explore elsewhere, but the fact is there are damned few campaigns in which a consultant or manager can say, "I made the difference."

The Shapp primary in Pennsylvania in 1966 is one in which I believe I can honestly say, "I made the difference."

And from an incredible upset in the spring of 1966, Shapp—and I—crashed to defeat in the general election that year.

There are several reasons why I intend to treat the Shapp campaigns of 1966—primary and general election—in some detail. The Shapp primary victory was the forerunner of other media-oriented campaigns in which a total unknown smashed to a primary victory, chiefly through the effective use of television, only to lose in the general election. Two similar cases that come to mind im-

mediately are Howard Metzenbaum in Ohio, who knocked off heavily favored astronaut John Glenn in the Senate primary in 1970
only to lose the general election to Robert Taft; and Richard
Ottinger, who rode the tube to an impressive victory in the New
York Senate primary's multicandidate contest in 1970 and then
lost to Conservative candidate James Buckley in a three-way general election.

I first met Milton Shapp in my Washington office in January 1963.
He arrived with a big scrapbook, a fat briefcase, and a tall assistant
named Leonard Randolph. Ironically, by the time Shapp actually
did run for office, three years later, Randolph was writing speeches
and handling press for Shapp's opponent.

"I want to run for the United States Senate," said Shapp.

"From where?" I asked.

He explained that he lived outside of Philadelphia, had developed the first successful cable television system in the United
States, had made a lot of money, and now wanted to run for office,
specifically the United States Senate seat held by Republican Hugh
Scott.

We chatted for a while and, because I had another appointment,
I asked him to leave the scrapbook for me to look at. That evening,
by pure chance, I ran into him on my way home in an airplane
from Washington to Springfield, Massachusetts, that made a stop
in Philadelphia. We sat next to each other and talked for an hour.

I was impressed with Shapp as a person, if not, at that time, as
a candidate. We agreed to enter into a modest retainer that called
for me to go to Philadelphia three or four times a month to meet
with him and his staff to review what they were doing and evaluate
it politically. In addition to Len Randolph, the other member of
his staff was a bright young man named Richard Doran, who
also, when Shapp eventually made the plunge, was with the opposition, although not in so active a role as Randolph.

Shapp's problem in 1964 (and 1966 and 1970) was that the
Democratic organization in Pennsylvania simply wouldn't accept
him. He spent most of 1963 trying to make friends with the party
organization, but they weren't having any. They'd attend his meetings and his parties, eat his food and drink his booze, but they
weren't about to give their blessing to this independent, free-thinking
businessman.

As the end of 1963 approached, Shapp was undecided about taking the gamble. The Pennsylvania Democratic party does not hold a state convention to select candidates for governor, senator, and other major offices. It has a State Policy Committee, composed of approximately 120 persons (including, as a representative from Montgomery County, Milton Shapp). The policy committee meets usually in January or February and "recommends" certain candidates for the various offices at stake that year. This is tantamount to official endorsement by the Democratic party organization.

There is nothing, however, to prevent any candidate who obtains the necessary signatures from opposing the organization choice in the primary. (In 1964, 1966, and 1970, the organization choices for governor and senator were defeated in the primary, although until that breakthrough, organization nominees invariably won the primary.)

In 1964 it looked as though the party would nominate Judge Michael Musmanno, from Pittsburgh, to be the Senate nominee, a disastrous selection for many reasons. Also seeking the nomination was Genevieve Blatt, Pennsylvania's Secretary of Internal Affairs and the protégée of the reform group led by Senator Joseph Clark.

I urged Shapp not to seek the endorsement of the policy committee, but to tell them to go to hell and plunge straight into the primary and run against the organization.

Everyone else in the state told Shapp he would be crazy to do this, and I was crazy for suggesting it. What did I know about Pennsylvania politics, anyway? Not much, I am willing to admit—but enough to know that the organization was so fat and flabby it couldn't possibly survive a tough campaign.

Shapp listened to the "experts" who told him, "You can't beat the party in a primary," pleaded his case at the policy-committee meeting, received a sharp rap on the knuckles for his efforts, and decided the organization was too tough to buck.

Now, Milton Shapp wasn't a very impressive candidate, as candidates for United States senator go, but Musmanno was incredibly bad, and Genevieve Blatt, not exactly a glamour girl, decided to make the challenge in the primary with Senator Clark's backing.

Shapp stayed home; Miss Blatt took on Musmanno, and in a campaign so bad you wondered if either side could win, edged

Musmanno by a few hundred votes. Shapp, incidentally, in the interests of "party harmony" (whatever that is) had supported the organization choice, Musmanno, against the renegade, Miss Blatt. Maybe he thought the party would reciprocate in 1966. Fat chance. Then she achieved the virtually impossible feat of losing to Senator Scott by forty-nine thousand votes while Lyndon Johnson was carrying Pennsylvania by 1,700,000. It wasn't only that Genevieve Blatt was a poor candidate, but also that she ran a poor, and poorly financed, campaign.

There was no doubt in my mind then, nor is there to this day, that if Shapp had made the run in 1964 he would have defeated both Musmanno and Blatt in the primary—by a big margin—and could easily have ridden Lyndon Johnson's 1964 long-length coattails into the United States Senate.

Shapp later agreed that if he had run his 1966 campaign in 1964 he could have won, but pointed out that his business, the Jerrold Corporation, was having problems in 1964, and there was no way he could have devoted the time to the campaign in 1964 that he did in 1966. He's the only one who can make that judgment; from a pragmatic political point of view, the 1964 election would have been much easier to win than the one he attempted in 1966.

I stopped my weekly visits to Philadelphia after Shapp decided not to make the 1964 run, saw him briefly at the Democratic Convention in Atlantic City in August 1964, and didn't hear from him again until January 1965.

"I'm thinking of running for governor next year," he said. "Can you come in and talk with me about it someday?"

I could and did, and soon resumed my periodic visits to Philadelphia. This time it became clear that Shapp was serious, and was going to run regardless of what the organization did. He still hadn't got rid of the idea that he could sell himself to the organization, and he spent a lot of time (or wasted a lot of time, to be more accurate) courting members of the policy committee.

In the summer of 1965 I met with Dick Stolley, then Washington bureau chief of *Life* magazine, and asked him if he would like to do a story on the evolution of a candidate. He agreed, and every month or so Stolley would spend a day or so with us in Philadelphia, or make a swing to another city with Shapp. Stolley's impression of Shapp was similar to many: a lovable guy, but not such a hot candidate.

In the summer and fall of 1965 most political observers in Pennsylvania said 1966 would be a Republican year in the state. Governor Scranton had become a national figure through his attempts to capture the Republican nomination for President in 1964, and after some sharp initial criticism when he increased the sales tax from 4 per cent to 5 per cent, his administration had won general approval from the public. The unprecedented month after month of uninterrupted national prosperity also had benefited Pennsylvania. Increased demands brought about by the Vietnam War kept the steel mills busy. There appeared to be no major crisis, no major scandal—and no outstanding Democratic candidates.

In the fall of 1965 Milton Shapp was hospitalized. He looked pale and was exhausted because of unwise dieting. Mentally sharp and alert as always, he dictated endless memoranda and letters from his hospital bed and, later, from his home.

There was serious doubt in his doctors' minds that he would be physically able to withstand the rigors of campaigning in a state as large and complicated as Pennsylvania. (Ironically, on November 8, 1966, after months of virtually non-stop campaigning, Milton Shapp was tired but physically fine.)

Many names were suggested as potential Democratic candidates for governor: State Senator Robert Casey of Scranton, former Governor George Leader, Mayor Joseph Barr of Pittsburgh, U.S. ambassador to Chile Ralph Dungan, attorney Philip Kalodner and athlete Jack Kelly, both of Philadelphia, and State Senator William Sesler of Erie.

In the fall of 1965 Milton Shapp agreed to decide, by the first of the year, whether or not to be a candidate. We conducted a poll which led us to believe that he had a chance of winning the nomination for governor—not because it showed him running ahead, but because it showed that all the candidates, with the exception of George Leader and Mayor Barr, were virtually unknown.

Shapp spent the late fall recuperating and holding meetings with county chairmen and Democratic leaders throughout the state. Most of them liked Milton Shapp as an individual; few of them took him seriously as a candidate. By the end of the year Shapp had pretty much decided to seek the Democratic nomination for governor

—provided that George Leader was not a candidate for the nomination. On the night before Shapp announced his candidacy, in Harrisburg, he and I met with Leader at the Locust Club, in Philadelphia.

"I'm holding a press conference in the morning to announce my candidacy for governor," Shapp told Leader. "If you tell me that you are going to run, I'll hold the press conference and announce that I'm not running but that I am supporting your candidacy. But if you tell me that you are not running, I'll announce my candidacy and then I'll be in the race to stay."

Leader thought for a moment and then said, "Milt, as of this time I'm not a candidate and my inclination is not to run."

As 1965 ended and 1966 began, it was apparent that Shapp was not going to be the choice of the Democratic leadership. Late in 1965 and early in 1966 Shapp issued statements and called upon the party leadership to forgo the policy-committee meeting in 1966 and encourage all candidates interested in the nominations for governor and other offices to enter an open primary. Such a primary, Shapp believed, could be conducted without acrimony, and would serve the useful purpose of obtaining badly needed exposure for potential Democratic candidates. Also, he felt, there would be no disruption within the organization if the party itself encouraged an open primary. Shapp is a pretty good salesman, but the party wasn't buying.

Shapp announced his candidacy at press conferences in Harrisburg and in Philadelphia the third week in January 1966. In the meantime, we had begun to activate a campaign organization. Shapp's office had been moved from the Suburban Station Building to 1424 Walnut Street, in downtown Philadelphia, where a string of offices designed like a railroad train would serve as headquarters not only in the primary but through the general election as well. Staff, at this time, was minimal, and there was very little volunteer or other assistance. At the end we faced several major problems, including these:

1. Getting the people to take Shapp seriously.
2. Getting Shapp better known.
3. Deciding the best course to oppose the organization in the primary.

The policy-committee meeting was scheduled in Harrisburg on

St. Valentine's Day, February 14. As the day of the meeting approached, it became clear that the organization had settled on State Senator Robert Casey of Scranton as the candidate for governor. Casey was an attractive, vigorous candidate, but his age, thirty-two, and corresponding lack of experience, weighed against him. He had waged a vigorous campaign to win the policy-committee endorsement, and had impressed many county chairmen with his credentials as a candidate. And, by that time George Leader, the personal choice of most of the top organization people, had decided not to run, perhaps because he, too, saw 1966 as a Republican year in Pennsylvania.

While the pre-policy-committee discussions were taking place, I had engaged the film producer Guggenheim Productions, then of St. Louis, now of Washington, to make films and television spots for the campaign.

It was decided that Shapp would go to the policy committee and request permission to read a statement calling for an open primary. If his request were denied, as we were certain it would, then he would leave the meeting room and go directly to a press conference, where he would reaffirm his intention of taking his case directly to the people.

Casey won the policy-committee endorsement. The rest of the ticket consisted of State Senator Leonard Staisey for lieutenant governor, our old friend Genevieve Blatt for the position she held, Secretary of Internal Affairs, and Judges Clinton Budd Palmer and Juanita Kidd Stout for judges of the Superior Court.

Other candidates for governor still in contention at the time were Kalodner, an articulate, issues-oriented lawyer with a strong ADA background; Erwin Murray, a state representative who also was angry at the organization; and Harvey Johnston, a McKeesport real-estate dealer whose presence was to prove an important factor in the race.

Because my main intention here is to analyze the general election, which we lost, I will merely skim over the highlights of the primary campaign. As the deadline for filing and withdrawing from the primary drew near, Kalodner withdrew, leaving Murray, Shapp, Johnston, and Casey as the candidates for the Democratic nomination. A day or two before the deadline, Shapp met with Johnston in Pittsburgh after Johnston had held several discussions with a

Shapp representative who later left the staff many weeks before the primary.

Shapp knew Johnston only as a man who had received 162,000 votes, against Richardson Dilworth, in the 1962 Democratic gubernatorial primary. Shapp believed that he would have a better chance of defeating Casey in a two-man race than he would if there were other candidates in the contest to diffuse whatever anti-organization vote existed in Pennsylvania. I was not present at the meeting. According to Shapp, he asked Johnston to withdraw from the race and offered to hire him to work on our staff handling two areas of particular interest to Johnston—and, for that matter, to Shapp: highway safety and conservation. In his 1962 campaign, Johnston had prepared and mailed throughout the state thousands of giant postcards on highway safety. He had preserved his mailing lists, and these, Shapp believed, would be of some value in the campaign.

In any event, Johnston withdrew, and Shapp subsequently paid him a total of fifteen thousand dollars in three separate checks, of six, five, and four thousand dollars. Later, when Johnston's background was revealed, there were charges that Shapp paid him to drop out of the race and not for any services he might perform. Shapp was incredibly naïve to pay Johnston by check and later to report paying him fifteen thousand dollars when he filed his financial report for the campaign. Shapp also offered to hire Murray as an area co-ordinator for his campaign if Murray decided to drop out of the race. This made good sense, because Murray had been around Pennsylvania, and while not the smoothest operator in the state he appeared to be a hard worker. Murray was determined to stay in the race, and wound up with almost one hundred thousand votes. The Johnston involvement was to come back to haunt Shapp many times over in the general election.

Another act that came back to haunt Shapp was one in which he was a completely innocent victim. During the primary campaign, Randolph Holmes, a black in his mid-forties, was hired at seventy-five dollars a week. His chief function was to act as a messenger and to distribute campaign materials. Holmes, a former basketball player at Long Island University, also claimed to have close ties with black athletes throughout the state. From time to time during the primary, Holmes would bring in some of these men; I remember meeting Timmy Brown, the Philadelphia Eagles halfback, on one occasion.

One afternoon I walked into the office and saw a man I had never met but who was not difficult to recognize: Wilt Chamberlain, the seven-foot-tall NBA basketball star. There were photographers, including the Guggenheim film crew, in the hall. I asked what was going on and was told that Chamberlain, Timmy Brown, and Ira Davis, an Olympic sprinter, were there to endorse Shapp and have their pictures taken with him. I was busy with other campaign activities and went into my own office, closing the door on the commotion in the hall. Perhaps twenty minutes later Shapp called me into his office, which was next to mine.

"Do you know anything about any agreement to pay these people?" he asked.

"What people?"

"These athletes."

"Pay them for what?"

"For endorsing me."

I told Shapp I knew nothing at all about it. Shapp said that after the pictures had been taken, Holmes had asked to see him privately and had told him the athletes were waiting to be paid fifteen hundred dollars. I called Holmes into the office and asked him who had authorized him to pay anything to anyone. He blandly replied that he had cleared it with "the agency."

At that time we were using the Firestone Advertising Agency, in Philadelphia, primarily to buy time and space and to make layouts. (Firestone's work was not satisfactory. The agency was discharged at the end of the primary. Later the agency ran an advertisement in Philadelphia newspapers pretty much claiming credit for Shapp's primary victory. In the ad they also referred to other "winners" represented by the agency, including tuna-fish and dog-food manufacturers. The Republicans picked this up in the fall and used it against Shapp.)

Although we were less than satisfied with Firestone's handling of the Shapp account, I doubted that anyone at the agency had given Holmes authority to pay anyone anything. A telephone call to the agency executive handling the account elicited the information that Holmes had asked him if he thought it would be a good thing if he could get the endorsement of Chamberlain, Brown, et al. The account executive, naturally, said yes. He was proceeding under the assumption, as was Shapp, as was I, that these endorsements would be freely offered. There never was any discussion of paying the athletes anything, until *after* the films and photographs had been made.

So there was Shapp, in his office, with the three athletes waiting outside for money they had been promised by Randy Holmes. The athletes were acting in good faith. Apparently Chamberlain had made a special trip to Philadelphia for the session, and the others had been told they would be paid. All three assumed that Holmes was representing Shapp and had authority to make commitments.

Shapp, with characteristic generosity (and no one who knows him well will have any difficulty understanding this), agreed to pay the athletes "because they had been told by someone from this office that they would be paid and they had no way of knowing that Holmes had no authority to make commitments." The money was paid by Shapp to the advertising agency and the agency paid the athletes.

It was a sorry and unproductive incident. Ironically, none of the film ever was used. One still photo of Shapp, Chamberlain, and Brown was used in a brochure aimed at black voters in the primary and discarded for the general election.

After the filing date had passed, the three candidates in the race for the Democratic nomination were Casey, Shapp, and Murray, with Casey the heavy favorite. Shapp was given virtually no chance by anyone until practically the eve of the election, and even then there were few who conceded that he would do better than make a "good showing."

Exactly one week before the primary, on Tuesday, May 10, Senator Joseph Clark held two press conferences with Casey, in which he predicted Casey would win every county and roll up a plurality of two hundred thousand. Dick Stolley, of *Life,* had been following the Shapp campaign and the evolution of Shapp as a candidate since the summer of 1965. His piece on the making of a candidate was scheduled for *Life*'s May 6 issue. Closing date for the issue was April 20. That morning Stolley called to tell me, ruefully, that the New York editors had killed the story because they had checked sources in Pennsylvania and were convinced Shapp had no chance at all of winning the primary. Using the story, they felt, might embarrass *Life* if Shapp was smothered by Casey in the primary. Stolley spent primary night at Shapp headquarters, and at 3 A.M. sent a two-word telegram to his New York editors: SHAPP WON. He hastily revised the story and *Life* revamped its makeup for the May 27 issue to publish Stolley's comprehensive report of how Shapp won the primary.

Shapp spent the spring traveling through the state. Speaking engagements were hard to come by, because we didn't have the forum that the organization provides. Organized labor did give him considerable support in the primary (and in the general election), and a patchwork statewide organization that was long on enthusiasm but short on experience was assembled. In some areas our field organization was excellent. In the northwest corner of the state, for example, Harvey Thiemann did an excellent job of co-ordination, and Bob Tullio was extremely helpful in the city of Erie. Shapp wound up winning Erie, a city of 125,000, by more votes than Casey won Philadelphia (population two million).

Shapp also acquired a running mate in the spring, a handsome Irishman named Jim Kelley from Greensburg, in Westmoreland County, a Democratic stronghold in the southwest corner of the state. (Dick Stolley's comment on first meeting Kelley: "He looks as though he was sent over by central casting.") I personally was opposed to the concept of Shapp having a running mate, on the theory that it is easier to run a campaign for one man than it is for two. Shapp felt that Kelley, an Irish Catholic, would give his ticket balance. My objections, incidentally, were not to Kelley personally, but to the concept of running a team. They were expressed long before I had ever met Kelley. I still feel it would have been better for Shapp to run alone, although I will readily concede that Kelley's organization in Westmoreland County helped produce a solid Shapp victory there, something I had considered highly unlikely.

In the meantime, Guggenheim was following Shapp around and shooting film clips of him all over the state. These eventually were assembled into the thirty-minute motion picture *Man Against the Machine,* still the best thirty-minute political film I have ever seen. There is no doubt that it was the single most important instrument in Shapp's primary victory. The film was directed and narrated by the late Shelby Storck.

After discussing with Guggenheim the films and radio spots, which he also was producing, we decided on a late, intensive media campaign that had five major prongs: a mass mailing of a sixteen-page brochure, newspaper ads, television spots, radio spots, and the television film. The brochure, also entitled *The Man Against the Machine,* went into the mails the third week in April and was mailed to approximately one million Democrats. We aimed at reaching all Democratic households, but fell short of the goal.

The media campaign was intensive and calculated to start so late that by the time the organization realized it was in trouble it would not have enough time to react. I'd like to take credit for the slogan "Man Against the Machine," but it was Shapp's creation, and it was ideal for the type of campaign we waged. Shapp finally had learned that what the organization understands is clout, not wheedling.

The brochures began hitting around April 20, with the last ones not delivered until May 13 or 14. We relied on volunteers to do the addressing and mailing. In the general election we turned this assignment over to a mailing house, which did the job somewhat more efficiently and, surprisingly, cheaper than we could have done it with volunteers.

During the third week in April 1966, we also completed a statewide poll, which produced these results:

Casey	29%
Shapp	6%
Murray	2%
Undecided	63%

Remember, this was in April, when not many people were paying very much attention to the primary and hardly any could identify the candidates. A Casey poll taken about the same time showed about the same results.

Our media campaign, which has since been termed a "blitz," began May 2. On that day we ran our first newspaper ads. The next day, Tuesday, May 3, we began our radio spots. Television spots began Friday, May 6. We had one showing of the film on Saturday, May 7, and started its regular schedule on Monday, May 9, just eight days before the primary. (We showed the film thirty-five times in all, including ten showings on the night before the primary.)

Our campaign was geared to peak Shapp's candidacy on May 17, primary day, and we were successful.

We had been told time and time again that it was impossible to persuade Democrats to vote in a primary through the use of mass media, that we needed bodies to drag voters to the polls. One of the most meaningful statistics in the primary was the fact that we succeeded in increasing the turnout of voters by 15 per cent over the 1964 Blatt-Musmanno battle. In that contest, approximately 995,000 voters cast ballots; in 1966, nearly 1,150,000 voted. Roughly, Shapp received 550,000 votes, Casey 500,000, and Murray 100,000. There is no question in my mind that these extra voters were motivated to vote by our media campaign, and particularly by the film.

Shapp's primary victory caught the state by surprise—including the Democratic party and Raymond P. Shafer, the lieutenant governor and Republican nominee for governor.

Shafer was the candidate picked by the party chieftains (ironically, Shafer was more the "hand-picked candidate of the political bosses" than Casey, but for a number of reasons, including the fact that Shapp felt it was important we make peace with the organization, we decided not to make this the major issue of our campaign) and had only nominal primary opposition in the person of perennial candidate Harold Stassen. On May 17, Shapp had performed a political miracle in Pennsylvania—beating the young, attractive, vigorous organization candidate in the Democratic primary. Could he move on to a second miracle in less than five months?

On balance, Milton Shapp has to be rated a good-to-excellent candidate. He had his deficiencies; so does every other candidate I've ever met (to say nothing of campaign managers). But his attributes outweighed his deficiencies. The pluses exceeded the minuses. First let's look at the man.

At fifty-four, Shapp had accomplished more than most men accomplish in a lifetime. He had started with a few hundred dollars after the war and created a corporate complex that by mid-1966 employed over twenty-one hundred persons in five factories and a research laboratory. When the company had been in trouble a couple of years earlier, at the time Shapp was thinking of running for senator, he had shifted from political activities and devoted full time to business long enough to see the price of Jerrold stock quadruple.

As a *person,* you couldn't find a better guy. As a *candidate,* Shapp had these liabilities:

a. Despite several years of writing about Pennsylvania's economic and social problems and heading the drive to get a new constitution for the state, Shapp was not well known to the voters when the campaign started. As a matter of fact, he really wasn't terribly well known until after the primary media blitz. After the election he probably was the fourth-best-known man in the state, after former President Eisenhower, William Scranton, and Raymond Shafer. (Even before the election, Shapp ran several points ahead of Senators Clark and Scott in name recognition among voters.)

b. He bucked the organization in a state where this usually is political suicide. Shapp took the Democratic party apart in May, put it back together again by October. In my opinion, the Democratic organization worked as hard for Shapp as it could. I believe that the county chairmen, including the Philadelphia and Allegheny organizations, did everything they could to help Shapp win. I detected no signs of cutting. The fact is that the organizations were bucking the tide just as much as Shapp was. It also is true that some county organizations are better than others—and it also is highly probable that the old organizational style of campaigning is on its way out, in the rest of the country as well as Pennsylvania.

c. He is Jewish. I don't think that being Jewish in itself cost Shapp the election—but I'm pretty sure it didn't help him very much. There are some pretty clear signs that in a few Pennsylvania German strongholds the anti-Semitic vote hurt Shapp considerably. If the election had been decided by ten thousand or twenty thousand votes, then Shapp's Jewishness might have been pin-pointed as the cause. As the first Jewish candidate for governor in Pennsylvania's history, he did well.

d. He is divorced and remarried. Again, I don't think this was much of a factor in the over-all picture, but I suspect Shapp didn't gain any votes because of his marital situation.

e. His physical appearance is not impressive. If Shapp's body were proportionately as big as his brain, he'd weigh 250 and stand six feet five. As it is, he is small in stature, stoop-shouldered, and when he smiles he wrinkles his nose like a rabbit. Late in the campaign the Republicans distributed a picture of Shapp and Shafer that, at the moment the shutter clicked, showed Shafer in a much more favorable light than Shapp. The caption read, "Which man looks more like a Governor?" Imagine what they could have said about Franklin Roosevelt in his wheelchair, or Abraham Lincoln with his warts.

f. Shapp was not the best speaker in the world when the campaign began. Or when it ended, for that matter. But he did improve considerably, as the campaign progressed. Shapp has a tendency to prolong a sentence instead of making a point and cutting it off sharply. Effective speechmaking comes with practice and experience—and this was Shapp's first campaign.

g. No base of power. Shapp started out with no base of power at all, either geograhical or organizational. He had a small coterie of devoted followers, but no big power bloc. (Casey, for example, had Lackawanna County in the primary, and his home county delivered him a whopping majority of twenty-two thousand over Shapp.)

h. An unquenchable desire to attack Scranton. Whether the acceptance of Scranton as a good governor by the public in Pennsylvania was justified or not, the fact remains that the feeling existed. The Republicans deliberately put Scranton out front in their campaign, knowing that he was more popular than Shafer, as well as being a better campaigner. Nothing could dissuade Shapp from taking a dig at Scranton whenever possible, and I believe these hurt Shapp much more than they hurt Shafer.

i. An unfortunate tendency to shoot from the hip. (Or, as someone later said of Hubert Humphrey, "from the lip.") Most of the time, Shapp was excellent in question-and-answer sessions; much better, by far, than Shafer. But often Shapp would overanswer a question, and late in the campaign this got him into real trouble.

Balanced against these negatives were these very real positives:

a. Shapp is an extremely intelligent candidate with a thorough grasp of the issues. He probably knew the problems of Pennsylvania better than any person in the state.

b. Shapp has a creative, imaginative approach to problems and is willing to try new ideas. Maybe this really isn't much of an advantage in Pennsylvania; Shapp probably was ten to fifteen years ahead of his time.

c. Shapp was willing to spend his own money to support his ideas. In a way, Shapp's biggest weakness as a candidate was his unwillingness to ask people for money. He did provide the funds that were needed when they were needed, out of his own pocket, and from experience in many campaigns I can emphatically state that knowing that sufficient money will be available to meet the needs of the campaign is a tremendous asset.

d. Shapp worked hard. From the first of the year until November 8, he devoted all his time to the campaign. Even when he was in Europe on a postprimary vacation, he would telephone almost every day with suggestions and ideas. His day-to-day schedule was more rigorous than Shafer's. (At least, a comparison of schedules indicates that Shapp's was much fuller.)

e. Shapp was willing to listen. Many of his slogans, ideas, and proposed positions were impractical. In most cases, he could be dissuaded from adopting these positions.

f. Shapp is a decent human being, with a real concern for people, and this shows through when he is exposed to people. His interests lie in areas far removed from those of most (if not all) politicians: music, art, theater. Shapp lives modestly; his idea of a big night out is to take his wife to a concert.

So far as Shafer's assets and liabilities are concerned, I have only a superficial knowledge. I met Shafer only once, briefly; saw him at the television studio the day of the debate; saw him debate Shapp at a meeting of Associated Press editors; and watched him on television several times. I also studied his background and voting record.

His assets, it would seem to me, were these:

a. He was running on Scranton's record, and most people in Pennsylvania thought that Scranton had been a good governor.

b. He was *physically* more impressive than Shapp—tall, athletic.

c. He read and memorized speeches well, although his delivery was sometimes wooden.

d. He had the support of the party right from the start, and had a good hatchet man, Hugh Scott, and a father image, Scranton, chipping away at Shapp.

e. He enjoyed a very friendly press. Newspapers in Pennsylvania are basically Republican, and they were helpful to Shafer. They gave greater play to his issues.

f. He avoided making mistakes, either because he was carefully coached or because he was naturally conservative.

g. He had been through campaigns before and had acquired the ability to answer questions with pious platitudes and generalities that often avoided the question but also precluded getting himself into trouble.

h. He gave the outward appearance of being a highly moral man —for motherhood and against sin. One of the more perspicacious newsmen covering the campaign dubbed Shafer "Dudley Do-right." He did not intend it as a compliment. And so far as morality is concerned, it was well known that there was a woman in Shafer's life, and that he had had family problems. Shapp knew of this situation from the start of the campaign but refused to take advantage of it.

i. He was amply financed. Shafer is not a wealthy man, but there appeared to be no shortage of funds in his campaign, despite the Republican's pious complaints about the state house not being for sale. (Figures filed after the campaign indicate Shafer outspent Shapp well over two to one.)

So far as Shafer's liabilities as a candidate are concerned, I would list these:

a. He did not think quickly on his feet and, when pinned down, had difficulty with tough questions.

b. His program, and the Republican party platform, contradicted his voting record and positions he had taken in the past.

c. The Republican party's conservative position (and basis of financial support) tied Shafer's hands on some issues that Shapp could and did speak out on loud and clear. It would have been unthinkable, for example, for Shafer to come out and take Shapp's positions on requiring the public utilities to pay local real-estate taxes on their operating property.

    d. Shafer seemed to lack confidence in himself, and sometimes
this showed through. Reporters who followed the campaign
noted that after a speech or a television show, members of
Shafer's staff would invariably thump him on the back and
reassure him that everything was all right and "You're going
to win, baby!"

    e. Despite his eight years in government, I don't believe Shafer
had the grasp of the problems in Pennsylvania that Shapp had.
At least, he didn't appear to demonstrate the depth of knowledge on state problems that Shapp had at his fingertips.

    The Republicans had two major issues in the campaign: Scranton's
record and image, and destroying Shapp's credibility. Their campaign was far more negative, personally, than Shapp's campaign.
They began attacking Shapp's credibility immediately after the
primary. One week to the day after the primary campaign, Senator
Scott held a press conference and blasted Shapp's claim that he
was instrumental in persuading President Kennedy to start the
Peace Corps.

    At the press conference Scott showed excerpts from our primary
film, *Man Against the Machine.* Where he got this film remains a
mystery. If its unauthorized use was not illegal, it certainly was unethical. All television stations had been requested to return the
film after it was shown; one, obviously made it, or a print, available
to Scott.

    The gist of Scott's argument was that the concept of the Peace
Corps was proposed by many other persons, including Hubert
Humphrey, many years before Kennedy became President. He
clearly indicated that Shapp was a liar for claiming any part in
the creation of the Peace Corps.

    The Philadelphia *Inquirer* made this its banner headline the
next morning. It was a sample of things to come, because the
Inquirer never gave Shapp an opportunity to reply to Scott's charges
before they printed them. When Shapp did reply to the charges, at a
press conference two days after Scott's, the *Inquirer* buried the
response on an inside page.

    In his press conference Scott deliberately refrained from mention-
ing a few things that were brought to the attention of the press at
Shapp's press conference two days later—but, as always, the re-

buttal attracted nowhere near the attention or the play that the charges received.

Among the things that Scott neglected to mention were these:

1. He himself had inserted into the Congressional Record a copy of a Drew Pearson column in which Shapp is credited with persuading President Kennedy to start the Peace Corps.
2. Shapp never, under any circumstances, ever claimed credit for originating the *idea* of the Peace Corps. He claimed only to have been instrumental in persuading President Kennedy to use it in his campaign.
3. The narrator in the Shapp film clearly states that the concept of the Peace Corps "is as old as the first missionary" and that proposals to start such an organization "have been kicking around the halls of Congress for years."
4. Several statements that appeared in a memorandum prepared by Shapp for Robert Kennedy in 1960 appeared virtually verbatim in the San Francisco speech by John F. Kennedy in which he called for the creation of the Peace Corps.
5. Vice-President Humphrey and Theodore Sorensen both remembered speaking with Shapp about the Peace Corps idea before it was presented by President Kennedy.

And the climax was a statement by Senator Robert Kennedy that we used as a television spot late in the campaign, in which Kennedy recalls the role Shapp played in making the Peace Corps a proposal in the 1960 presidential campaign. At the end of the campaign, voters were given the choice of believing Hugh Scott when he said that Shapp played no role in starting the Peace Corps, or Bobby Kennedy who said that Shapp did have such a role.

Unfortunately, Shapp's explicit repudiation of every charge Scott made did not receive anywhere near as much attention as Scott's accusations, and there is no question that Scott had done Shapp damage. This was the first blow in destroying Shapp's credibility, and no matter what the truth was, Shapp was hurt by the incident. The Republicans maintained this attack on Shapp's integrity and credibility through the summer and fall. There is no doubt that this was one of the chief factors in Shapp's defeat.

Under Pennsylvania law, candidates and political committees must file a financial report of expenditures within thirty days after the election. Shapp filed primary expenditures of $1.4 million, Shafer of $239,000. I have reason to believe both these reports were wrong.

I think Shapp is the first candidate in political history ever to report more than he actually spent on his campaign, and Shafer, like most candidates, reported less than he spent.

After the primary it was clear that the Republicans were going to accuse Shapp of "buying" the election. Shapp's accountant and chief financial adviser, Ralph Fratkin, sincerely believed that Shapp should account for every penny of expenditure to make certain that no audit of his account could disclose unreported expenditures. Legally and fiscally, there is no question that Fratkin was right, and the financial report filed by Milton Shapp was without question the most detailed I have ever seen filed, and may be the only true report ever filed in a political campaign.

My quarrel was not with the ethics of filing the report in this way, but with the political consequences, and in addition I said at the time and believe to this day that many of the items listed on Shapp's financial report should not have been reported because they were not proper primary-campaign expenses. (Shapp isn't the only candidate who has suffered because of sharp pencils wielded by accountants: in May 1971 it was revealed that Governor Ronald Reagan of California had paid no income taxes for 1970 because of personal business losses. The revelation came a few days after Reagan had announced, "Paying taxes should hurt." To me, it was the most politically damaging incident that had occurred to Reagan in his more than four years as governor, and I am sure it was caused because some smart lawyer or accountant did his job the best way he knew how and figured out a way that Reagan could—legally—avoid paying income taxes for 1970. That's business and logic—but not politics. It would have been a lot cheaper for Reagan to have had his return calculated in a manner that would have required him to pay a few thousand dollars in taxes— and I think if the lawyer or accountant who did the return really tried he could have found a way. This is what happens when non-political people get involved in important decisions concerning candidates without considering the political implications. I'm certain that if any of Reagan's political aides had known about the tax return before it was made public, he would have found a way for the governor to pay some taxes.)

During the primary we had signs in every room in Shapp head-quarters that read: WILL IT WIN VOTES IN THE PRIMARY? So far as I am concerned, only expenses with a direct bearing on the primary campaign should have been included in the report. For example, in the winter of 1965–66 Shapp published two *Shapp Reports*. One was on the general condition of Pennsylvania's economy, the other on what Shapp considers an impending crisis in the steel industry in Pennsylvania.

These reports ran to forty pages or more apiece, and were filled with charts and illustrations. Each was mailed to approximately fifty thousand persons. Nowhere in either report is Shapp's candidacy mentioned, nor is the recipient urged to support Shapp or vote for him.

The total cost of preparing, printing, and mailing these reports was approximately one hundred thousand dollars. This money was reported as a primary-campaign expense. I thought this was a mistake at the time, and I am even more convinced now that it was a mistake. I am willing to accept the blame for not working harder to have it, and many other similar expenditures, scratched from the financial report.

Milton Shapp had been fighting the merger of the Pennsylvania and the New York Central railroads for years. He was still fighting the merger after he lost the election. This is ample proof that his opposition to the merger is not politically motivated. It is something he would have done whether he ever became a candidate. Yet Shapp's financial report of primary expenses listed legal fees for fighting the railroad merger, the cost of newspaper ads he had taken out opposing the merger, the fees paid to a Washington representative who was fighting the merger, and other merger-related expenditures.

During the late fall and early winter of 1966 Shapp entertained county chairmen and other Democratic leaders at a series of meetings and receptions. He showed a film he had made two years before, *War on Poverty,* and attempted to alert chairmen and other party officials to what he considered the crisis in Pennsylvania. Shapp might have had notions of running for governor at the time, but there was nothing done at any of these meetings calculated to win him votes in an open primary, but the costs of these receptions were reported on his financial statement.

There are many other, similar expenditures. While I have not gone over the report with a fine-tooth comb, my offhand guess is that Shapp reported at least a quarter of a million dollars of expenditures that had nothing to do with his primary campaign, and perhaps the figure is higher than that. If a question had been raised, Shapp certainly could have claimed that he did not consider them primary expenditures. In any event, Shapp reported spending $1.39 million, all of which was his own money with the exception of roughly three thousand dollars in contributions.

Incidentally, despite the hue and cry, this does not seem to me to be an abnormally large expenditure of money in a state of more than 11 million people—particularly when Shapp performed the unprecedented feat of upsetting the Democratic-organization choice for governor in an open primary. Compared with the costs of the Florida primary that year, in which Mayor Robert King High of Miami upset Governor Hayden Burns, or the 1965 mayoral race in New York, the cost of the Pennsylvania primary appears almost modest. Shapp's biggest fault was his honesty.

If there were errors in the Shafer reporting, they were in the other direction. And this is not really a criticism of Shafer, because very, very few candidates ever report the true amount they spend. Shafer was just following tradition and common practice. I am not saying that this is right, just that it is so. A few days after Shafer announced his candidacy, in January 1966, and received the blessing of Governor Scranton, Senator Scott, and other bosses of the Republican party, John Scotzin, considered the dean of state-house reporters in Harrisburg, wrote a Sunday feature in which he said Shafer's announcement ritual had "the sweet smell of money" about it. On the day he announced for governor, Shafer puddle-jumped across the state in a rented turbo-prop, a not-inexpensive piece of aircraft. To coincide with his announcement, Shafer mailed, first class, to Republicans around the state a brochure entitled "The Next Great One" (a slogan, incidentally, that he inexplicably dropped soon afterward). His campaign aides reported that 420,000 brochures had been mailed.

At five cents apiece, that makes a postage bill of twenty-one thousand dollars. In June, when Shafer filed his financial report, he reported a total expenditure for postage of less than fifteen thousand dollars. When this discrepancy was called to the attention of the court in the postfiling audit suits that were brought by both sides, the judge, by coincidence a Republican, informed Shapp's attorneys that the purpose of the hearing was to investigate the expenditures that were reported, to make certain they were legal, and not to investigate any expenditures that were not reported.

On the last hour of the last day to challenge the financial report, the Republicans filed a taxpayers' suit demanding an audit of the Shapp report. This had been anticipated, and a countersuit asking for an audit of the Shafer report was filed. The suits were heard during the first two weeks in August. Shapp was on the witness stand part of three days. The suits attracted much attention, particularly the Harvey Johnston payments, which will be considered next, and the payments to Negro athletes, reported earlier, and to Negro ministers. Throughout the audit the Philadelphia *Inquirer* in particular was vicious in its treatment of Shapp. After the general election, as had been expected, both suits were dismissed. The audit proceedings did succeed in embarrassing Shapp and putting a strain on his credibility.

Harvey Johnston received 162,000 votes in the 1962 Democratic gubernatorial primary. Shapp felt his chances of winning would be better if Johnston were not in the race. And about this he probably was right. When Harvey Johnston withdrew as a candidate and joined the Shapp campaign, Shapp paid him fifteen thousand dollars in three checks. These checks were reported as part of Shapp's financial report in the primary. They may have been the costliest checks Shapp ever wrote.

About two weeks after Shapp had paid Harvey Johnston, we learned that Johnston was president of an organization called the National Association for the Advancement of White People (NAAWP) and also had been chairman of Democrats for Goldwater in Pennsylvania in 1964.

Shapp maintains that he knew nothing of either affiliation at the time he hired Johnston, and I am sure such is the case. I certainly knew nothing about these associations, and neither did Oscar Jager, Milt's press secretary. When we learned of Johnston's background, through newspaper reports in Pittsburgh, Johnston was quickly repudiated—privately in a telegram and publicly in a press release that was sent to every newspaper, radio station, and television station in Pennsylvania. The repudiation was clear and firm, but the damage had been done.

We also learned, later, that Johnston had headed a committee for the election of William Scranton in 1962, and as a result of his efforts had received a "Dear Harvey" letter from Scranton in which Scranton noted, "Mary and I are grateful" for the work Johnston had done. This was before Johnston became president of NAAWP, but apparently his racist views were known, at least to many people, before he went to work on Scranton's behalf. So far as I know, Scranton never has repudiated Johnston.

The Republicans hopped on the Johnston incident and used it in black areas throughout the summer, the early fall, and in the heat of the closing days of the campaign. They reproduced a check for fifteen thousand dollars ostensibly signed by Milton Shapp and accusing him of paying a white racist. Radio spots on two Negro stations in Philadelphia began on August 12, and continued through the election. Many of them urged blacks not to vote for Shapp because he had given fifteen thousand dollars to the white racist Harvey Johnston. Several other pieces of literature were distributed in Negro neighborhoods, some of which came close to calling Shapp himself a racist. Late in the campaign the Republicans distributed in black neighborhoods something marked OFFICIAL SAMPLE BALLOT, which showed on one side pictures of thirteen Negro candidates for various offices in Pennsylvania, and on the other side called to the attention of Negroes that Milton Shapp had paid a white racist $15,000.

The single most important factor in Shapp's winning the primary was the thirty-minute film produced by Charles Guggenheim. The first time I discussed the campaign with Guggenheim, in December 1965 in New York, he expressed some doubt about anyone's ability to effectively utilize films to win two tough races in less than six months. We knew that Shapp faced a tough primary fight; we also knew that if he didn't win the primary he wouldn't get a chance to run in the general election. The primary film produced by Guggenheim is a masterpiece. Without seeing that film, it is impossible to understand how Shapp won the primary.

At the time of the primary I still was on speaking terms with Joe Miller of the Philadelphia *Inquirer,* and I urged him several times to make it a point to see the film. He never did. The day after the primary he wrote an "interpretive" article telling how Shapp won the election, and missed the mark by a mile or so. Former Governor David Lawrence, a true professional, was in Washington during the primary and did not see the film either. If he had, I am certain he would have realized its effectiveness and attempted to prod the organization to greater efforts.

Shapp did not see the primary film until it was shown on television. In one of the retrospectively amusing incidents of the primary, Guggenheim flew the film from the California laboratory to Cleveland one night, rented a car and drove one hundred miles or so to Erie, where Shapp was making a talk. The plan was for Shapp to see the film in a motel room about midnight. His meeting took longer than intended, and at one o'clock in the morning he called Guggenheim to tell him he simply was too exhausted to go to the motel and see the film, and that he would watch it on television.

We caught Casey and the Democratic organization unawares in the primary, and by the time the blitz was over Shapp had won.

In the general election we had to make some policy decisions on whether to make another thirty-minute film, and, if so, what kind of film it should be. The decision was made early to make the film, and the specific tone or content was left to be decided later. Eventually we all agreed (Guggenheim's people and I) that the film should attempt to show Milton Shapp as the warm, sincere person that he is. We also agreed that we should again run the film late, on the theory that the idea would be to have someone watch the film and then walk straight into a voting booth. In retrospect, I think we made the wrong decision.

We had difficulty buying prime half-hour times in the Philadelphia and Pittsburgh markets, although we did pick up additional prime half-hours in Pittsburgh in the last week. All told, we ran the half-hour general-election film, titled simply *Shapp,* about seventy times. The film was good. My personal opinion is that it was not as good as the primary film, and I fully recognize the difficulty, if not the impossibility, of repeating the emotional impact of the primary film. People who had not seen the primary film were more impressed with the general-election film than those who had seen both.

Again we decided to run our television spots late, starting eleven days before the election. The film was first shown eight days before the primary. In addition to the film and the spots, we also had a fifteen-minute cutdown of the primary film, which captured many of the highlights while eliminating all the material pertinent only to the primary. This fifteen-minute version, retitled *The Man Against the Odds,* was shown thirty times. The spots in the general election were excellent; better, in my opinion, than the spots in the primary.

While we had one half-hour program in the general election, the Republicans had four, one a live telecast of the opening of their campaign on September 8. Two of the others were shown in October, and the final (and most effective) one the night before the election. (They had ten showings of their film that night; we had thirteen, including several on UHF stations.) Their first film was patterned on our primary film, and was a combination biography of Shafer and panegyric of the Scranton administration. I didn't think it was particularly effective, although some of our staff people were more impressed. Their second film had very little Shafer in it—but a lot of Scranton and Scott. This made sense, because both Scranton and Scott are more effective than Shafer on television.

This one was a real hatchet job on Shapp, as the Republicans did everything to impugn his credibility. They brought up the Peace Corps charge again, even though it had been refuted, the Harvey Johnston incident, the primary spending, and an old anti-trust suit involving the Jerrold Corporation, and hit Shapp's proposal for tuition-free higher education because it would "bankrupt the state." The final Republican film was shown the night before the election, and, until Shafer appeared in it, was very effective indeed. The film opened in a television studio, where paid professional actors pretending to be newsmen brought in election-eve "reports" from different sections of the state. The format was effective and believable, although not as effective as it might have been if it had been more subtle. The only flaw in this film was Shafer, who made what seemed to me—although, obviously, not to the voters—a rather dreadful, wooden appearance at the finish.

It is interesting to note that although the Republicans shouted for months about the Shapp television blitz, they spent just about as much money on television as Shapp did, and ran a total of fifty to sixty half-hour shows compared with our seventy or seventy-five. In addition to the film, we also had Shapp on four or five 30-minute "Meet the Press"-type shows, in which he was asked unrehearsed questions by local newsmen. This is a format in which Shapp does well.

Both sides had effective radio spots. After an early fund-raising radio jingle, which apparently did not go over well with anyone, Shafer's people began using basically the same type of radio spot we had been using: a good speaking voice delivering a message. Guggenheim handled our radio spots as well as television spots and films. In the primary he picked David Wayne, an actor, to cut the radio spots, and the choice was excellent. In the general election Guggenheim selected Ed Binns, also an actor, to do the radio spots. While Binns was good, I think Wayne was better. Wayne did do the narration on half the television spots and the thirty-minute film in the general election.

The Republicans spent more money on radio advertising than we did. They started earlier and ran at least as heavy, perhaps heavier, at the finish. Radio and television expenditures are a matter of public record, and the FCC requires that the station make this information available to anyone who seeks it. Some stations, however, refuse to give out the information by telephone or mail, requiring that the interested party personally visit the station to examine the books. With more than two hundred radio stations and about twenty-five television stations in Pennsylvania, this can be quite a chore. If anyone is seriously interested, however, the information is there for the asking.

Our radio spots came in three sizes (60-second, 30-second, 10-second) and two varieties: anti-Shafer and pro-Shapp. We began with the anti-Shafer spots and mixed in the pro-Shapp spots in the final two weeks of our five-week radio campaign. The anti-Shafer spots were specifically designed to meet a gap in our campaign. We were giving voters reasons to be *for* Shapp, but no reasons to be *against* Shafer. Shafer's spots were almost entirely anti-Shapp. Harry Muheim wrote our radio spots, and they were very good. One line from Muheim's fertile pen still is quoted in political circles: In one of the spots, he wrote, "If you liked William Penn, you'll love Milton Shapp."

Our newspaper ads had more variety and more punch than Shafer's, and we used them more extensively. We used newspaper ads on the television page to promote our television programs, particularly the half-hour show. In fact, I would guess that we spent as much to promote the programs as we did for the time it cost to show them.

The so-called Negro vote posed a delicate problem. Democrats all over the country, not only in Pennsylvania, did not get as high a percentage of the Negro vote as had been expected in 1966. One reason for this undoubtedly was a protest against the national administration (a protest I personally believe was unjustified). The black vote poses problems in every election; it posed particular problems in 1966. There was real friction in Philadelphia and other large cities throughout the country between blacks who are resentful at being confined in ghettoes, and whites, particularly ethnic minorities in the lower and lower-middle income brackets (and consequently those living nearest the ghettoes) who are upset about what they consider the encroachment of blacks into their neighborhoods. Blacks voted solidly Democratic in 1964, probably out of fear of Barry Goldwater more than any other reason.

The Johnson administration had produced much meaningful civil-rights legislation, and there were solid reasons for blacks to vote Democratic again in 1966. But having won so much of the Negro vote in 1964 put the Democratic party in a precarious position: it could gain no more of the black vote; the best it could do was hold its own.

The Republicans, on the other hand, had a great opportunity to go after black votes. They had nothing to lose and, in Pennsylvania at least, the Republican party and the Republican candidate for governor were infinitely more conservative than their Democratic counterparts, party platforms notwithstanding.

The Republicans did go after the black vote, hard, and there is no doubt that the majorities for Shapp in the black wards were less than anticipated. How much of this is due to the Republican campaign and how much to the national mood is hard to judge.

Shapp won some Negro wards by 2–1 or 3–1 that we had expected to win by 4–1 or 5–1. I am not certain whether this resulted from a shift of some blacks to Shafer, or the fact that many black Democrats simply did not vote; I suspect it was a combination. On the basis of record, Shapp should have won thumping majorities among the blacks.

Shapp long has been a leader in the field of civil rights and civil liberties. Many organizations have honored him for his activities in these areas. Long before it was popular (or required), Shapp was hiring blacks (and other minority groups) for his office staff as well as for his factory. For years Shapp's personal secretary has been a black woman, Mrs. Catherine Boyd, and it would be difficult to find a better secretary, white, black, or green, anywhere.

Shapp started a scholarship program chiefly to help Negro youngsters get into college. He was the chief financial backer of the Berean Institute, a vocational school attended mostly by blacks. He has made generous gifts of equipment and cash to Negro schools and projects. The only flaw in Shapp's appeal to the Negroes was the Harvey Johnston incident. The Republicans seized on this and made it *the* major issue in their appeal to blacks.

Shafer's public record on civil rights, on the other hand, was, to be charitable, undistinguished. Among other things, he voted against a bill providing for better housing and supported Scranton's position on unemployment-compensation legislation that in practice, if not in intent, discriminated against the Negro. Certainly nothing in Shafer's background qualified him as a champion of the black man.

And on top of everything else, Shafer had done two things (which we exploited in a late campaign piece aimed at black voters) that should have caused concern among blacks. In one case he dismissed as without foundation charges by black civil-rights demonstrators that state police had been brutal in their treatment of blacks in a disturbance in Chester. Only "reasonable force" had been used, Shafer said following an investigation. Shapp had done some investigation of his own, and came up with a photograph of state police beating a black man with clubs that is one of the most brutally frightening pictures of its kind I have seen.

The other thing Shafer did was accept a deed to his home and to other property in Meadville that contains a restrictive covenant. The deed limits sale and occupancy of the house (except for servants) to "Persons of the Caucasian race." These deeds were conveyed in the fall of 1964, while Shafer was lieutenant governor. He also is a lawyer, and had been a district attorney. While restrictive covenants are not enforceable, it certainly was careless, if nothing more, of Shafer to accept such deeds.

There are a couple of observations I wish to make about the

black vote and the black community in Philadelphia. I am doing so because I feel they should be said, and in full recognition of the fact that it would be more tactful and probably politically safer to leave them unsaid. Tact is not one of my strong points, although candor may be. It is more difficult to get blacks to vote than it is to get white people to the polls. It is more difficult to get blacks to register to vote. I know the socioeconomic reasons for this difficulty. I am well aware of the relationship between the lack of education and civic responsibility (in whites as well as blacks), but the fact remains that blacks often require special incentives, special efforts to get them to the polls. They do not vote in proportion to their population—and in Philadelphia this certainly is not because they have been denied registration. Negroes in Philadelphia in 1966 lacked effective political leadership. There were some competent black officeholders, but there also were many black self-proclaimed leaders and spokesmen who appeared much more interested in how much money they could make in a political campaign than in how much good they could do for the people they ostensibly represented. Let me not leave the impression that I think political corruption is confined to the Negro; obviously it is not. But in Philadelphia the situation is exaggerated among blacks.

The black press in Philadelphia is the most venal I have ever seen anywhere. One black newspaper had the audacity to ask Shapp for forty thousand dollars to "buy" the paper in the primary. When I refused, and rather decisively, the paper, *Nite Life,* ran some of the most scurrilous cartoons and comments I've ever seen—but they were right back in the general election looking for money to influence their news columns as well as for advertising. We bought no space. I don't mind spending money on advertising; I refuse to be held up.

This is of small personal concern to me—but I think it should be of major concern to responsible blacks and to politicians of both parties who must live with, work with, and deal with the black community in Philadelphia.

I detest being put in a position where I must complain about the treatment given to my candidate in the press, but the coverage by the Philadelphia *Inquirer* in 1966 was beyond belief. Perhaps it would be best merely to reprint some comments made in the *Greater Philadelphia Magazine,* a highly respected monthly publication that devoted long stories to Shafer and Shapp in its October 1966 issue. Included in the Shapp piece were these paragraphs:

"Within days after the primary, the panic flags were up. Senator Hugh Scott, aided by one-sided coverage in the *Inquirer,* charged that Shapp's campaign claims about originating the Peace Corps were phony. Scott used strong language, saying, 'Not one word pertaining to the Peace Corps or Milton Shapp's relationship to the Peace Corps is true.' He warned that since Shapp had misrepresented this position, he could be expected to do the same on other subjects.

"The truth is that some of Shapp's literature did give the impression he thought up the Peace Corps, although he later said his only claim was that he convinced JFK that it would make a forceful campaign issue. He angrily produced testimony from a number of sources, including Vice-President Humphrey, which credited him with a major role in the Peace Corps. He also made Scott look silly by producing a copy of a tribute Scott had entered in the Congressional Record which credited Shapp with selling JFK the Peace Corps idea. Scott's entry was made, of course, before Shapp loomed as a potential candidate.

"Although Shapp exaggerated his Peace Corps role, Scott went much further to the other extreme by making Shapp appear a total liar. The *Inquirer,* which gave unbelievably prominent coverage to the charge, played down Shapp's rebuttal. It was just the beginning of a summer-long campaign against the Democratic candidate by the paper. Strong editorials, consistently slanted news stories, distortions and some outright untruths were obviously designed to picture Shapp as an irresponsible, intemperate man, drunk with the lust for power. *It was pure character assassination, and if a Pulitzer were given for yellow journalism, the* Inquirer *would have it wrapped up.* [Italics mine.]

"When a minor Shapp primary-campaign worker was arrested, *Inquirer* headlines repeatedly used the term 'Ex-Shapp Aide.' *Inquirer* readers also got the impression that Shapp had called the Pennsy's respected board chairman, Stuart Saunders, a 'robber baron.' That stemmed from a Shapp claim that the railroad merger 'was a legalized multimillion-dollar swindle which put the robber barons of old to shame.' No mention of Saunders. An *Inquirer* editorial promptly chastized Shapp for likening Pennsy officials to robber

barons. Then, in its Sunday news roundup, the Inky reported that
Shapp had called Saunders a robber baron. The fact is that Shapp
has great respect for Saunders and said at a press conference in
June that the Pennsy would never have gotten in the financial
trouble which precipitated the merger if Saunders had been running
the railroad since 1950, instead of only the last few years.

"*Paper Barrage*. The *Inquirer*'s coverage of the audit of Shapp's
campaign spending was a masterpiece of selective reporting. It
printed only what made Shapp look bad. *Inquirer* readers got the
impression that Shapp was being roasted for buying hundreds of
Negro ministers as well as a white supremacist. The *Bulletin,* which
has treated Shapp with its characteristic fairness, reported an entirely different trial. *Bulletin* readers were informed, accurately,
that the judge threatened to throw the case out of court because
the petitioners were unable to summon a single witness to substantiate some of their charges."

A couple of other examples will suffice to demonstrate the extent
of the *Inquirer*'s virulence:

Early in this report I mentioned a man named Randolph Holmes,
who had been hired as a messenger and got us involved in the
problem with the black athletes. Holmes was released from our
campaign on May 17. Three months later, during the second week
of August 1966, Holmes was arrested for trying to bribe a juror.
There was absolutely no connection between the crime and the
Shapp campaign—but the eight-column banner headline in the
Inquirer the next morning screamed: "EX-SHAPP AIDE AR-
RESTED ON BRIBE CHARGE."

I was astounded (although by that time nothing the *Inquirer* did
should have surprised me) to pick up the *Inquirer* one morning
and read Page 1 headlines that declared Shapp was asking voters
whom they preferred between Hubert Humphrey and Robert Kennedy if President Johnson died, so that he would know which one
to curry favor with.

The article, by Joseph Miller, contained a quote from the *Inquirer*'s favorite anonymous Republican spokesman to the effect
that this was the "most cynical political act I have ever encountered."
The story described a Shapp poll, including a distorted question, in
which voters were asked their preference if Johnson died in office.
The next day the *Inquirer* carried an editorial headlined "Beneath

Contempt," in which they described a question purportedly asked in our survey and then commented caustically about the lack of ethics involved.

As usual, there was a germ of truth in the *Inquirer* article. We did take a poll, and we did ask the voters to express a preference between Humphrey and Kennedy.

This is how the *Inquirer* said the question was worded: "If President Johnson dies in office, would you prefer Hubert Humphrey or Robert Kennedy as President?"

This is how the question actually was worded: "Suppose something were to happen to President Johnson or he chose not to run in 1968—who do you think would make the best President— Hubert Humphrey or Robert Kennedy?"

This was a standard question asked in many surveys around the country. Many of the results were sent to President Johnson's staff and to the Vice-President. We never received a word of criticism about the question, the wording of the question, or the ethics of asking the question, from the White House. (And, prophetically, President Johnson did elect not to run in 1968.) Apparently we offended only the *Inquirer* and its anonymous Republican spokesman.

The *Inquirer* also sent reporters to Cleveland and other cities to interview Shapp's first wife, former in-laws, and others who knew him before he moved to Pennsylvania. One of Shapp's relatives who had been interviewed called to say it was odd that the reporter did not seem to take any notes at all when she told him of the many good things that Shapp had done, but seemed interested only in pressing for information about any business difficulties he might have had, trouble he might have been in—in other words, anything unpleasant.

The *Inquirer* made it a point to mention often that Shapp was the first Jew running for governor of Pennsylvania, and saw fit to deny three times in five days that he had ever been in a mental hospital. Unfortunately, the *Inquirer's* slanted, distorted coverage of Shapp and the gubernatorial campaign had some effect—possibly enough to sway the outcome.

On one of our polls we asked voters which newspapers they read regularly. Those who regularly read the *Inquirer* had a much higher percentage of undecided voters than those who did not read the *Inquirer:* 50.3 per cent of *Inquirer* voters were undecided, and 43.3 per cent of those who did not read the *Inquirer.*

Shapp lost the election by 232,000 votes. In the six counties outside of Philadelphia city, in the circulation area of the *Inquirer,* Shapp trailed Shafer by 233,000 votes: Chester, 25,000; Cumberland, 15,000; Dauphin, 26,000; Delaware, 66,000; Lancaster, 38,000; and Montgomery, 63,000. If you put a compass on a map of Pennsylvania, with the point at Philadelphia, and draw a line delineating the *Inquirer's* circulation area, you find a sharp difference in the vote outside the line.

Apparently President Nixon doesn't feel as strongly about the *Inquirer's* policies as some of us, because after his election he appointed its publisher, Walter Annenberg, United States ambassador to England. More than a few people found that one a little hard to swallow.

By and large, the rest of the newspapers in Pennsylvania treated Shapp fairly. Most of them are Republican controlled and Republican oriented and endorsed Shafer editorially, but that is their privilege and we had no quarrel with it. If a newspaper reports a campaign fairly and accurately in its news columns, I believe it is fulfilling its obligations to the public. By and large, with the exception of the *Inquirer,* newspapers in Pennsylvania played the campaign straight in their news columns. My personal complaint, or perhaps observation is a more accurate word, about the Pennsylvania press is its lack of initiative. Some important issues were raised by Milton Shapp in his 1966 campaign, issues such as the tax exemption enjoyed by public utilities on their operating property, the reason Pennsylvanians have to pay more for the same milk than neighbors in other states, the desirability of tuition-free higher education.

For the most part, the press placidly accepted our statements and Shafer's violent criticisms. Seldom indeed did the press do any digging of its own to determine the accuracy of claims and counterclaims by each side.

Take the matter of campaign spending. The Republicans charged over and over again that Shapp was trying to "buy" the election, that he was spending millions on television and radio and other advertising. On October 20, I had Paul Weinberg, my assistant, run a check of every television station in Pennsylvania to find out how much we had spent on television and how much Shafer had spent.

I knew that Shafer's spending far exceeded ours at the time, because he had started his major television campaign and we had not. The exact figures showed a greater disparity than I had anticipated: Shafer had spent $73,430, Shapp had spent $5935. This was through midnight, October 19, 1966.

At that time, Shafer had outspent Shapp on television by twelve to one. I knew, of course, that as the campaign progressed and we launched our television campaign, the figures would even out or that we would go slightly ahead of Shafer in television expenditures, but the fact remained that as of October 19, Shafer had spent $73,000 on television and Shapp $6000. I issued a press release to this effect in my name.

Papers gave it some play; they gave a bigger play to a rebuttal by Shafer's campaign manager, Robert Kunzig, calling me a liar. The *Inquirer* headline, as might have been expected, said flatly that I lied. I'm not blaming Kunzig for the statement he made, although it was not true nor is it my style of campaigning.

But it would not have been a difficult task for the press to check the twenty-five television stations in Pennsylvania and find out for themselves who was right. This was a clear-cut opportunity for the press to determine who was telling the truth—Shafer's staff or Shapp's—on a matter of fact that could be easily determined. I even suggested in my press release that newspapers do this. None did. Some used my statement, some used Kunzig's rebuttal without using my statement, some used both, some used neither, none checked the facts on its own.

More campaigns are lost than are won. Every candidate makes mistakes during a campaign, particularly candidates who are not content to play it safe, and who come to the political arena brimful of ideas and programs. And candidates in their first campaign are more likely than seasoned campaigners to make mistakes. Shapp made his share, maybe more than his share. Some of the things that I consider mistakes, he might not, and I am sure I did some things that in my political judgment were sound but that he now feels were mistakes. These are what I would consider the major mistakes in the campaign, in order of their importance:

1. *The "bribe" charge*

About twelve days before the election, Shapp was interviewed on television. As is inevitable, a question was asked about campaign spending, how much Shapp intended to spend in the campaign, and where the money was coming from. Shapp answered the questions routinely until he was asked if he had had any offers of campaign contributions from persons who sought special favors. Shapp, apparently not aware of the booby trap in the question, answered that someone had offered him one hundred thousand dollars for his campaign if he could have the privilege of naming the insurance commissioner if Shapp were elected. Shapp said he had, of course, turned down the offer. Reporters' ears perked up, and the interviewer, smelling a story, probed further. Shapp reported two other offers of contributions-with-strings-attached, for appointments to the Public Utilities Commission and the Highway Commission. The *Inquirer* headlined the story "Shapp Reports $175,000 Bribe Offers," and other newspapers played the story big. There was nothing wrong with this; it was a good news story. The Republicans, scenting blood, immediately moved in and demanded that Shapp reveal the names of the persons who had made the bribe offers. They said he had a "legal obligation" to do so. (Actually, offering a candidate a bribe is not illegal in Pennsylvania, even though it should be.) Each day, Shafer, Scranton, Scott, Broderick, or some other member of the Republican staff would issue a new statement demanding that Shapp reveal the names of the people who had attempted to bribe him—"if, indeed, such people actually exist." The bobble played right into Republican hands, because their whole campaign had been based on impugning Shapp's credibility, and right at the end of the campaign he had handed them a hot issue. On the other hand, we were caught in a bind. We considered several alternatives, including going to the state attorney general (a Republican) and telling him the names. Shapp's lawyer said no crime had been committed, but there was nothing to prevent the attorney general from passing the names on to the appropriate district attorney, who could convene a grand jury and have Shapp called as a witness. Election-eve headlines screaming "Shapp

Called Before Grand Jury" would have done little to help our cause. We finally decided to sweat it out.

This was a most unfortunate mistake by Shapp, but it should be placed in perspective. Shapp had been campaigning virtually without letup for more than ten months. He was tired, and he is a naturally candid person. The question caught him unawares and he answered it honestly, whereas a more skillful politician would have fluffed off the question.

2. *Harvey Johnston*

This was an early mistake, but a costly one. It hurt Shapp not so much among blacks as among whites, particularly liberal whites, who saw this as one more piece of evidence that Shapp's credibility was in doubt.

3. *Filing Primary Expenses of $1.4 Million*

I firmly believe that the primary filing should have been pared to the absolute essentials directly connected with winning votes in the primary, because this would have deprived the Republicans of one of their major campaign issues.

There were other day-to-day mistakes, of course, but these, to my mind, were the three big ones, and they cost us votes. Enough to swing the election? I don't know. Perhaps.

The Republican campaign was pure character assassination, aided and abetted by the Philadelphia *Inquirer.* Ben Franklin of the New York *Times,* who covered the campaign, said he had talked with several people who used the expression "arrogant little Jew" in describing Shapp. These were people who didn't know Shapp, hadn't ever met him or seen him; their impression was based entirely on what they had read or heard about him. Shapp isn't very big, and he is Jewish, but he certainly isn't arrogant, and nothing like the insidious impression conveyed by the expression "arrogant little Jew." The chief hatchet man for the Republicans was Scott. He does it so much better than Shafer, maybe because he's had more practice.

The Republican county chairman in McKean County sent out a letter referring to the Democratic candidate as "Milton Shapp (Shapiro)." Envelopes used to arrive at our office rubber-stamped DON'T VOTE FOR SHAPP-IRO.

There were other indications that anti-Semites were at work in this campaign. How much effect they had, I don't know. In some counties, Columbia, for example, it would seem that Shafer picked up about six thousand anti-Semitic votes. There may have been some subsurface anti-Jewish feeling among Democrats who didn't want to vote for a Republican but didn't want to vote for a Jew either, so they just stayed home. The only sure comment is that being Jewish didn't help Shapp in this election—but he managed to win in 1970 without changing his religion.

I wore two hats in the Shapp campaign. Not only did I manage the campaign, but my organization also took the polls for Shapp. Our first poll for Shapp was made in January 1964, when he was thinking of running for the United States Senate. We were still doing telephone polls on Election Day 1966. First let's look at some of the figures and then my interpretation of what these figures meant. Here are the percentages for name recognition on Shapp and Shafer:

	Shapp	Shafer
January 1964	3.3	(Not included)
April 1965	3.3	14.0
January 1966	5.2	27.5
April 1966 (Democrats only)	20.5	30.8
July 1966	65.5	59.1
September 1966	70.9	66.8
October 1966	78.2	74.4

There are some interesting things here. Note that Shapp's recognition factor was unchanged between January 1964 and April 1965, and did not pick up much between April 1965 and January 1966. However, as Shapp became involved in the primary against Casey, his recognition jumped more than fifteen points between January and April 1966, and after his spectacular primary victory on May 17, it leaped forty-five points from the April to the July surveys. Shafer started off with a better-known name than Shapp, which was to be expected because he was the lieutenant governor of the state. After Shapp's primary victory, however, Shapp was the better known, and maintained his name-recognition lead over Shafer right up to the election.

Now let's look at what happened when we matched Shapp and Shafer head to head (and also the comparison with the Casey-Shafer vote in three surveys):

DEMOCRATS ONLY

	April 1965	Jan. 1966	April 1966	July 1966	Sept. 1966	Oct. 1966
Shapp	14.3	19.1	48.3	32.0	26.8	28.5
Shafer	21.4	34.8	4.8	27.5	28.0	29.8
Undecided/ refused	64.3	46.1	46.9	40.5	45.2	41.5
Casey	16.0	21.0	57.3			
Shafer	22.7	35.4	3.9			
Undecided/ refused	61.3	43.6	38.8			

The pattern is interesting. Shapp, and Casey, both run behind Shafer in the early polls, which really don't mean much because neither was known. Our April survey, which, of course, was just before the primary and in which we were concerned only with Democrats, showed Casey getting a higher percentage of the Democratic vote against Shafer than Shapp, but it must be remembered that this was before we started our media blitz. (The same poll showed Casey running ahead of Shapp, 29 per cent to 6 per cent, with Murray getting 2 per cent and the balance undecided.) Shapp jumped out ahead of Shafer in our July survey, which came on the heels of his primary victory. At the time that that report was written, however, I noted:

"There is no reason to believe that Shapp's percentage of the vote has gone up since this survey was taken. If anything, it probably has gone down as the result of the adverse publicity on the court suit, and it probably will drop some more before we launch our major fall campaign.

"Even so, at this stage of the campaign, with more than three full months to go, it would appear that Shapp is *no worse than even* with 40 per cent of the vote undecided.

"This means that the campaign will be won or lost as the result of what happens in the fall."

Our September statewide poll showed Shapp down 5.2 per cent, Shafer up only .5 per cent, and undecided up 4.7 per cent.

My comment then was:

"This means that many voters who in early July thought they would vote for Shapp now are undecided—but they have not decided to switch to Shafer."

We did one other survey in which we interviewed over fifteen hundred voters. This was not a representative statewide cross section, but was concentrated in those Democratic counties in which we knew we had to do well to win, and a couple of Republican counties we were certain to lose.

The over-all results are meaningless, but here are the party breakdowns, which do have some meaning:

	Democrats	Republicans
Shapp	46.9	5.9
Shafer	4.1	49.8
Undecided or refused	48.9	44.3

These results, as well as the October results, created a dilemma for me personally. As a *pollster,* I would have to say that the surveys showed Shafer leading and likely to win. As a *campaign manager,* I had confidence (misplaced, as it turned out) in my ability to swing that massive undecided vote to Shapp in the final ten days of the campaign. I also should note that the undecided vote was the highest I have ever encountered so late in an election in any campaign in any state where I have conducted polls.

I attributed the high undecided to the fact that the Republicans had succeeded in picturing Shapp as the "arrogant little Jew" Ben Franklin heard about—but I felt that our campaign film, which was to be shown seventy times in eight days, would blunt this fear by picturing Shapp as the warm, human person he really is. Unfortunately, the undecided vote did not break the way we expected —largely because it now appears that they were undecided for reasons quite different from what we had assumed.

Results throughout the country indicated a dissatisfaction with the national administration and the national situation in the big-city states *on the part of those voters who normally and ordinarily vote Democratic.* The returns in other large states, as reported in the first section of this report, indicate how widespread this dissatisfaction was. Our polls were accurate; our interpretation of our ability to sway the undecided vote was off. Also, a quarter of a million fewer persons voted in 1966 than in the 1962 race for governor. And most of these, voter-registration lists indicate, were Democrats. It made a big difference.

I believe we did as much for Shapp in 1966 as we could have done, all things considered. Since the election, I have been racking my brain trying to think of things I would have done differently, things we didn't do that we could have done, things that we did that we shouldn't have done. Most of the time I draw blanks.

We could have made some technical switches here or there, but none, so far as I can see, that would have been particularly meaningful. I am convinced it is impossible to change a candidate, although it may be possible to change his image somewhat over a long period of time, and, anyway, I rate Milton Shapp as a very good candidate.

A campaign manager, perhaps more than any other person who is not a member of the candidate's family, is in the best position to see the warts and weaknesses of a candidate. Milton Shapp was frustrating to work with at times, but so am I, and so is every candidate I ever worked with. Milton Shapp came out of the campaign with my respect as well as my sympathy. Reasons for his defeat? I would list them as follows:

1. *The Republican tide*

When I told Ben Franklin of the New York *Times* that Shapp lost because of a "cyclical imperative," I wasn't joking. The Republicans won twelve out of thirteen contests for senator and governor in the ten largest states in 1966. Of the twelve losing Democrats, Shapp came closest to winning, on the basis of percentage, and was the *only* Democrat in those twelve contests to improve on the Democratic party's showing in the 1962 elections.

2. *Dissatisfaction with the national administration*

Justified or not, there was dissatisfaction, not only in Pennsylvania but in other states as well, with the national administration. Our evaluation studies of President Johnson reveal a sharp decline in his popularity in the year before the '66 elections. Some of this rubbed off on Shapp and other Democratic candidates.

3. *Republican success in impugning Shapp's integrity*

Republicans had one theme in this campaign: destroy Shapp's integrity image. I don't think they succeeded in destroying it, but they cast enough doubt on it to cost Shapp thousands of votes.

4. *The Philadelphia* Inquirer

The slanted stories of the *Inquirer* certainly hurt. In Pittsburgh, the newspapers endorsed Shafer editorially but played news of the campaign straight. Shapp won Allegheny County by thirty-eight thousand votes, a remarkable showing in the face of the Republican tide. Dilworth had *lost* the county in 1962. Shapp did better in Allegheny County outside of the city of Pittsburgh than Governor Lawrence did running for re-election. (Lawrence lost the county outside Pittsburgh by twenty thousand votes, Shapp by only seventeen thousand.)

5. *Being the first Jewish candidate for governor*

I don't think this was *the* reason for Shapp's loss—but I do think it was *a* reason.

6. *The necessity to wage two tough campaigns within six months*

I have won campaigns in which we had an easy primary and a tough election, and when we had a tough primary and an easy election. This time we pulled off a near miracle in the spring and stretched our luck trying to repeat in the fall. The primary forced us to tip our hand on techniques and methods, and also took some of the juice out of our second half-hour film. We rattled the Democratic party, and no doubt a few nuts and bolts shook off.

It is reasonable to ask me, "How come Shapp lost in 1966 when you were managing his campaign and won in 1970 when you had nothing to do with it?"

When Ben Franklin asked me the first part of that question on the day after the election in 1966, I told him it was a "cyclical imperative." Someone else in my cubicle-that-I-called-an-office burst into laughter, and it wasn't a very cheerful day.

"Wonderful," he said. "Some guy is going to crawl out of a coal mine in Scranton this morning and ask who won the election, and they are going to tell him Shafer, and he is going to say, 'How come?' and the shift boss is going to say, 'It was a cyclical imperative!'"

Still there is no doubt that a Republican tide swept the United

States on November 8, 1966, and one of its victims was Milton Shapp. Comparatively speaking, Shapp didn't do badly in the 1966 general election, except that in politics, unlike horse racing, there is no pay-off for finishing second. He did come off the race strong enough to run again—and win—four years later.

In the ten largest states there were thirteen races for governor and United States senator in 1966. Republicans won twelve of the thirteen. The only Democrat to survive was Governor John Connally of Texas, who had been heavily favored.

Of the other twelve contests in the ten largest states, Shapp ran better than any other Democratic candidate for senator or governor. In addition, he was the only Democrat to improve on his party's performance compared with the previous off-year election.

Shapp chopped more than a quarter of a million votes off the margin William Scranton had won Pennsylvania by in 1962. In every other one of the ten largest states, the Republican margin was substantially improved over the previous off-year elections for the highest statewide offices.

In the ten largest states, the Republicans won all five Senate seats that were up, picking off one Democratic seat (Illinois) and seven of the eight governors' chairs that were contested, netting two (California and Florida).

These figures help put the Pennsylvania election in perspective. One other national phenomenon in 1966 deserves attention:

The power base of the Democratic party outside the South has been in the cities. The larger the city, usually the more Democratic it is in registration. The Democratic base has been composed largely of ethnic minorities (Irish, Italian, Polish, Puerto Rican) and the blacks.

The painful friction that has erupted between white ethnic minorities and their black city neighbors was just coming into focus in 1966. Lower- and lower-middle-income white became concerned about black encroachment, and frequently, in 1966, complained to pollsters that the Johnson administration was giving preferential treatment to blacks and not paying any attention to poor whites. Blacks, on the other hand, resentful and frustrated after years of oppression and becoming conscious of the powers for change inherent in violence and rioting, also were venting their anger at the men at the top—and in 1966 this was the Johnson administration.

Thus was created an explosive condition that found both ethnic white minorities *and* blacks demonstrating their resentment against the party in power—the whites because they felt blacks were going too far too fast, and the blacks because they felt they were not going far enough fast enough.

In city after city in 1966, Democratic candidates did not receive their usual majorities in lower- or middle-class white neighborhoods, *or* in black wards. In Philadelphia Shapp did as well as or better than Democratic candidates usually do in white middle- and upper-middle-class independent swing wards, but much poorer than expected in the Italian, fringe, and black sections of the city.

Republicans gained from both groups (and causes); Democrats lost from both.

There are fifteen states in the country that have cities of 750,000 or more persons; the ten largest states, plus Georgia, Maryland, Missouri, Wisconsin, and Minnesota. Over all, in these fifteen states there were nineteen elections for governor or senator. Republicans won sixteen and Democrats three.*

The only Democrat to survive outside the South in 1966 in states with cities of more than 750,000 was Senator Walter Mondale, of Minnesota, and even here his running mate, Governor Karl Rolvaag, went down to resounding defeat.

In the South, in addition to Connally, Senator Richard Russell was re-elected, and he was unopposed.

The Democratic power base in the cities was fractured in 1966. Some examples:

In 1962, Nelson Rockefeller had lost New York by 203,000 votes; in 1966, he lost it by only 65,000.

In 1962, George Romney had lost Detroit by 207,000 votes; in 1966 he lost it by only 37,000.

In 1962, John Volpe had lost Boston (a city that is 3–1 Democratic in registration) by 52,000 votes; in 1966 he *won* Boston by 11,000.

In 1962, the Republican candidate for senator had lost Chicago by 243,000; in 1966 Charles Percy lost it by only 132,000.

* In Georgia, the Republican candidate for governor, Bo Calloway, defeated Lester Maddox by three thousand votes, but because he did not receive a majority, the election went to the Georgia House for a decision, and this heavily Democratic body picked Maddox over Calloway to be governor.

In 1962 the Republican candidate for governor of Maryland had lost Baltimore by 63,000; in 1966 Spiro Agnew *won* the city by 24,000.

In 1962 Richard Nixon had lost Los Angeles to Pat Brown by 111,000; in 1966 Ronald Reagan *carried* the city by 335,000.

At dawn on Election Day 1966, there were thirty-three Democratic governors and seventeen Republicans. At dawn the next day the Republicans had twenty-five governors, the Democrats twenty-four, and the Calloway-Maddox contest in Georgia was still up in the air.

So in 1966 Milton Shapp bucked the Republican tide and was drowned. He was running against the representative of a popular administration, and voters elected to settle for the status quo. The climate was different in 1970. As we had suspected—and predicted—Raymond Shafer proved to be a lousy governor. A lot of the warnings Shapp had sounded in his 1966 campaign proved to be true.

It is reasonable to ask why I was not involved in the Shapp campaign in 1970. The honest answer is, "I don't know." I have my suspicions, and one gets back to Napolitan's rule for campaign managers: if the candidate wins, it is because of his personal appeal; if he loses, it's the campaign manager's fault. I suspect that within a month or two after the election in 1966 some of Shapp's followers, and perhaps Shapp himself, were convinced that I had made the wrong decisions in 1966, that if I had done things differently Shapp would have won. This kind of logic is difficult for me to accept—and impossible to refute. Shapp called me in 1970 to tell me that he was going to announce his candidacy. I wished him well, and that was the last conversation we had during the campaign.

In our 1966 primary film, Milton Shapp's mother, an aged and beautiful woman who unfortunately did not live to see her son elected governor, said, "Whatever Milton goes after, he gets." Time proved her right.

Unfortunately for Shapp, he took over a state on the verge of bankruptcy, and one of the first things he had to do to keep the ship of state afloat was impose a state income tax. But fortunately for Shapp, a law passed by referendum in the 1966 election makes it possible for a governor of Pennsylvania to succeed himself, so he now has a crack at serving for eight years instead of only four.

It's too early to tell what kind of governor Milton Shapp will make, but I'll make this prediction: His administration won't be dull. You'll hear more from this violin-playing governor before his term is out.

7

THE TEXTBOOK CAMPAIGN . . .
And Its Sequel That Sent Us Back to the Drawing Board

IT STARTED with a telephone call just before Thanksgiving Day 1966.

"Anchorage, Alaska, calling for Mr. Joseph Napolitan," said the operator.

I admitted my identity and heard a voice say, "Joe, you don't know me, but my name is Mike Gravel and I want to run for the United States Senate and I'd like you to help me."

We talked. I learned he was a Democrat, former speaker of the Alaska House of Representatives, and a defeated candidate in the Democratic primary for Congress earlier that year.

"I'm going to be in Chicago on December 2," Gravel said, "and I'd be glad to fly to Washington or Springfield and meet you there on December 3."

"That's fine," I replied, "except that on December 3 I'll be in Tripoli."

"Hell," he said, "I don't mind chasing you around, but I can't chase you to Africa. Where do you go from there?"

"Rome, Milan, Paris, London, and home."

"That's okay. You can stop in Anchorage on your way home."

"You mean stop in Alaska on my way from London to New York? Isn't that a little out of the way?"

"No, not at all," said Gravel, with that peculiar logic that successful candidates inherit or develop, "you just go over the pole and then swing back through Chicago."

"Insane," I said; "Okay."

Three weeks later I stepped off an airplane in Anchorage into an 18-degree-below-zero chill to begin a love affair with that craggy state and to participate in two political campaigns, one of which left me feeling I knew quite a bit about running campaigns, and the second of which made me doubt everything I thought I knew.

Waiting to greet me was a tall, dark, good-looking guy in his late thirties wearing a black fur Russian hat and a grin that covered half his face. As we walked to his car he told me he was from Springfield, too, and had divided his childhood between Springfield and Worcester.

"I even went to college in Springfield for a while before going to Columbia to get my degree," Gravel told me.

"Which college?"

"A small one—American International."

"When were you there?"

"In the fall of 1951."

"Great," I said, "I was there at the same time."

That night, after dinner, Gravel assembled in his living room a handful of people who were to help create political upheavals in Alaska—and although none of us suspected it at that time, precipitate the sequel campaign that still has us scratching our heads.

Among those present were Larry Carr, a huge, quiet man with a keen mind and shy manner; Barney Gottstein, Carr's more-gregarious business partner and friend; Joe Rothstein, then managing editor of the Anchorage *Daily News,* the smaller and weaker of the two Anchorage dailies, and a skinny Brooklyn transplant named Michael Rowan, who was city manager of Bethel, Alaska (population, 3000).

The events leading up to that meeting were quickly related: Gravel had come to Alaska ten years earlier, worked on the railroad, in a gas station, at anything he could, went into the real-estate business, had some ups and downs, got elected to the House of Representatives of Alaska and within two years became its speaker, and a few months before, in the summer of 1966, had challenged Alaska Congressman Ralph Rivers in the Democratic primary and lost, 52.5% (17,042 votes) to 47.5% (15,404 votes).

Rivers subsequently lost to Howard Pollock in the November election. Pollock (who since has perfected the art of being the right person at the wrong time) was returned to private life four years later.

But now Gravel's eye was on bigger game: the man they called Mr. Alaska, Senator Ernest Gruening.

Few people in American public life can match Gruening's record of public and private service. By coincidence, he also was from Massachusetts, where, among other things, he was the last editor of the old and mourned Boston *Transcript.* Later he became editor of *The Nation,* was appointed territorial governor for Alaska in pre-statehood days, and had served in the United States Senate ever since Alaska became the forty-ninth star on the American flag.

The next morning and afternoon, December 12, 1966, in a conference room on the second floor of the Anchorage Westward Hotel, we laid out a plan that took twenty months to prepare, nine days to execute, and sent Ernest Gruening into retirement.

The plan was simplicity itself:

–Take polls and determine what needed to be done to beat Gruening.

–Gravel would play a very low-key role for the next year or more, making no political statements, and not appearing to pose any great threat to Gruening.

–Blitz Gruening at the finish with the best television materials ever produced and shown in Alaska, which is a long way from Madison Avenue.

And that's exactly what happened—except for one postprimary complication none of us had anticipated: after losing the primary in Alaska's biggest political upset, Senator Gruening decided to run in the general election as an independent and rolled up 14,118 votes, or 17.4 per cent of the total cast.

If, on that December day in 1966, any one of us had had a crystal ball and could have known that Gruening would get 17 per cent of the vote in the general election, Mike Gravel would have gone back to building houses on the Kenai Peninsula, Larry Carr and Barney Gottstein back to their grocery business, Joe Rothstein to writing editorials, Mike Rowan to driving garbage or whatever it was he hauled in those vile-smelling trucks in Bethel, and Joe Napolitan back to running campaigns in warmer places.

And we would all have been dead wrong, because if Gruening hadn't run, and hadn't piled up that many votes, Gravel might well have lost the general election.

But November 1968 is a long way from that overheated meeting room in the Anchorage Westward in December 1966. We did our first poll in February 1967. It showed Gruening *could* be beaten, that he was in some trouble, that he had a net popularity rating of +21.4 compared with Senator Bob Bartlett's +57.2, and that twice as many voters had unfavorable comments about him than about his Senate colleague, Bartlett.

This was useful information, but nothing on which to assume that anyone actually *would* beat Gruening. The same poll, for example, showed George Romney, then governor of Michigan, running nearly two to one ahead of President Lyndon Johnson, while Johnson was running ten points ahead of a New York lawyer named Richard Nixon.

Perhaps the most important bit of information we acquired in this poll, aside from the possibility of Gruening's vulnerability, was that the matter of most concern to Alaskans was the lack of job opportunities in the state.

Also important, we learned that Gravel had the image of a brash, aggressive, impulsive, arrogant young man—traits all of us, including Gravel, were convinced had to be softened if he actually were going to pull off this coup.

And there was opposition to the idea, within the room, of Gravel taking on Gruening, especially if Howard Pollock were the Republican candidate.

At that time, February 1967, Pollock's popularity in the state was second only to that of Senator Bartlett and was higher than that of newly elected Governor Walter Hickel, and many people thought Pollock would be the Republican challenger to Gruening.

There also was this problem: after just having been burned in Pennsylvania, where Milton Shapp had earned a stunning and unprecedented victory over the Democratic organization candidate for governor in the primary, only to lose in the general election, we knew we had to conduct a campaign that not only would allow Gravel to win the primary, but at the same time be so positive in its approach that it would not alienate Gruening supporters and shove them into the Republican column in the general election, only ten weeks after the primary.

So we began, slowly and softly.

The first step was to get Gravel some exposure, so we arranged for him, as outgoing speaker of the Alaska House, to create and be the moderator of a weekly fifteen-minute television program, *Capitol Comments,* in which he discussed state issues and invited Democrats and Republicans in the Alaska House and Senate to debate their differences.

"They'd shout and argue and get angry," Gravel remembers, "and I'd sit back and smile."

The program continued through the legislative session, and helped foster the softer, more-positive image of Gravel that all of us thought would be better for the campaign.

We moved slowly through 1967. I would go to Alaska every two or three months for four or five days, meet with Gravel and his people, talk about organization, and analyze political developments over which we had no control.

Toward the end of 1967 we launched a new campaign gimmick: a monthly newspaper magazine insert, *Today in Alaska.*

The reason was simple: Large portions of Alaska in those days did not receive television. Newspapers were delivered to all sections of the vast state.

Today in Alaska was a full-color newspaper supplement, privately financed and printed, and made available free to all the newspapers in the state. Advertising was sold, and many of the articles, not every month but frequently, mentioned or showed a picture of Mike Gravel.

One issue was called "Mr. Speaker" and reviewed the accomplishments of the various speakers of the Alaska House. The objective analysis clearly showed Gravel to have accomplished more than any of the other speakers.

(This is the issue that carried a disclaimer that noted that although the cover photograph was of a Republican, *Today in Alaska* was non-partisan and should not be considered a Republican puff piece. The only reason the cover picture was of a Republican, we explained, was because he happened to be speaker at the time.

The center spread, conveniently, featured a Democrat—none other than Mike Gravel.)

Another issue featured "The City Builders" and emphasized the development of the Kenai Peninsula, and whose handsome mug should show up in big pictures but that well-known real-estate developer Mike Gravel.

You get the idea.

The funniest thing about the whole *Today in Alaska* operation was that it may well have been the only political publication the opposition helped finance: as the newspaper grew (it became, in a matter of months, the newspaper with the largest circulation in Alaska), Senator Gruening's advertising people thought he should be involved in it, so they purchased some full-page ads about Gruening for the final pre-election issues.

A year passed. Gravel stayed loose. It began to look more and more as though Howard Pollock would run for the Senate, and there was only one among us, Gravel, who felt Gravel could defeat Gruening in the primary and come back ten weeks later and beat Pollock.

In March 1968 we took another poll. In the Senate general-election test, Pollock ran well ahead of both Gruening and Gravel:

Gruening	37.5
Pollock	57.1
Undecided	5.4
Gravel	31.2
Pollock	59.2
Undecided	9.6

Thus Gravel trailed Pollock by two to one in the general election, and also ran behind Gruening in the primary matchings.

The Alaska primary is difficult to poll, because it is an open primary. All the candidates for Senate, for example, are listed on the ballot. Voters of all political persuasions—Democrats, Republicans, and independents—can vote for any of the candidates on the ballot, with the Democrat and the Republican with the highest number of votes becoming their parties' nominees.

We indulged in the usual guessing games about who would run

in the primary, but failed to hit on what eventually proved to be the four-man field.

But some of the observations were interesting:

In a four-man race among Gruening, Gravel, Elmer Rasmuson, and Pollock, Gruening and Pollock were easy winners. Rasmuson, who, as we shall see, eventually became the Republican candidate, was then mayor of Anchorage, president of the largest bank in the state, and considered by all to be the wealthiest man in Alaska.

In a four-man race without Pollock but including a Republican stand-by, John Butrovich, Gruening and Rasmuson were the winners, but in this test Gravel was running only five points behind Gruening, compared with fourteen points in the four-way fight involving Pollock.

Interesting and disturbing, because, if Pollock decided to run, it looked then as though he would be a certain winner.

(I've often wondered if Pollock was polling at this time, and if he was, why he didn't run, or if he wasn't, why he wasn't, because his decision not to make this challenge seems a serious mistake.)

We began making some moves in the spring of 1968. Mike Rowan moved from Bethel to Anchorage to run the campaign. Rowan at twenty-six was sometimes abrasive, sometimes irritating, sometimes wrong, but full of ideas and the ability to execute them, and an extraordinary fast learner. How Rowan got to Alaska is interesting in itself. He had been editor of the college newspaper at St. John's University, in Brooklyn. In one issue he wrote an editorial critical of the college administration, and was expelled. This was before the days when college students showed their displeasure with the administration by burning down buildings, barricading doors, and kidnaping deans.

Sitting in a bar on Third Avenue, a friend pulled out a handful of job applications he had obtained from the federal government for teaching positions at government installations around the world —Guam, the Panama Canal Zone, Alaska. Rowan filled in an application for Alaska. Three weeks later he was accepted and sent to Bethel to teach school. A year or so later he became city manager at the age of twenty-five, and kept that position until he left to run the Gravel primary campaign.

To say that the staff was small in somewhat overstating the case. It consisted of Gravel, the candidate; Rowan, the campaign manager; and a secretary who handled both Gravel's real-estate business and whatever political work was required. In the summer, another full-time person, Adelaide Blomfield, a petite mother of eight with political contacts throughout the state, was added.

And, so far as staff is concerned, that was about it for the primary.

Carr, Gottstein, Rothstein, attorney Stan Reitman, former IBM executive Joe Wiley, and one or two others sat in on strategy sessions, but as the long Alaska winter brightened into spring, the big question remained: what was Pollock going to do?

Though we were waiting, we did not sit idly by. For one thing, we brought Shelby Storck into the picture, and in many ways Shelby became the most important figure in the campaign, because he produced the half-hour documentary film *Man for Alaska,* which made the difference in the campaign.

Shelby Storck is dead now. He died unexpectedly in his sleep in April 1969 of a heart attack, a few hours after telling me he was turning down an offer to handle a candidate in the New York mayoral election, "because life is too short to get involved in a mess like that."

But in April 1968, Shelby was healthy and fit. And quickly became enchanted with Alaska.

In the spring of 1968 Storck brought one of his partners, Art Fillmore, an extraordinary cinematographer, and what he always referred to as his No. 1 crew—Bob Bauer, Don Matthews, Art Moser—to begin putting together the Gravel half-hour and spots, all of which were edited by another partner in the firm, Pierre Vacho, back in St. Louis. And Wilbur Phillips spent several months in Alaska doing research for the film.

This Storck/Fillmore/Vacho team is the same one that later in the year produced the documentary *What Manner of Man* for Hubert Humphrey.

In August the Storck film would prove its merit in Alaska. But in April and May we still were wondering if Pollock would run, and what Gravel should do.

Some people thought that if Pollock ran for the Senate, Gravel should run for Pollock's seat in the House. Gravel didn't say much, but quietly resisted these ideas, and I am convinced that even if Pollock had decided to go for the Senate, Gravel would have said, "What the hell," and gone for it anyway.

The March 1968 poll reinforced a finding of the February 1967 survey: namely, that voters in Alaska were primarily concerned about lack of job opportunities.

So, with the assistance of Rowan, Gravel wrote a book, creatively entitled *Jobs and More Jobs*.

It never became a best seller, but it was displayed in an attractive counter stand in drugstores, newsstands, bookstores, and supermarkets all over Alaska.

I can confess now that I've never read the book—and I'm not sure many other people did either—but that's beside the point. The book served its purpose by being published and displayed—a perfect example of the medium being the message.

The book was supported by full-page ads in *Today in Alaska*. Mike Gravel was interviewed on television and radio. Chapters in the book were serialized in legitimate Alaska newspapers. Gravel did, in fact, become an authority on the unemployment crisis in Alaska, and directed his research toward finding ways of creating new jobs in the state. This was not political expediency so far as Gravel was concerned; it was something he believed in, a problem he wanted to do something about. By the end of the campaign there was no doubt that Gravel knew more about the problems of the jobless in Alaska than any of the other candidates, in or out of office, and this knowledge led him to useful rapport with those out of jobs or insecure in the jobs they held.

Memorial Day 1968. Nearly sixteen months had passed since our first meeting in the Westward Hotel. Mike Rowan and I were driving back to Anchorage from Palmer, a small city about thirty miles away, where Gravel had been a guest at a picnic. The early-afternoon news carried the announcement that Howard Pollock would run for re-election to Congress.

Rowan flashed me a big toothy grin. We were in a race for the United States Senate against Mr. Alaska.

That night we assembled in Anchorage: Gravel, Gottstein, Carr, Rothstein, Reitman, Rowan, Napolitan. The decision was "go."

Shelby's crew was called in, and we made plans for a television press conference for the announcement.

It was quite a press conference.

We rented a room at the Anchorage Westward. Anchorage, like so many cities in America, has its Democratic and Republican hotels. In Anchorage, Democrats tend to hold their functions and meetings at the Westward; Republicans go to the Captain Cook. Maybe the fact that Wally Hickel owns the Captain Cook has something to do with it.

The three Anchorage television stations were there, with crews. Several radio stations had reporters there with tape recorders. Both Anchorage newspapers covered, with reporters and photographers. Gravel read his announcement statement, concluded, and said, "That's the end of my formal statement. I'll be glad to answer any questions."

Silence.

"Doesn't anyone have any questions?"

Silence.

"Okay, I guess that's it."

Not a single television, newspaper, or radio reporter posed a single question. No one asked, "What makes you think you are qualified to run for the Senate?" No one asked, "What makes you think you can defeat Senator Gruening?" No one asked, "What issues are you going to campaign on?"

But they do some strange things in Alaska.

The introduction to the March 1968 poll contained this message:

"The information contained in this report is intended only for the private use of Mike Gravel. It is strongly recommended that only those persons with a policy-making interest in his campaign be permitted access to the report."

I went to Alaska when the poll was ready, to interpret the results and discuss the findings with Gravel, Carr, Gottstein, et al.

Barney Gottstein asked if I would mind coming to his home to discuss the results with a group of people interested in the political situation in Alaska. I said I wouldn't mind doing so, but that it was rather unusual to share the results of a confidential poll with other people.

"That's okay," he said. "Sometimes we do things a little differently up here."

He wasn't kidding. One of the twenty or twenty-five people who gathered at his home that day was Senator Gruening's campaign manager. This, of course, was several months before Gravel had decided definitely to run against Gruening, but it wasn't much of a secret that he was thinking about making the challenge.

Anyway, since Carr and Gottstein were raising the money to pay for the poll, and this is what they wanted, I went along, and proceeded to brief everyone there—including the opposition—on what we had learned.

We played it straight, too. There was no fiddling with numbers or juggling percentages. I told them honestly that I thought Gruening would be beaten either in the primary or the general election, and that the best hope the Democratic party had of holding onto the seat was to nominate a younger man in the primary.

The Gruening people weren't buying this. They felt that their man could survive both the primary and the general election.

"He may be old," they said, "but he's tough."

They were right about that: During the campaign the 81-year-old Gruening challenged 37-year-old Gravel to a swimming race in the Arctic Ocean.

"Are you kidding?" responded Gravel. "You'd kill me."

Gruening was a physical-fitness fetishist; one of his posters was a near-life-size photo of himself doing push-ups.

Once Gravel decided to run, we determined *how* he would run. The plan was not at variance with the original concept laid out in December 1966.

It would be a simple campaign.

First, and perhaps most important, we had to present Mike Gravel as a *respectable alternative* to Ernest Gruening. We knew that Gruening had some soft spots, but it takes someone to beat someone, particularly an incumbent United States senator.

Second, we decided to run a low-key campaign right up to the time of our media blitz. By "low-key" we meant no billboards, no posters, no bumper stickers, no handouts, no wild assortment of position papers and brochures, no early media.

From our polls we knew that the biggest thing working against Gruening was his age—81.

Gruening also was among the most dovish members of Congress. He was one of two senators who voted against the Tonkin Gulf resolution. (A decision, in retrospect, that makes Gruening look pretty good.) The national press tried to interpret Gravel's victory over Gruening as a hawk-versus-dove duel. Nothing could be further from the truth. Gravel certainly wasn't to the left of Gruening (there was very little room there), but his inclinations and later Senate votes are anti-war, anti-military establishment.* He was one of the leaders in the anti-ABM fight, and his attitudes toward Vietnam certainly were closer to Senator Gruening's than to Lyndon Johnson's or Richard Nixon's. Gravel did not attack Gruening's position in Vietnam; it was an issue seldom mentioned in the campaign.

One area where we did feel that Gruening was vulnerable was his deep and active interests in foreign affairs—an appealing arena for a man of his personal inclinations and intellect, but also, as other ex-senators have learned, one that is full of pitfalls if you fall out of touch with the people back home.

Gravel made the point, repeatedly, that if the voter's primary interest was in foreign affairs he should support Gruening, but if he was primarily concerned with what was happening in Alaska, then he should think about voting for Gravel. It was a persuasive argument.

Although Gravel had announced early in June, he was still playing very low-key and doing little in the way of overt campaigning. His attractive wife, Rita, Mike Rowan's equally attractive wife, Irene (a full-blooded Tlingit Indian), Adelaide Blomfield, and some other women in the campaign were doing a lot of door-to-door campaigning and obtaining a favorable response, but even the tip of the iceberg in our real campaign had not begun to show.

Gruening, on the other hand, was campaigning vigorously, much harder than anyone, except perhaps his own people, had anticipated. He was good at it, too, and there is no doubt that he picked up points during June and July.

Some people expressed disappointment in Gravel's campaign. He was soft-spoken and positive in his public appearances, and had no media campaign at all.

The press, particularly in Anchorage, was with Gruening. While Joe Rothstein of the *Daily News* was personally friendly to Gravel,

---

* In 1971, Gravel led a filibuster against extending the draft, and risked disciplinary action by the Senate when he became the first—and only—United States senator to disclose and decry information contained in the Pentagon Papers. It was a courageous act, one that none of the presidential candidates dared to do, although several of them had the same access to the papers as Gravel.

his publisher, Larry Fanning, was an old and strong supporter of Gruening. The larger Anchorage *Times* gave little space or attention to Gravel, and going into the final month it looked as though Gruening would win with a substantial majority.

I remember walking out of the Westward Hotel with Gravel one afternoon and bumping into Gruening on the sidewalk.

"Ah, my opponent," said the senator, smiling. Introduced to me, he gave me a patronizing pat on the back and said he hoped I enjoyed my visit to Alaska.

And while Gruening was well liked by many people, let me hasten to add that the feeling was not unanimous. The first time I met Senator Bartlett, who was to die an untimely death a few weeks after the general election, was in his Washington office. I didn't know much about his relationship with Gruening, but assumed that because they had both been so active in Alaska affairs for so long that they were pretty good friends. I went to see Bartlett because Barney Gottstein wanted me to bring him up to date on what was happening in the Gravel campaign and let him know what we were doing.

I started by saying something like, "Senator, I want you to know that I have nothing against Senator Gruening personally, but I am working for Mike Gravel . . ."

Bartlett interrupted me.

"Do you know Gruening well?"

I admitted I had never even met him.

"He's a double-dealing, no-good son of a bitch."

So much for where Senator Bartlett stood.

While Gravel and Gruening were preparing for the primary, so, too, were the Republican candidates, who were banker Elmer Rasmuson and State Senator Ted Stevens.

Stevens was to lose to Rasmuson, blame Gravel's campaign for his loss, and through a quirk of fate, wind up a United States senator before Gravel did.

A classmate of Mike Gravel's, a Massachusetts realtor named Dick Thomas, came to Alaska for the final month of the campaign as a volunteer worker for his friend. Accustomed to the hoopla of Massachusetts politics, Thomas was amazed and discomfited on a Sunday afternoon three weeks before the primary when he learned that the only event scheduled that day was a cookout for eighteen or twenty friends of the Gravels at their home.

Thomas called me aside.

"Look, Joe, I know that this is your business. But shouldn't we be doing *something?*"

I told him to relax, all was well.

In truth, we were putting all our eggs in one very small basket, Shelby Storck's film.

And it was important to us that the Gruening people not take Gravel too seriously until it was too late to do much about it. Despite Barney Gottstein's mania for sharing information, only a handful of us knew about the film and our hopes for it.

The greater-Anchorage area represents about 30 per cent of the vote in Alaska. It clearly is the key city in any Alaska election. Mike Rowan developed a straw-vote-poll procedure to use at shopping centers throughout the Anchorage area. There was nothing very scientific about these polls, but they did measure voter intentions in the same areas over a twelve-day period.

And anyone who asks whether television really can affect the outcome of an election should study the Anchorage figures carefully.

We took straw polls in Anchorage every day but one, for the last twelve days of the primary. On the twelfth day, the eleventh day, and tenth day, the polls showed Gruening leading Gravel by about two to one. On the ninth day, a Sunday, we did not poll.

But that night, from 10 to 10:30 P.M., on all three Anchorage television stations, we ran a simulcast of Storck's half-hour documentary *Man for Alaska*. It was the first time the film had been shown, and the only time it was presented in simulcast. Simulcasting can be effective, but it is dangerous; you always run the risk of getting voters so irritated at your candidate for blocking out all other television programs that they might vote for your opponent just out of spite. My recommendation is never to use a total simulcast—i.e., complete blackout of everything else—more than once in a campaign, and then only if the program you are putting on is good enough to hold the viewer's interest.

The film traced Mike Gravel's career from his taxi-driving days in New York City while he was at Columbia, through his trip to Alaska when he lived on peanut-butter sandwiches and arrived in the territory with less than a dollar in his pockets.

It showed him working on the Alaska Railroad, working for military intelligence in Europe, entering Alaska politics.

Research for the film also uncovered, as good research almost always does, a bonus film clip no one knew existed but that added emotionally to the film.

Storck was going through some old footage taken on the night Alaska achieved statehood. One of the scenes showed a pretty girl, trembling slightly as she climbed a ladder to pin the forty-ninth star on a huge American flag.

"My God," said Shelby. "That looks like Rita Gravel."

It was. A former beauty queen, Rita Martin had been selected to climax the statehood ceremony by adding the forty-ninth star. This pleasant sequence, maybe forty-five seconds long, added a nice touch to the film.

The film wasn't all froth and fireworks. There were solid sequences in which Gravel explained his solution for Alaska's problems, and expressed unequivocally his stand on native land claims and protection for the environment.

There was substance to the film—but it was *interesting* substance, not dull and dreary.

Although the film did, of course, carry a disclaimer that it was a paid political program, some viewers called Gravel during and after the show to tell him about the great film the networks had made about him, or how well he had come out in the film.

The film over, we kept our fingers crossed, Gravel & Co. in Alaska, Shelby and I in the Lower 48, as Alaskans refer to the contiguous United States.

Gravel called, ecstatic: the Monday poll, on the eighth day before the primary, showed Gravel running ahead of Gruening 55–45, the first time Gravel had ever run ahead of Gruening in Anchorage.

And the only thing that had happened between Saturday, when Gruening had led two to one, and Monday, when Gravel led 55–45, was the film!

This is the best example I know, of how effective television, and half-hour films, *can* be, not necessarily will be, but can be in a campaign.

We played hell out of the film in the next eight days, and also phased in our television and radio spots and some newspaper ads. A large brochure also was mailed to everyone in the state.

Our nine-day blitz worked: Gravel defeated Gruening by 1956 votes, with 52.9 per cent of the vote cast between the two men.

Even as the blitz was reaching its peak, most politicians still didn't take it seriously. They were reacting to their conversations with other politicians, a form of mental masturbation that causes some interesting upsets. Late in the week before the primary, Gruening's people realized that something was happening, so they hired a pickup truck and a post-hole digger and went around Anchorage putting up signs that said RE-ELECT SENATOR GRUENING. Talk about the differences between the old politics and the new politics!

By primary day in Alaska I was at the Democratic National Convention, in Chicago. During the day, just about the time the polls were opening in Alaska, I was at a meeting in Orville Freeman's suite in the Conrad Hilton Hotel. Someone asked how my campaign in Alaska was coming. I said I thought we'd win.

One of the men present, later introduced to me as a former attorney general in Alaska, gave me a self-satisfied smile and said I didn't understand Alaska politics if I thought the voters there would reject Gruening for Gravel. I conceded he might be right about my not understanding Alaska politics, but I thought I knew something about voter reaction. We bet a steak dinner on the outcome, and I'm still waiting to collect.

But let's look now at what was happening on the Republican side. As I mentioned earlier, all four names were on the ballot, two Democrats and two Republicans, and the Democrat and the Republican with the highest numbers of votes would be the nominees.

The Republican nomination went to Elmer Rasmuson, the banker candidate, whose campaign had been guided by Spencer-Roberts, a top-flight California political counseling firm. Ted Stevens, the Republican loser, was furious—at us.

He was convinced that the film and Gravel's last-minute television/radio barrage had pulled votes away from him and over to Gravel. He may be right, but that really wasn't our worry.

We felt pretty good after the primary. Gravel had scored the biggest upset in Alaskan political history, and although he had a deficit and was running against the wealthiest man in Alaska, we felt he could outcampaign Rasmuson. And we were proud of the fact that we had deliberately not been harsh with Gruening and really hadn't bruised anything except his ego.

But we were wrong.

Under ordinary political procedure, Gruening would have sulked awhile, nursed his wounds in private, and then endorsed Gravel. But this irascible old man, apparently convinced Gravel's primary victory was a fluke, decided to run as an independent write-in candidate in the general election.

At first we weren't concerned, but as the campaign progressed it was obvious that Gruening was going to do much better than we had anticipated. He eventually received 17.4 per cent of the vote in a three-way race, extraordinarily high for a write-in candidate.

The irony, however, was that Gruening's supporters, and there are so few voters in Alaska that a senator knows a high proportion of them by name, were so bitter that they probably would have voted *against* Gravel in the general election out of sheer vindictiveness.

No one will ever know for certain, but in retrospect it now appears that if the pro-Gruening, anti-Gravel voters had not had an opportunity to vote for Gruening in the general election, they might very well have gone for Rasmuson, and if they had, Rasmuson would have defeated Gravel in the final.

Elmer Rasmuson is an enigma. Clearly bright, married to the former Mary Louise Mulligan, who held a high position in the Women's Army Corps in World War II, eminently successful in Alaska, accumulator of a vast fortune, he seemed to have everything going for him.

Everything, that is, except himself.

I still don't understand why he ran such a poor campaign. One big mystery is the Spencer-Roberts role. This firm has a fine reputation in the political counseling business, and I can't believe they would have willingly let Rasmuson conduct the kind of campaign he did. Either Rasmuson overruled their recommendations (in which case the sensible thing for Spencer-Roberts to do was resign the account) or someone other than one of the principals was assigned to the campaign and didn't realize how bad the situation was.

Rasmuson had one tremendous advantage: money.

He had literally unlimited resources, while Gravel's purse was more than empty; it had a hole in it.

Looking back on my memoranda to Gravel for the 1968 campaign I find these comments:

June 8, 1967: "Without doubt, the most important thing you can do this summer is raise funds for the 1968 campaign."

June 3, 1968: "The most important thing you can do in the next five or six weeks is concentrate on raising funds."

August 4, 1968: "In my opinion the best use you can make of your time in the remaining three weeks is:

"a. Raising money.

"b. Personal contact with voters through visits and door-to-door campaigning."

Gravel tried, but he never managed to raise all the money needed. In fact, at this writing, three years after the election, Gravel still has a campaign deficit that he is gradually reducing. Maybe by the time he runs for re-election in 1974 he'll be clear with the board.

Rasmuson used television extensively in his campaign, too, but he had failed to learn an important lesson about the use of television in politics: you can *lose* votes on television as well as win votes.

Rasmuson didn't have Shelby Storck, and he wasn't Mike Gravel, with his innate sense of how media can be used effectively. He outspent Gravel by a lopsided margin.

But Storck had revised the half-hour film and produced some new television and radio spots, and Gravel pumped every dime he had into the media campaign.

During the general-election campaign, Gravel accompanied Shelby Storck to the Waverly, Minnesota, home of Hubert Humphrey, where Storck was filming Humphrey for the epic documentary *What Manner of Man.*

Relaxed, Humphrey chatted with Gravel about the responsibilities of a senator and offered this advice:

"Give four years to the Lord, and then start worrying about being re-elected. Don't even think about campaigning for the first four years. Just concentrate on being the best damn senator you can be."

Gravel took the advice to heart. In the winter of 1971 one

observer of the Washington political scene noted that the only two senators whose votes were totally unpredictable in advance were Margaret Chase Smith and Mike Gravel.

It was a hard campaign, complicated by Gruening's third-party presence, but Mike Gravel hadn't come that far down the pike to blow it at the end, and he didn't. The final vote was:

Gravel	36,527	45.1%
Rasmuson	30,286	37.4%
Gruening	14,118	17.4%

And then the biggest tragedy, and biggest irony of all: Senator E. L. Bartlett, of whom I have heard no man speak critically, was stricken with a heart attack late in the fall and died before Christmas.

Walter Hickel already had been designated Secretary of the Interior, but, at the time of Bartlett's death, still was governor of Alaska, and, as governor, had the right to name a senator to replace Bartlett.

Instead of selecting the recent Republican nominee and winner of the Republican primary, Elmer Rasmuson, he by-passed the banker and named the man Rasmuson had beaten in the primary, Ted Stevens.

Thus Stevens entered the Senate before Gravel, became the senior senator from Alaska, and left Gravel to enter the Senate as No. 100 in terms of seniority, since Senate seniority is determined by a complicated formula that takes into consideration such factors as previous offices held, number of votes received, etc.

"That's okay," said Gravel. "Worse than being No. 100 is being No. 101. I'm very happy where I am."

My Alaskan friends and I were pretty pleased. We had achieved a great victory in the Senate, but already we were thinking of the 1970 election for governor, an election of extraordinary importance because of oil discoveries on the North Slope of Alaska.

In September 1969 the state of Alaska auctioned off parcels of land on the North Slope to oil companies interested in developing those properties. More than *$900 million* was collected, *in cash,* as a result of that auction.

This put Alaska in the position, probably for the first time for any state since the Union was founded, of having enough money in the bank to solve its problems. And, under law, Alaska's governor is a strong governor; he has more power within his own state than any other governor.

Long before the oil development, however, Democrats in Alaska were looking around for a candidate to run against Keith Miller, who had been elected secretary of state (Alaska had no lieutenant governor) with Walter Hickel in 1966 and ascended to governor when Hickel went into the Nixon Cabinet. The assumption was that Miller would not be a strong governor or a strong candidate in 1970. There was even speculation, early in 1968, that he might not be a candidate at all, or that he might well be defeated in the Republican primary in August 1970. Neither of these things happened.

In any event, even while I was working on the Gravel campaign, Gottstein, Carr, and other leading Democrats were seeking out a strong Democratic candidate. Several times I was asked to meet with potential candidates to size them up. One, high on Barney Gottstein's list, had lunch with us one day at the Westward. When he stirred his coffee with his knife, we began to have doubts about his ability to run a sophisticated campaign.

Bill Egan, who had been governor for two terms and was the first and only governor Alaska had had since acquiring statehood, was defeated by Walter Hickel in 1966 and ran what everyone conceded was a poor campaign. Egan moved to Seattle after the election and it was assumed he was out of the 1970 race.

After Gravel's victory, the people in his camp began making serious efforts to find a strong Democrat. One by one, candidates were considered and were either discarded or decided on their own to seek some other office. All three major offices were up in 1970 —governor, senator (the Bartlett-Stevens term expiring), and Alaska's lone congressman. The one unbeatable candidate appeared to be Howard Pollock, safely ensconced in his House seat, probably wondering why he hadn't made the run for the Senate, especially after Gravel proved that both Gruening and Rasmuson could be beaten.

By the fall of 1969 no strong candidate had emerged, and we began looking around the room at ourselves.

Slowly, but with the certainty of an Alaskan glacier, we all settled on one man: Larry Carr. The only reluctant holdout to this idea was Carr himself.

To understand this you must know a little about Larry Carr. He came to Alaska right out of high school in California and may be one of the few people in public life whose ambition was to be a successful grocer. His first job in Alaska was packing groceries in a small general store. From that he advanced to clerk and store manager. In the fall of 1969, at the age of thirty-nine, he owned the largest chain of supermarkets and shopping centers in Alaska, and was the largest private employer in the state. His Alaskan dream, unlike so many, had come true, and he was not disposed to plunge into public life. He has a pleasant home in Anchorage, a comfortable retreat in Palm Springs, and a family who is as proud of him as he is of them.

Besides which, Larry Carr is a shy, introspective man.

But he has what Barney Gottstein calls "a mind like a steel trap," and I have no doubt that Larry Carr would come out on the high end of any intelligence test. During the campaign, he once had a meeting with a group of university professors who were concerned about Larry's lack of educational credits. They discussed the problems in Alaska and Carr's proposed solutions to them. The professors left the room talking to themselves. There is no doubt in my mind, even today, that Larry Carr knows more about the problems of Alaska and what should be done about them than any person there.

We all thought up arguments why Larry should run, and they were persuasive:

1. While not as physically attractive as Gravel, or as good a speaker, his mind was brilliant and he would have the benefit of the entire Gravel campaign team.
2. We knew, or thought we knew, a lot more about campaigning than we had when Gravel had become a candidate, and we had the experience of the Gravel campaign to fall back on.
3. While a long way from Elmer Rasmuson's financial position, Carr was in a position to finance and raise money for his campaign, and these funds would allow him to retain the best research, media, and organization people around.
4. There was no one else.

Finally Carr agreed, and I must say I never have seen a

candidate zero in on a campaign with as much zeal as he did. From the day he announced his candidacy until the election was over, he never set foot in his business office. He turned the day-to-day operations of the Carr supermarkets over to Joe Wiley, who by this time had left IBM and joined the Carr organization. During the campaign, when a Carr employee was arrested for embezzlement, Carr learned about it by reading the newspapers.

He plunged into the campaign as he had gone into business: all the way.

A huge man, six foot five, Carr was overweight. He immediately went on a diet and shed forty pounds. At the urging of his children he even let his hair grow longer. He changed his glasses. Far more important, he set about learning what was wrong in Alaska and how it could be corrected.

And we began bringing in people to help.

Bob Squier of the Communications Company, in Washington, D.C., came aboard to help improve Larry's television appearances. Carr's extraordinary shyness and slow, deliberate manner of speaking led many people, especially those who didn't know him well, to believe he was cool, aloof, unapproachable. I'm sure he instilled fear into the heart of more than one Carr employee just strolling through the store, although I've never met a man whose employees were better treated. We felt we had to show the public the *real* Larry Carr, and not the one they knew from casual observance, and we felt Squier was the man to do the job.

Tom Lantos, Ph.D., a Hungarian-born economist of inordinate intelligence, was retained as a research consultant and to explore and develop programs for Carr to use in his campaign.

Walter Davis, an experienced political campaigner and former radio announcer with strong labor ties, was hired to direct the organization.

Medion, the San Francisco television producer, was retained to produce a half-hour documentary film.

Tony Schwartz was hired to do radio spots.

Other key people in the Gravel campaign pitched in.

Gravel himself broke precedent in Alaska and actively campaigned for and openly supported Carr in the Democratic primary.

I was there, along with Mike Rowan, who, by this time, after a six-month stint as legislative assistant to Senator Gravel, had joined Public Affairs Analysts, Inc., in Washington, D.C. Joe Rothstein, Gravel's administrative assistant, devoted as much time as he legally could to helping.

A hell of a team, no doubt.

Now let's look at what the other guys were doing:

Bill Egan had moved back to Alaska and was planning to run for governor.

Governor Keith Miller definitely was going to be a candidate.

And our old friend Congressman Howard Pollock was making noises about running for governor, for senator, or for re-election. If he ran for either governor or senator he would have to run against a Republican incumbent in a primary, Miller for governor or Stevens for senator.

The indecisiveness of the major candidate left a host of less-well-known candidates hanging. Mayor Red Boucher of Fairbanks, an early contender for governor, eventually decided to run for lieutenant governor. (And won.) Nick Begich, a school administrator defeated in the 1968 Congressional primary, also was a Democratic possibility for governor. He eventually ran for Congress when Pollock cast his lot elsewhere. (And also won.)

We began taking polls. The results were interesting. They showed Larry Carr to be reasonably well known—but not very well liked. They showed Pollock strong—but Miller stronger than had been anticipated.

And they showed Bill Egan to be very popular.

Egan presented a problem for us. It's hard not to like Bill Egan. He's a pleasant person, but had been something less than a howling success as governor, although everyone conceded that he was a simple, honest, sincere person.

Honest. Sincere. A man of integrity. Likable.

Good qualities. But Alaska had nearly a billion dollars in cash to invest, to improve the state, to make it hum.

Could Bill Egan successfully manage this amount of money? Or, put another way, could we persuade voters that Larry Carr, with his broad and successful business background, was better equipped to manage that money for them than Bill Egan?

We thought we could.

We were wrong.

Pollock eventually jumped into the race for governor, giving up a sure seat in Congress. In 1968 Pollock made a mistake by not seeking higher office; in 1970 he made one by doing it. Some people just can't win.

So it came down to a four-man primary—Egan and Carr, Democrats, and Miller and Pollock, Republicans.

Egan, Miller, and Pollock all had been elected to statewide office, Egan and Pollock more than once. Carr had never even run before.

But we, disciples of the new politics, thought we could do it. After all, when you compared Egan and Carr in terms of ability, wasn't Carr clearly the more successful?

Here we made the mistake of ignoring one of our dicta: more people vote on the basis of emotion than on the basis of logic.

Logically, Carr was the better man. Emotionally, people were with Egan.

There is an interesting parallel in their non-political careers. Egan was a modestly successful grocer in his home town of Valdez, and remained modestly successful. Carr began as a modest grocer and developed, by the time he was in his mid-thirties, the most successful chain of supermarkets in Alaska.

We used techniques in the Carr campaign that probably were more advanced than those used in any campaign outside of Nelson Rockefeller's in New York.

We had a half-hour film, issues-oriented television spots, good media, individualized computer letters, a statewide mailing of an attractive sixteen-page brochure, specialized mailings, a batch of position papers, question-and-answer radio and television programs, newspaper ads, utilization of McLuhan's "instant information" theories, a top-flight television coach, brilliant research, creative and innovative programs, and some gimmicks that have never been used anywhere, such as this one:

Most native villages in Alaska do not receive television. They could, if the state launched a communications satellite that would permit it to pick up signals from stations in the Lower 48. (The satellite also could serve a variety of other useful purposes— transmittal of medical information, for example: Electrocardiographic and electroencephalographic reports can be transmitted by satellite to specialists outside of Alaska for diagnosis—much quicker than mail, for instance.) Carr had a plan to develop a communications satellite program for Alaska.

As he visited the tiny villages in the Alaskan bush, he brought to each a small, inexpensive television set (net wholesale cost of these was around forty dollars). Each was inscribed, "A gift to the children of _____ from Larry Carr."

Carr also carried a portable videotape unit he used in his television coaching sessions, and played, on the gift set, some tapes—usually of natives in a near-by village that the inhabitants of this village recognized.

He told them that as governor he would launch the communications satellite, and then they would be able to receive live television all the time.

When Carr left the village, the set remained.

A lot of Eskimos in Alaska are going to get their first look at live television courtesy of Larry Carr, one-time candidate for governor.

The whole program cost less than four thousand dollars, and I'm sure brings Carr some satisfaction, even if he didn't become governor in 1970.

On paper, everything looked fine. But we lacked something, and if I had to give a one-word description of what this was I would have to say "emotion."

We decided early in the campaign not to personally attack Egan. First of all, this style of campaigning is contrary to Carr's nature. Secondly, there wasn't a lot to attack, although every public figure who has served in office as long as Egan has some points of vulnerability.

There was another problem: fear of a Gravel/Carr/Gottstein monopoly that would take over the state. At first I was inclined to doubt this fear, although Barney Gottstein was very sensitive to it. In retrospect, he probably was right.

Gottstein is a native-born Alaskan—and one of the most urbane men I know. He's about as far away from the average American's impression of a sourdough or Alaskan frontiersman as you could imagine. I have never known him to perform a dishonorable act;

if anything, he bends over backward to avoid the taint of dishonorableness. Despite this, one of the reasons voters give for voting against Carr is his association with Gottstein.

If we had the campaign to do over again—the forlorn hope of every losing manager—then I would have given Gottstein much more exposure on television and let everyone see the kind of decent, respectable person he is. Gottstein also is more articulate and personable than Carr, and I'm sure could have done a great deal to dispel the fear that had been created about their relationship.

While our decision was not to attack, the Egan forces were on the offense. They ran large newspaper ads criticizing Carr for trying to buy the election (he spent a fraction of what Elmer Rasmuson had, although admittedly much more than Egan) and insinuating the threat of the Carr/Gravel/Gottstein troika.

Some of our material looked better on paper than it did on tape.

Carr's announcement, for example, was videotaped and distributed around the state. Carr improved significantly on television as the campaign progressed and he acquired confidence and sophistication. But he was pretty bad in the early stuff, and we made a mistake in using him on camera so early. Here's a case where a mimeographed press release would have done us more good than a widely distributed paid videotape announcement.

Medion produced two superb 30-minute films in 1970, one for Governor John Burns of Hawaii in a campaign in which I was involved, and the other for Jack Danforth in Missouri, who challenged and almost defeated Senator Stuart Symington.

But the one they did for Larry Carr wasn't up to those standards. It lacked an essential ingredient: emotional punch. We compounded the error by overexposing the film, and probably running it too soon.

Our success with the Gravel film in 1968 caused us unexpected problems in 1970: *everyone* running for office went on television, some of them with long films, and the airways were crammed with political material. We reasoned that with so much late competition, it was important for us to get on much earlier with the Carr film. So we did. I believe, and some of the straw polls showed, it had some effect, but we were guilty of overkill.

In Alaska, where many communities can receive only one television signal, seeing the same film three or four times can be deadly.

It's possible our initial reasoning—to get on early—was sound. But it seems now that what we should have done was get on, get off, and stay off until the very end.

There are lessons to be learned in this campaign.

Our polls were interesting. None of our statewide personal-interview polls ever showed Carr running ahead of Egan. But the straw polls, which we took weekly for the final ten or twelve weeks, showed Carr moving into the lead after the initial showing of the film. These polls also showed Miller with a consistent lead over Pollock, which surprised everyone.

Suddenly, with a couple of weeks to go, the bottom fell out of our polls, and Carr began to slide. What appears obvious is that we had peaked too soon by utilizing the film beyond its capacity to influence votes, and that we were doing nothing to counteract the negative campaign that was being waged against Carr. Our final straw polls, sadly, were pretty accurate, and simple, honest, sincere Bill Egan won the nomination. On the other side of the ticket, Keith Miller scored a solid victory over that man in the wrong place, Howard Pollock.

If we learned anything in the Carr campaign, it was a reinforcement of a view that we always have held: issues don't mean a hell of a lot in a campaign.

Let me cite two examples from our postprimary survey:

First we asked, "What would you say were the main issues in the campaign for governor?"

These were the responses:

Oil money ($900 million)	33.6
Pipeline road	27.3
Native land claims	9.1
Natural resources (fishing)	3.6
Conservation/pollution	3.2
Education	2.8

Carr spent more time talking about the oil money and the need to manage it properly than the other three candidates combined.

The whole issues priority list looked like our check list of campaign issues.

Another question: "Regardless of whom you voted for, which candidate do you think raised the best issues in the campaign for governor?"

Carr	27.3
Pollock	21.4
Miller	17.7
Egan	8.3
Not sure	25.5

So what happened?

Carr and Pollock, who raised the best issues, both lost in the primary. And Egan, who scored lowest on the issues question, not only defeated Carr in the primary, but then went on to whip Miller in the general election.

Alaska, a microcosm of the country, taught lessons screaming to be learned.

And one thing it taught us above all others: don't take *anything* for granted in a political campaign.

8

THE CONVENTION—
It's Over Before It Begins

THERE IS A SHARP, and little understood, difference between convention politics and election politics. Even many of the people in this business don't appreciate or understand the difference.

In a campaign, you try to influence tens of thousands, or hundreds of thousands, or even millions of voters; in trying to win a convention you are concerned with hundreds, or at the most a few thousands, of individuals.

The two people I know in this country who understand convention politics best are Larry O'Brien, the Democratic national chariman who ran John F. Kennedy's successful, and in many ways unprecedented, convention victory in 1960, and F. Clifton White of New York, who engineered Barry Goldwater's nomination in 1964. Goldwater's victory was a classic, and White documents it in his book *Suite 3505*, which should be required reading for anyone attempting to win a nomination at a convention.

The key to success in winning a convention is easier to say than to do—but if you do this, you will win:

Elect your own delegates to the convention.

Even today, candidates still try to influence delegates *after* they have been elected, instead of making an all-out effort to get their own people elected delegates in the first place. Eugene Burdick fostered this theory of influencing delegates after they have been elected in his interesting but naïve novel *The 480*, which describes a computerized effort to win the presidential nomination at a national convention.

Actually, national conventions and the nomination of presidential candidates represent the last bastion of political-party strength. In general elections, and even in primaries, parties are becoming less and less important. But party bosses (leaders, if you prefer) continue to have an important voice in nominating candidates for President.

Even here, their power is being eroded, and I think this is a gain for the country and the average voter. The Democratic National Committee changed its rules in 1971 so that all delegates to the national convention in 1972 must be elected. Previously, in many states some or all of the delegates were appointed by party leadership.

This meant that a very few men controlled sizable blocks of delegate votes and could wheel and deal at conventions.

Qualifications for becoming a delegate vary from state to state. In some states a delegate must be a member of a county committee or a state committee before he can be elected a delegate to the national convention. This means that if you want to get your people elected you must start very early in the game—sometimes more than a year before the actual convention—in order to make certain that you are not locked out of electing your own delegates because the time has passed for them to be eligible for nomination to the lesser committees to which they must be elected before they can seek positions as delegates to the national convention.

If I were advising a candidate running for President, in either party, the very first thing I would do would be to assemble the state regulations governing the election of delegates to the national convention. This gives you a timetable to begin delegate operations.

Some states have presidential primaries that bind the delegates to the winner for one or more ballots at the national convention; some states have non-binding primaries; some have no primaries at all. But every state now has some procedure for electing delegates.

Delegate elections usually attract small turnouts, and these are campaigns in which organization is infinitely more important than media, because you are concerned with small numbers of (usually) politically oriented voters.

The same strategy holds true in state conventions to nominate governors, senators, and other statewide candidates. These nominees can be challenged in primaries, and more and more frequently are being defeated. My personal preference is for *all* candidates to be nominated in primaries, thus giving full power to the people—at least, full power to the people *if they use it,* which they often don't.

Usually delegates are elected by slates—sometimes on a district basis, sometimes statewide, sometimes on a combination of both. Sometimes the candidate for President favored by the delegates is indicated on the ballot; sometimes it is not. There is no standarization of nominating procedures for delegates, which is all the more reason for an early start and expert advice on how to go about selecting, nominating, and electing delegates favorable to your candidate.

Delegates you are looking for should have two major qualifications:

1. They must be committed to your candidate, come hell or high water, until he releases them.
2. They must be reasonably electable.

Finding a committed potential delegate who doesn't have a prayer of being elected is about as bad as electing a delegate who may decide to wander off the reservation and play games after he has won his seat in the convention hall.

The Kennedy nomination in 1960 was the first in which the process of electing your own delegates was fully developed, and Goldwater's people perfected the model in 1964.

At the 1960 Democratic National Convention in Los Angeles I can remember Lyndon Johnson, then majority leader of the United States Senate, wandering around collaring delegates, and depending upon his friends in the Senate to shift blocks of delegates in his direction. No way.

Kennedy went into that convention with just about as many delegates as he needed to win, with a large chunk of the remaining delegates still uncommitted, according to our figures.

O'Brien had assigned a co-ordinator to every state delegation, always someone from another state who would not be part of any warring factions within the state. The co-ordinators literally lived with the delegations—stayed in the same hotel, ate, drank, talked, and did other things with them. The co-ordinators were under strict instructions to telephone our headquarters in the Biltmore Hotel any time of the day or night when a delegate switched, in any direction: from undecided to Kennedy or someone else, from someone else to Kennedy, from Kennedy to undecided or to someone else.

In addition they were to assemble at the Biltmore every morning at eight to review the activities within their delegation with Robert Kennedy, O'Brien, and Ken O'Donnell. Those who have participated in political conventions on the national level will appreciate the feat of getting political types to a meet at eight in the morning, every morning, during the convention. For most of them, it was the middle of the night, and they looked it: but they were there. Or they were gone.

Because of the tremendous preconvention effort made by O'Brien and his people, and Kennedy's success in the presidential primaries, Kennedy needed only a handful of votes to clinch the nomination. We weren't announcing this to the press, of course, because it almost always is better to publicly underestimate your strength, in case of defections or error.

On the night of the actual balloting, I was closeted in a trailer alongside the Convention Center with Robert Kennedy, Pierre Salinger, and Hy Raskin, a Chicago lawyer. When the roll call got to Wyoming, State Chairman Tino Roncalio announced that the delegation was for Kennedy, giving him enough votes to put him over the top, and the count I had prepared was off by just three votes: we went into the Wyoming delegation with three votes more than we had anticipated. If you are going to make a mistake in counting delegates, that's the way to do it: err on the conservative side.

Put another way, by the time we got to Wyoming, our figures were off by less than one half of one per cent; you can't figure them much closer than that.

Goldwater's effort in 1964 was even more impressive, because he had an absolute lock on the nomination before the delegates assembled in San Francisco, and he had a solid, loyal, committed (some might even say fanatic) group of devoted delegates who were unshakable in their support. That's why William Scranton's frantic, last-minute, bumbling effort, and Nelson Rockefeller's eleventh-hour speech to the delegates were meaningless exercises in political futility.

Sometimes, of course, candidates can place too much stress on winning the convention and ignore the fact they must also win an election. This is what happened to Humphrey in 1968; he and his staff placed so much emphasis on the convention—which they could not lose after Robert Kennedy's assassination—that they did absolutely no postconvention planning, and with the convention as late as it was in 1968, this, as much as anything else, played a large part in Humphrey's defeat.

Clif White had an interesting delegate operation going for Ronald Reagan at the 1968 Republican convention in Miami Beach, and although Nixon carried the nomination on the first ballot, White assures me that Reagan's strength, based in large part on conservatives who had supported Goldwater in 1964, was much greater than the press or public realized, and that the switch of a few critical votes in key states might have prevented Nixon's first-ballot victory. When it became apparent that Reagan was not going to have the strength to stop Nixon on the first ballot, White released the delegates, a good political move, because if Nixon was going to win the nomination there was no point in having him upset at a Republican delegate and party functionary who he might not have realized was not solidly with him.

The best convention efforts are quiet, unpublicized; you don't really want anyone to know what you are up to, or how successful you are at what you're doing. That's why candidates and their managers hold back the announcement of commitments until these announcements will achieve maximum impact.

Lining up convention delegates is a long, slow, dull, painstaking job—perhaps the toughest and least glamorous in politics. Many of the delegate candidates have had little or no political experience, particularly if you are running against the party favorite, and need constant guidance and direction.

Finding delegate candidates requires hours of interviews, scanning names, ferreting opinions, long nights, and frequent trips to some pretty drab places. There's none of the media excitement of Madison Avenue, no glare of Kliegl lights or whirr of television camera: just plain hard work, skillfully directed.

But once you have your delegates in place, if you have selected carefully and elected properly, you have a rock-hard core of support that no one can take away from you, and even if you aren't successful in carrying the convention, you have some pretty good cards to play when the deal comes your way.

It's not always possible to elect your own people. When you don't, then you begin another difficult job: persuading uncommitted delegates to move toward your candidate, or, even tougher, trying to pry delegates away from another candidate.

This is the real world of power politics, and fortunately, I think, it is in its twilight stage. In state conventions the game often is rougher than at national conventions, with the carrot and the stick very much in evidence. I have seen delegates come to candidates, literally with tears in their eyes, to tell them they had to switch to the opponent to protect their job, or that of their brother-in-law, or to make certain someone in their family was appointed to a position he wanted or was moved into a housing project. This is raw, nasty politics, but it goes on, and, because state conventions are invariably not covered as penetratingly by the press, much of the arm-twisting and eye-gouging goes unnoticed.

The stakes are high. Even in states where the convention nominee can be challenged, and frequently is defeated, winning the convention usually means some kind of advantage, such as having your name placed first on the ballot, or the right to call yourself the "official" party nominee.

In many states the conventions are controlled by the old-line party machinery, and often the best advice a manager can give his candidate, particularly if the candidate starts late and has no way of electing his own delegates, is to boycott the convention and go directly into the primaries "so the people can pick the candidate."

This is fine in state elections, but there is no way—yet—that you can become the Democratic or Republican nominee for President without winning the convention.

And even if you won *all* the presidential primaries, you still would fall short of the required number of committed delegates. This leaves you the choice of being in the (preferred) position of electing your own delegates, or of trying to sway delegates in whose election you had no voice.

So don't be misled by all the meanderings and statements of the candidates for President every quadrennium: if they really are doing their job properly, their organizations are diligently working and quietly attempting to elect committed delegates.

And if any candidate for President fails to do this, his chances of winning the nomination are minimal.

9

CAMPAIGNING ABROAD

_____

IT LONG WAS my suspicion that there was no reason why the political techniques and technology learned and developed in the United States could not be transferred to other countries, and when I got the chance to prove it I was pleased that my expectations were justified.

There are some delicate areas in campaigning abroad, because politicians in many countries are fearful of the reaction in their own countries to the use of American consultants. This isn't true in some countries—but in others the feeling is strong indeed. The British are paranoiac about it, and my personal opinion is that they can use American technologists more effectively than any other country, because of the common language.

As a matter of fact, I have used a British film producer, Midge McKenzie, to make films and spots in an American campaign, in Alaska in 1968, and, as you can imagine, with no concern to anyone. I'll go into the British situation in some detail later, but let me first report on the foreign campaign in which I was most deeply involved. This was the campaign to re-elect President Ferdinand E. Marcos in the Philippines in 1969.

There was a peculiar challenge here: no president of the Philippines had ever been re-elected. Of course, they had not had all that many of them, because the country didn't attain its independence from the United States until after World War II.

Three American friends, at different times in the spring of 1969, called me to ask if I would be interested in working in the Philippine election. I told all of them I would, and in mid-June I received a call from Benjamin Romualdez, governor of Leyte and brother of President Marcos' glamorous (and tough-minded) wife, Imelda. Some people believe that Imelda, a lovely combination of beauty and brilliance, is a better politician than her husband, and they may be right.

I lunched with Romualdez at the Metropolitan Club in New York and agreed to fly to Manila a few days later to meet with the President and his campaign staff. The Manila campaign is another indication of how modern campaign counseling would be impossible without jet airplanes. Manila literally is halfway around the world from the Eastern seaboard. Elapsed time from New York, with the best connections, is more than twenty-four hours; I got to know the run pretty well, because I made it five times in the next few months.

I had read a biography of Marcos before I left, and even disregarding the panegyrics of the biographer, one could not help but be impressed with this man's record. He is one of the world's legitimate war heroes, and while the expression is trite, if ever a man was destined to be president of his country it was he.

Often I tell people in this country that I have no interest in government, that my interest is entirely with the political process, the art of getting a man elected to office. This is certainly the case in campaigning abroad. This is not to say I would accept any candidate in a foreign country, any more than I would accept any Democrat in this country. I'm not likely to take on a quasi-Fascist dictator or even a Fidel Castro-type Communist as a client, if any ever asked me, which they haven't and which I don't think they will. But I find too many people here who tend to criticize the government or programs of another country without really knowing much about the situation.

Marcos certainly has had his problems since his re-election. (For that matter, so have Lyndon Johnson, Richard Nixon, Georges Pompidou, Edward Heath, and just about anyone else you care to name.) But I was impressed with him as a man, more than impressed with him as a candidate, and convinced that he was a far better candidate for his country than his opponent, Sergio Osmena. In fact, it is difficult for me to imagine how Osmena seriously expected to win, because he had been convicted of collaboration with the Japanese in World War II, not exactly the kind of activity one would want to base a campaign on. To his credit as a candidate, however, Osmena also was a superb campaigner, a smooth articulate speaker who apparently, from his actions, ran his campaign on the hopes of capitalizing on dissatisfaction with inflation and other issues.

His was an entirely negative campaign, not bad strategy considering the circumstances.

My first impression of Marcos was extremely favorable. He is bright, knowledgeable, handsome, charismatic—the kind of candidate you like to work with. He also is decisive; one example will suffice: I had breakfast with President and Mrs. Marcos at Malacanang, the Filipino White House, one morning on my first visit. I had seen some of the television and film materials that had been produced for him, and was singularly unimpressed. Most, perhaps all, of these materials were the product of the government press-relations office, and they looked it.

I strongly urged him to scrap what he had, scour Manila, and come up with the best film producer available, even if he had no previous political experience. This was on June 23, 1969.

A few weeks later, on my next visit, accompanied this time by television producer/consultant Bob Squier of Washington, we viewed three ten-minute films in rough cut. I had told Squier how poor I thought the initial material I had seen was, but both he and I were favorably impressed with these films, even in their early stages, and I complimented the producer, Manuel Escudero.

"Well, thank you," he said, "but we really could have done a much better job if we had had more time. You must remember we have only been working on this campaign since June 23."

"What time on June 23?" I asked, curious.

Escudero obviously was puzzled by the question, but thought a moment and replied, "Early afternoon. When I returned to my office from lunch that day there was a message for me to call the

President's office, and when I did they asked me to come over and talk about films for the campaign."

I nodded. I had left the President on the twenty-third about 10 A.M. Apparently his people had found out who the good film producers in Manila were in the next couple of hours, and by lunchtime had initiated a call to Escudero and his crew.

What I wouldn't give for some American political candidates who responded to advice that quickly and decisively!

We handled our counseling role in the Philippine election precisely as we would have handled it in the United States. The first thing I insisted on was a poll, and I wrote the questionnaire before I left Manila.

In my first memorandum to Marcos I noted:

". . . the President has an excellent opportunity to be the first President in the history of the Philippines to succeed himself. However, and this is important, *the stakes are too high to take anything for granted.*

"One of the cardinal rules of politics is to assume nothing, no matter how far ahead you may appear to be. (I am not suggesting that the President is complacent about the election; to the contrary he displays precisely the kind of electoral instincts required to ride down the overconfidence that may appear in some areas. It is not really the President's attitude that I am concerned about, but rather those of some of his supporters who may believe he is a sure winner and will not work as hard because they feel he is going to win anyway. This is an attitude not to be tolerated.)"

Elsewhere in the memorandum I noted:

"The biggest obstacles to re-election, in my opinion, are:

"—The tradition that no incumbent ever has been re-elected.

"—The gullibility of the people who (in every country, not only the Philippines) are willing to believe the worst about politicians in office. Senator Osmena gives clear indication that he plans to conduct a campaign of character assassination, replete with wild charges and smear attempts. The theory behind this is as old as politics: throw enough mud and hope that enough of it will stick.

"It always has been my experience that you should never underestimate the intelligence of the voters, *nor overestimate the amount of information they have.*

". . . there may well be a communications gap in this administration. That is, there are indications that the accomplishments of the President may not have been fully communicated to the voter. President Marcos may well have done more for the people of his country than any other President—*but if the voters are not made aware of his accomplishments they may well believe he has accomplished little or nothing.*"

And later:

"President and Mrs. Marcos are their own best salesmen, *but they have not been used to their maximum effectiveness* in the films shown to us.

"I have a fetish about *quality* in the production of campaign materials, and with two such outstanding personalities to work with, it would be criminal to impair the message they have to deliver to the voters through technical incompetence.

"There is too much at stake to settle for less than the best."

Marcos is a good listener, and he acts on recommendations he believes are useful.

The poll was taken, and here are some of my comments and recommendations, verbatim from the report I prepared for the President:

"Here are the potential danger areas in the poll results, as I see them:

"High Undecided Vote

As a rule of thumb, a high undecided vote *late* in a campaign tends to work *against* the incumbent and *for* the challenger. I think the undecided vote will drop significantly between surveys. Even now, if you succeed in holding on to your own vote, Osmena would have to win virtually all the undecided vote, which he is not likely to do.

"Concern About High Costs

This complaint occurs repeatedly in the survey, and must be considered the major issue in the campaign at this point (or, perhaps more accurately, the major weakness in the Marcos position).

Some examples of how concerned voters are about this issue:

Q. Why do you think Macapagal was a better President than Marcos? [Asked of voters who said they preferred Macapagal, the previous President, to Marcos.]

A. High prices/cost of living—25 per cent.
Q. What are the major problems facing the Philippines today?
A. Cost of living—25 per cent.
Q. What are the things you don't like about Marcos?
A. Cannot solve high prices—24 per cent.
Q. Which promises do you think Marcos failed to keep?
A. High prices—41 per cent.
Q. What would you say have been the major failures of the Marcos Administration?
A. High prices—34 per cent."

In every case, the answer on prices was mentioned by the highest number of voters.

Another major issue in the Philippines in 1969 was peace and order, probably more familiarly known in the United States as law and order. Our comments here:

"At the moment, this isn't bad—but it is the explosive threat of what may happen that causes us concern. If anything does develop, it is essential that quick, firm action be taken by the President. We already have recommended a television spot in which the relatively mild situation in the Philippines is compared with the destructive and bloody riots in Ireland, Indonesia, Japan, and the United States." [After the election, the situation in the Philippines deteriorated considerably.]

The poll also revealed that the United States is surprisingly popular in the Philippines, and that there is a real fear of communism among Filipinos.

We also learned that radio "is by far the most useful of the paid advertising media, and the best creative efforts should go into producing quality radio spots and longer programs. . . ."

The reason for this, of course, in the Philippines is that, at the time, only about 20 per cent of the population, those who lived in and around Manila and one or two other large cities, could receive television—but everyone had a transistor radio, and there were radio stations scattered all over the country. Everyone with an inexpensive pocket-size transistor could pick up radio signals; only one in five lived in an area and had the equipment to receive television.

Interestingly, for all his attributes, Marcos and his key advisers suffered from the same lack of appreciation of what a political poll is supposed to do as many candidates and campaign managers in the United States, the people who lock the poll results in the bottom drawer of the desk.

In a memorandum dated August 21, 1969, I wrote:

"At our meeting earlier today President Marcos asked me what was being done wrong in the campaign. Upon reflection, the major criticism I have of the campaign is the apparent lack of co-ordination and communication between those who are directing the campaign and the media team you have assembled to translate directives into votes.

"As noted in the memorandum presented to the President today, I am favorably impressed with the media team that has been assembled for the campaign. These are bright, competent, creative people—but they will not be able to produce the best work possible on behalf of the President unless they are taken into the confidence of the campaign leadership.

"I understand the need and desire for security, but certainly the issues material in the poll, and the geographic and demographic breakdowns—if not the entire poll itself—should be given to at least the leader of the media team. They are the people entrusted with the responsibility of producing persuasive and motivational material, and the President will not receive the excellence of material he can get and is paying for unless the media team has the tools to work with."

In another memorandum, dated September 11, I approached the importance of a candidate using television as a *positive,* not a *negative,* medium (a recommendation as valid in America as it is in Manila):

"President Marcos should emerge on television as a warm, popular, progressive, dynamic leader—not as a hatchet man. He can criticize Osmena all he wishes at rallies and meetings, but not on our paid television. The President already has Osmena on the defensive, an enviable accomplishment for an incumbent, and I agree that we should continue to put pressure on Osmena to keep him on the defensive. But we can use other people to slice Osmena into little pieces, while the President continues to appear as a statesman and leader in his television spots.

"Manuel Escudero reports that one of the big difficulties his group has encountered is getting access to the President. This is a continuing and universal problem [in the United States as well as any-where else, I might add]—but someone who does as well as Marcos can on television, who benefits in comparison to Osmena every time they appear on television, who possesses charisma and charm and all the qualities of a leader, should make it his business to clear time for the film crews. The films they will make can be put to multiple uses—television, mobile units, movie houses, etc.

"More people will see the President in one television spot than he can possibly hope to see in person throughout the campaign. When such a precious talent is available, it should be used."

In mid-September, Osmena took to the air with a two-hour tele-vision program, to be followed the following night by a telecast of a giant rally he was having in a football stadium in Manila. I happened to be in the Philippines at that time, and here are some of my comments and criticisms of the Osmena performance:

"The camera work and direction were poor. It appears that Os-mena was content to use a studio director. We should insist upon having our own director whose primary job should be making certain the candidate appears at his best throughout the program. (For example, on one occasion the camera cut back to Osmena wiping his brow with a towel; this should never have been allowed to be shown on camera.)

"So far as Osmena personally is concerned—forgetting the con-tents of his remarks for a moment—he is better than I thought he would be. He is low-key, which always is effective on television, spoke softly, and never lost his temper or raised his voice. He used his material skillfully, and appeared in absolute command of him-self. For someone who faced such serious charges [we had been hitting Osmena hard about his collaboration conviction] this ability to 'keep his cool' is important.

"On the other hand, Osmena was kept on the defensive for almost the entire two hours. In my opinion, he made a mistake by de-liberately choosing to use his time only to answer the Marcos charges, and did not take the offensive in the same forum. He obviously plans to do this tonight at the rally—but it is quite possible there were people watching last night who will not see or hear him tonight, and he missed an opportunity to reach these voters when they were available. And two hours on the defensive, answering another man's charges, is a long time.

"I am certain you have people picking apart the contents of Osmena's statements for rebuttal (not by Marcos, who should not allow himself to go on the defensive on these charges), and I have some suggestions which I will present to you in the form of statements ready for release. For example, I am sure Osmena is the first political candidate in the history of the world who felt compelled to go on television with an affidavit from his mother saying she would vote for him."

(This last comment, about Osmena's mother, referred to an intrafamily squabble among the Osmenas, as a result of which it was widely rumored that even his mother would not vote for him, because she was upset at certain of his earlier actions. Osmena actually appeared on the program with an affidavit from his mother pledging to vote for him.)

At my suggestion, Marcos also retained Bob Squier as a television consultant and, later, to supplement the efforts of the Filipino film producers, a crew from Shelby Storck & Co. to do some spots and programs of the President and the First Lady.

Squier also produced a telethon the night before the election, based on the highly successful Humphrey telethon he had produced in the 1968 presidential election in America; only the one in the Philippines was three times as long.

Squier had difficulty persuading Mrs. Marcos to appear, but he can be a very persuasive guy, and eventually she did, and from all reports (I did not see the program), she performed very well indeed.

I should not overlook the role of Ben Romualdez in the Marcos campaign. Often a compaign consultant is only as good as the full-time, on-the-spot campaign manager he is working with, and Romualdez is superb in this role. He could step into any campaign in the United States and provide it with intelligent and imaginative direction. He's one of the best campaign directors I've ever worked with anywhere. (Despite his habit of materializing in the middle of the night—say 3 A.M.—and ringing from the hotel lobby to say something like, "Joe, can you be ready in fifteen minutes to go talk with the First Lady?" I don't know if Mrs. Marcos ever sleeps, but she certainly managed to keep some weird office hours during that campaign.)

On the day of the election I was on the Italian liner *Raffaello* crossing the Atlantic, and, after pestering the radio officer for several hours, finally learned that Marcos had won, big. More than a few passengers on the ship were surprised when I invited them to join me in a drink celebrating the re-election of the President of the Philippines.

After the campaign, in Washington, Ben Romualdez graciously credited Bob Squier and me with making the difference in the campaign. I don't know how Bob feels about this, but I'm convinced it's simply not true. I think Marcos would have won if neither of us had ever set foot in the Philippines.

But one of the reasons that he would have won is that he didn't leave any potential method of winning votes unexplored, and if this meant bringing in consultants from outside, that's what he did.

Getting us to work on the campaign wasn't a high-budget item: not counting the film-production costs, the counseling fees for Squier and me together totaled less than twenty-five thousand dollars, plus travel expenses. In a presidential election in a country of 40 million people that's not a significant expense.

In addition to my Philippine experience, I have worked on two campaigns in Europe, lectured to representatives of more than fifteen Latin American countries on a week-long seminar in American political-campaign techniques, met with spokesmen and leaders on two Caribbean islands, and visited with political campaigners in several Asian nations. Unfortunately I am ethically bound not to discuss these campaigns or reveal the countries, again because of the fear of what the opposition might do if it were known that an American was serving as a consultant to the other side.

Let me say that my experiences abroad have convinced me that:
   –It is possible to transfer American political techniques and technology to other countries.
   –It is possible for Americans to work quietly in other countries without causing any great internal upheaval.

Often when I am working on a campaign, or merely consulting with a political leader abroad, very few people know that I am involved in any way with the campaign or the candidate. This can happen in the United States as well, when candidates or their staffs are worried about the reaction of bringing in an out-of-stater, but the fear is dying out here because candidates are realizing voters really don't give a damn.

Some of the rules are different, of course. In many countries television and radio are controlled by the state, and only certain allotted segments are made available to each candidate. (Not, as a matter of fact, a bad idea; something I'll explore in the chapter on election reform in this country.)

This does not detract from the value of a consultant; if anything, it makes him more valuable, because with a limited amount of time available (and usually free) the consultant—not because he's smarter than anybody else, but merely because this is his business —can use the time more effectively and maximize the impact of the electronic-media operation.

Of all the countries where I have had discussions with parties or candidates or worked in campaigns, I find the British the most difficult to understand; maybe it's because I spend more time there than anywhere else. I've had an office in London since 1964, and the more I see of British politicians the less I understand them, and that goes for the British press, too.

They are frightened to death of giving the slightest impression they might possibly learn something from an exchange of ideas with people in the same business from other countries.

The reluctance to retain professionals in Great Britain is paranoiac. But I'm sure if the toilets stopped flushing in Labour party headquarters they'd send for a plumber quick enough, because that's his business and he might know what to do about it. With something like the government at stake, you'd think they might be interested in obtaining the best skills available, whether the possessors of these skills happened to be Armenian, Algerian, Afganistanian, or American.

In 1968 Michel Bongrand and I organized in Paris the International Association of Political Consultants. As the name implies, this is a group of men and women who work in political campaigns and public affairs throughout the world. Our idea was that these people would meet periodically to exchange ideas on techniques and advances in our field—as do lawyers, public accountants, dentists, and astrophysicists.

Our first meeting was in Paris, our second in Florence, Italy, in the fall of 1969. We were concerned over the lack of British participation (at the Florence meeting my associates in London were the only British present as delegates), so we scheduled the 1970 conference in London.

Even though we devoted a full day to the British political system —and it was a useful and interesting experience—the British political types virtually boycotted the meetings and the British press generally gave us a roasting. Yet at the London meeting we had political consultants from Italy, Germany, Holland, Denmark, Sweden, Belgium, South Africa, Portugal, Mexico, Norway, Canada, and France, as well as the United States, and many of them had useful comments to make.

Considering that the three-day conference was held a few months after the British Labour party had been soundly trounced in a major upset, you'd think some Labourites might have enough interest in what the rest of the world was doing to poke their heads inside the meeting room, but they didn't.

Maybe it's simply that they believe they know it all or perhaps it is because they feel that anything not produced in Great Britain can't measure up to their standards, but whatever the reason they all stayed home and sniped.

I know that I have learned a lot at every one of these conferences, and I may be one of the few people in the world who spends virtually all of his time on political campaigning in one form or another.

I also know this: some day one of the British political parties is going to crack out of its chauvinistic shell, assemble from a number of countries the best political skills available in the world, and whip the bejesus out of the opposition. That's a prediction, and I think the day of fulfillment is not far off. If we can use a British film producer in an American campaign, what's so bad about the British using a Frenchman or an Italian, or even, glory be, an American, as a consultant in one of their campaigns?

And it's not true, in case anyone ever had any doubts, that we have all the political brains in the United States. I know three or four political consultants in Europe who could work effectively in any campaign here, and there are several areas of the world in which specific techniques are used more effectively than they are here.

Take political posters, for one example. Latin American countries with high illiteracy rates and, in many cases, limited access to electronic media, use political signs and posters much more imaginatively than North Americans do. Their use of color is much better than ours.

Emilio Pucci, better known as one of the world's foremost fashion designers, is an active member of IAPC because of his involvement in Italian politics. At the London conference he spoke eloquently on campaigning without the use of electronic media. Many of the European countries do a better job in this area than we do in the United States, because they don't have as many vehicles for communicating their political messages as we do.

A good consultant, as I have said often in this country, can play by any rules that are established, so long as the other side is required to play by the same rules. Sometimes the games get rough on the other side of the Atlantic: France is a country of many political parties, but in his last presidential campaign Charles de Gaulle magnanimously gave his interpretation of equal time on television and radio for the campaign: half for the majority, half for everybody else, to be divided among them. Not exactly what I would call a sporting proposition.

The French, however, take a more enlightened view of outside consultants than the British; at least, they demonstrate an intense interest in learning what everyone else is doing, and how they can adapt it to their own situation.

The problems an American encounters in running a campaign abroad, with two exceptions, are essentially the same as he encounters in this country. The two exceptions are the fear—often legitimate—of what impact it might have on the voters if the opposition played up the fact that an American was being used by the other side, although I personally believe this fear of using outsiders is lessening each year, and the other, of course, is the language barrier. Americans are linguistic illiterates compared with most educated Europeans, Asians, and South Americans. But the mere fact that most of the people Americans will be working with do speak English means, in most cases, that work can be done effectively through an English-speaking member of the staff and/or interpreters.

Ferdinand Marcos happens to speak excellent English, but with a candidate like Marcos it wouldn't make a great deal of difference if he spoke only Martian, because he is quickly able to grasp what you are talking about and relate it to the solution of his specific problems.

Abroad, as here, the consultant must try to analyze what the problems are, try to define the messages that need to be communicated to the voters, and suggest methods of getting these messages across to the voters.

I said earlier that I knew of several Europeans who could easily handle campaigns here; I also know of half a dozen, maybe more, Americans who could work effectively in any country. Matt Reese, a talented consultant who works out of Washington and specializes in organization, already has conducted a successful referendum campaign in Puerto Rico, and while Puerto Rico technically isn't a foreign country, Spanish is the official language, and the problems one encounters there aren't much different from those you'd find in other Spanish-speaking countries.

In the Puerto Rican gubernatorial election of 1968, Luis A. Ferre used American consultants, effectively, in scoring an upset victory. I know of a French pollster who periodically tests the political attitudes in several African countries, and a French consultant who has done work in, of all places, Rhodesia.

What political leaders in other countries must realize is that utilization of outside consultants poses no internal threat to them, their country, or their party. It's just a question of getting the best man available to do the job, whatever his nationality, the color of his skin, or his religion.

You'll see more use of foreign political consultants as time goes by—in the United States as well as abroad.

10

CHANGING THE RULES OF THE GAME

THE IMPORTANT FACT to remember about any regulation limiting the expenditure of funds in political campaigns is that it is unenforceable.

If we start from that premise, then perhaps we can make some meaningful headway with election reform.

Naturally, I'm more interested than most people in any legislation that affects campaign spending—and it's not that any of the proposed or pending laws that I know of would hurt my business; on the contrary, all of them would force candidates to put a premium on quality, something we've been preaching for a long while, and would make the services of a competent consultant more valuable.

It *is* possible, of course, to limit the amount a candidate spends in a specific medium—television, for example—but as infrequently as I am likely to find myself in agreement with the network presidents, not to mention President Nixon, I believe they are right when they say it would be unfair and unwise to single out television and radio for limiting campaign expenditures.

Most of the formulas suggested for limiting electronic expenditures are based on so many cents per voter in the previous election; in the bill Nixon vetoed late in 1970, it was seven cents per vote, and there were a spate of bills introduced in 1971 with all kinds of proposals based on all sorts of sliding scales and allowable expenditure per voter.

Before making any criticism of the suggestions made by anyone, or offering some ideas of my own, let me say clearly that I, and others in my business, will live by any of the rules that are passed, so long as everyone is required to play by the same rules.

Take the bill, or any of the bills, that would limit the amount of money a candidate could spend on television to so many cents a voter. Agreed, this would limit the amount of money *spent on television,* but would do absolutely nothing about reducing over-all campaign costs. What *is* the object here? If it is to reduce the income of television networks and stations, fine; if it is a serious attempt to reduce over-all campaign expenditures, or to give a candidate who is not wealthy a more equitable opportunity to compete with richer opponents, then those proposals are meaningless.

Perhaps worse than meaningless, because they might well succeed in causing candidates with access to large amounts of money to use those funds in ways less obvious to the public, and at the same time deprive voters of seeing the candidates on television as often as they would under ordinary circumstances. Some voters, admittedly, would gladly have all political announcements ruled off television, but they might quickly find that this is a step backward, not forward, in their quest for an ideal society.

Suppose John Q. Affluent has a million dollars to spend on his campaign for the United States Senate. And suppose that in the normal course of events he would spend half of that on television and radio. But under some form of new regulation he is limited to spending only $250,000 on television and radio. Does this mean that his campaign will be a quarter of a million dollars less expensive? Hell no. What it means is that he will be able to spend that extra quarter million in areas that cannot be regulated (at least not without changing the Constitution of the United States), such as newspapers, direct mail, pamphlets, brochures, and for some of the newer electronic devices: computers, forced feed of radio news messages, telenews operations, electronic telephone calls with a tape-recorded message.

All laws like this do is cause the candidate to shift expenditures from one area to another. And I really don't think that the candidate who buys hoggish amounts of television always wins just because of his television buys. The examples of wealthy candidates who fail make a long list. I'm sure, although I have no figures to prove it, that sometimes voters vote against a candidate just because they're sick and tired of seeing him on television so often.

If you try to limit *over-all* expenditures, then you have a different set of problems. Again, there is no way you can enforce these rules if candidates are determined to evade them. You can call for full financial disclosure, but any candidate with a rudimentary knowledge of political campaigning can get around these regulations. How are you ever going to trace ten thousand dollars in small bills distributed by hand to election workers? Any law I've seen proposed on over-all limitation of funds contains as many holes as a chicken-wire fence.

Besides, such legislation gives incumbents a tremendous advantage, and I'm not sure this is a good idea; in fact, I'm damned sure it isn't a good idea.

There are financial-disclosure and maximum-contribution laws on the books now, but they're hardly ever enforced, and they have more loopholes than a rodeo full of lariat twirlers. When James Buckley ran for the United States Senate in New York in 1970, he had more than fifty different committees formed in Washington, D.C., for accepting and dispensing funds—in Washington, not New York. Some of these committees had imaginative names indeed; if you look closely you might even find something like Blue-Eyed Mothers with Children Under Five for Buckley. These committees were a subterfuge to prevent the press and other interested parties from learning who contributed to Buckley's campaign (and in this case the contributors were Republicans who didn't want to publicly go on record as supporting a candidate running on the Conservative line against the Republican nominee).

Does this mean that I am opposed to election reform? Not at all. It just means that I believe any law imposing restrictions on the amount of money that a candidate can spend is unenforceable and impractical.

I think the approach should be from a different direction, and in an area that we *can* do something about: making it easier and less expensive for candidates to get their message across to the voters.

We all recognize that in major campaigns, television is the most effective way of reaching voters. I agree. What we should do, then, is make television available to all candidates, free. There is nothing earth-shattering about this; most countries in the world with a democratic system do this as a matter of course.

We could do three things that would solve many of the problems:

1. Require that an equal and equitable amount of television time be made available without charge to all candidates for President, governor, senator, and congressman.
2. Limit the time frame in which candidates could use this time to a reasonable period, say three or four weeks before a primary or general election.
3. Put a ceiling on the amount of time a candidate could purchase in addition to the free time that he is allowed, or prohibit candidates from buying any time above and beyond what they are allotted free.

The same rules could apply to radio as well.

I know the networks and the local stations will scream, but I must admit I have very little sympathy for their position. Air time should be public property. The piece of paper issued by the FCC that permits a company to operate a television station is a license to print money.

If any television-station owners feel that such regulations would put them out of business, then I have a feeling there would be another individual or group or corporation in their community willing to snap up their license to operate the moment they decided to turn it in.

Newspapers are a different story. Anyone, at least in theory, can start a newspaper if he wishes to. We've done this, more than once, in political campaigns. In one election in Springfield, Massachusetts, in 1961, when the newspapers showed strong favoritism to the incumbent, we began a weekly newspaper for his opponent. Fifty thousand copies were printed each week and hand-distributed to every household in the city by volunteer workers. The challenger scored a major upset.

You can do this with newspapers, but not with television and radio. To operate these media, you need federal approval, and to say that it is difficult to obtain permission to start a new television station is understating the problem.

I would propose that the candidates be required to engage in at least one and perferably two or three debates. I would allow them a certain number of time segments of various lengths, ranging from 30-minute and 5-minute programs to 60-second and 30-second spots. The candidates could do what they wanted with these segments: appear personally and give speeches, or use films or structured spots. *How* they would use the time is up to them, but they would have the assurance that they would be on television as often as their opponent, and have at least a reasonable opportunity to communicate what they want to say to the voter.

In a general election this really doesn't pose any problem, because usually the fight is between the candidates nominated by the major parties. Occasionally a third-party candidate also is in the race, as an independent or a Liberal or a Conservative. These third-party candidates could be required to file a predetermined number of signatures on petitions to qualify for the free television or radio time. Signature drives require work and volunteers, not much money, and if a candidate can't get a reasonable number of people to sign his petitions, then he probably isn't a bona fide candidate anyway.

In multicandidate primary races, the problem might be more difficult, because it is not unusual in some states to have five or six candidates seeking the nomination from each party. Again, I would resort to the signature drive, and set a fairly high figure. In order to qualify, the candidate would have to devote some real effort to obtaining signatures on petitions of voters who say they want him to run. Candidates who can't get enough signatures become ineligible for the free time; this doesn't prevent them from running. In most states candidates have to obtain a certain number of signatures to get on the ballot, although this number is lower than the minimum figures I have in mind for qualifying for free television and radio time. One of the great and little-noted accomplishments of the 1968 presidential election was George Wallace's achievement of qualifying for the ballot in every one of the fifty states. This is a stupendous organizational effort, never before accomplished, and is a tribute to the Wallace workers.

I'd *like* to see newspapers be required to give space to candidates to use as they see fit, but because newspapers are not subject to federal regulation, and do not need permission to publish, I see no way of making them do this. Television and radio *are* subject to federal control, and if the people who make our laws are serious about election reform, then this is where they really have some clout.

If Congress wants to take another step toward making it easier for candidates to communicate with voters, they could provide each candidate for President, senator, congressman, and governor with a free mailing. England and other countries do this now. The major cost in a direct-mail campaign is the postage (unless, of course, you are sending out an elaborate and expensive brochure). If each candidate were given the opportunity, once in the primary and once in the general election, to send a letter or piece of literature free to every voter in his district, then he would have some assurance that he at least was getting some piece of printed material containing his views into every home. Whether the material is read or not depends on how attractively and interestingly it is prepared, and how involved the recipient might be in the election.

In a state with one million voters, the postage cost for a mass mailing runs around thirty thousand dollars at bulk-mail rates, a pretty good chunk of money. If congressmen and senators believe that the government can't afford this expense, then I suggest they take a step in economizing government expenditures by relinquishing their own franking privileges. If an incumbent congressman or senator can mail material free to his constituents as often as he wishes ("non-political" material, of course), then why shouldn't someone challenging him for his job have the opportunity of sending at least one piece through the mails free?

So there, in a nutshell, are my suggestions for equalizing the differential between rich and poor candidates:

--Give all candidates for major office a minimum (and reasonable) amount of free television and radio time.

--Give all of them an opportunity to mail one piece of literature free to every household.

While no one is able to compel newspapers to give anything, I'd like to see the American Newspaper Publishers Association adopt a policy encouraging their member newspapers to give each candidate in major elections a small amount of space to use as he wished—perhaps two quarter-page ads in a primary and three quarter-page ads in a general election. I suppose this is whistling in the dark, because newspaper publishers are not among the most charitable people I know; but since they are not hesitant to criticize the cost of campaigns editorially, maybe they'd like to support their sermons with a little action.

I'll say one thing for television and radio: while they may be callous, and point-blank refuse to sell candidates time, and often charge the highest rate on their card, at least they don't increase the rates for political candidates, as some newspapers do. I've often thought it was the highest (lowest?) form of hypocrisy for a newspaper to moan about the soaring costs of political campaigning on its editorial pages, while its advertising department has a special political rate that could be 50 per cent or even 100 per cent higher than its regular advertising rates. Not all newspapers do this, of course, and the practice is dying out, but it existed for a long time and still persists in some areas.

Reducing costs of campaigning, while a noble goal, isn't the only kind of election reform we should be working toward. My pet desire is to change the way we elect a President.

My ideas are simple—some will say simplistic.

Succinctly, I propose:

1. Direct nomination of candidates for President on a national primary day.
2. Abolition of the Electoral College.
3. Direct election of the President.

The second and third proposals are not new; they have been made by many political observers, and legislation that would accomplish these objectives is regularly introduced and just as regularly killed.

For the moment, let's look at the first proposal—nominating presidential candidates in a national primary.

The way we nominate presidential candidates now is crazy-quilt and hodgepodge. The candidates are nominated at quadrennial national conventions, the last bastions of the political bosses and power brokers. Some states have binding primaries, which require their delegates to cast their ballots at the convention for the winner of the convention, either for the first ballot or until released. Other states have primaries that are meaningless, because they really are only expressions of voter sentiment and not binding on anyone. Many states have no presidential primary, and the delegates are picked or elected by various means. The Democratic National Committee adopted some reforms for the 1972 convention, which, among other things, require that all delegates be elected by the people, abolishing the appointment of delegates by political bosses; a step in the right direction, but a long way from home plate.

I've been on the primary trail, from New Hampshire to Nebraska, Wisconsin and West Virginia, Oregon, and California. More states are having presidential primaries now, some of them, I think, just for the national publicity value. For candidates, these primaries can be brutal and debilitating—and solve little.

My idea is to have a national primary day in May. If no candidate wins 50 per cent of the vote cast, then there would be a run-off between the top two candidates four weeks later. The parties could still have their conventions, if they wished, to argue about planks and platform and all the other things that cause great hue and cry at conventions and are promptly ignored as soon as the convention ends.

A candidate could qualify for the primary by obtaining a reasonably high number of signatures from a variety of states in different sections of the country, and perhaps a minimal number in every state. This requires organizational effort, utilization of volunteers, citizen participation.

The candidates who qualify for the primary then would be allowed sizable chunks of time on the national television and radio networks. If the primary is national, and on one day, then it is so much easier for candidates to formulate and deliver their messages. They can campaign wherever they wish—but their mass appeals could be made over the national networks, because every state would be voting on the same day. Perhaps they could be permitted to purchase a reasonable amount of time above and beyond what they are given free; again, this could be network time, because they will be voted for in every state. The Republican and Democratic candidates would be named on the same day—and if any third- or fourth-party candidate qualifies, through the signature route, he also could win a place on the November ballot.

This would mean that the candidates would be named by mid-

June, at the latest, and would have the summer to recoup and prepare for the November general election.

Even if there were no law requiring networks to give time to candidates, and I think there should be, then it probably still would be cheaper for candidates to campaign once than under our present system, in which vast sums of money are poured into a series of small, medium-sized, and large states to achieve hollow victories. (In mid-1971, Senator Muskie announced he would enter all presidential primaries, a horribly expensive effort.)

If one party has a President in power, and he is not opposed, then he automatically would be on the ballot. A national primary would make it easier, of course, for a President to be challenged, and I think that's a good idea, too.

Or take the case of John Lindsay. I see no possibility of his winning the Democratic nomination in 1972 under our present system—but he certainly would be a formidable challenger in an open primary. (Not that I am convinced he would be a good President if he were elected.) There are other attractive potential candidates in our country, some of them not in public office, who might be lured into politics under such a system.

So far as the general election is concerned, if the Supreme Court is serious about its one-man, one-vote ruling, then it seems sheer hypocrisy to enforce it in minor elections for state legislature and offices like that, and ignore it in presidential elections. If ever there were a case to be made about the misrepresentation of voting power, then it is in the elections for President, which are heavily weighted in favor of voters from small and underpopulated states. A voter in Alaska or Nevada has several times the weight of a voter in California or New York when it comes to electing the chief executive of our country, and I believe there is something inherently unfair in a system that continues to permit such injustices.

I'm not so naïve as to believe that political leaders and elected officials are going to rush out and embrace, endorse, and enact these proposals, but it seems to me there is a basic fairness about them that should be considered. Under the present, Electoral College, system, a candidate for President can win California by twenty-five thousand votes and capture all of its votes in the Electoral College, and lose New York by a million votes and lose its total

Electoral College vote, and still wind up with more Electoral College votes than his opponent, even though nearly a million fewer voters marked their "X" for him than for his opponent.

There undoubtedly were good reasons for enacting the present system when it was conceived—but these reasons have long disappeared. And there is nothing inviolable about our election procedures: no one that I know of wants to return to the system of state legislatures naming United States senators, but it's only been a half century or so since this procedure was changed. I don't think we want to take the vote away from women, but this, too, is a comparatively modern innovation in our electoral process.

It seems to me that some of the citizens' groups that are working for change and improvement in our society might well start paying some attention to the way we nominate and elect our Presidents, and start devoting some of their efforts in this direction. How about this as a project for militant black organizations, national civic organizations, women's liberation groups, the League of Women Voters, or Common Cause? And with eighteen-year-olds now having the privilege of voting in federal elections (and I'll be curious to see what use they make of this privilege in 1972), election reform might be an interesting project for them to tackle.

It's doubtful that those in office will take the initiative in making these changes. Some of the more progressive or enlightened congressmen and senators *have* initiated solid proposals for election reform, but many of them are quite content with the status quo out of the not-unrealistic fear that if we alter the method of electing people to office they might lose their jobs.

National direct elections give every voter the assurance that his vote will count. It may well encourage greater participation in our presidential elections, an area in which we lag far behind many countries. But how much incentive is there for a Democrat in Iowa to cast his vote in the ordinary presidential election when he knows that except in special circumstances (Johnson versus Goldwater in 1964, for instance) his effort is meaningless, that the vote won't count at all, because the state is going to go Republican and the Republican candidate is going to swoop up all the electoral votes, no matter how skinny or how large his margin of victory? The same is true for Republicans in heavily Democratic states.

One of the arguments used against direct elections is that these would encourage cheating. I think this is a particularly specious and fallacious argument, because I believe just the opposite is true.

There is real incentive, under our present system, for a party machine to try to win its state in a presidential election by corrupt means, because it is a winner-take-all situation. In the 1960 presidential contest between Kennedy and Nixon, more controversy centered around the results in Illinois than in any other state. Some people believe to this day that Democratic wheelhorses in Illinois snatched the state away from Nixon. Maybe so, maybe not: I have no way of knowing, and truth is elusive. Under our present system, capturing Illinois, by fair means or foul, was critically important to John Kennedy, because it meant that he attained all twenty-six of Illinois's electoral votes, while Nixon got none. In 1968, if Humphrey had won California by a single vote, the election would have been thrown into the House of Representatives, and Humphrey might well have emerged as President. That's real incentive to vote the graveyard and juggle the figures.

But the importance of these winner-take-all contests is sharply minimized when the total vote goes into the national pot. The incentive to emerge from a state a few thousand votes ahead of your opponent is significantly diminished when the prize is just that—a lead of a few thousand votes—instead of a tremendous prize such as twenty or thirty or forty electoral votes.

It is clear that more votes are cast on the basis of emotion than logic, and the same holds true in election reform. Logic may be on the side of the reformers—but emotional involvement is on the side of those with the power, and they're not likely to relinquish it without a powerful mandate from the public.

11

HOW TO BEAT RICHARD NIXON IN 1972

As I WRITE THIS, in mid-1971, the only certainty about the Democratic campaign for President in 1972 is that there will be a candidate.

Preparing a campaign plan to unseat an incumbent President without knowing the identity of your own candidate is a risky business, but I believe there are a certain number of things, some of which I will outline in these pages, that the Democratic party can do to tool up for the 1972 election. I hope they are doing some or all of them already.

I start by assuming that Nixon can be defeated in 1972.

There are some elections that cannot be won—even on a presidential level. I'd put the 1964 Johnson victory over Goldwater in this category; I don't see any way that Goldwater could have beaten Johnson that year. But I do think Nixon can be taken in 1972—that's not to say he *will* be, only that he *can* be.

What happens between the time this book is written and published and the Democratic convention and the election in November 1972 certainly will have incalculable impact on the '72 campaign.

The status of the war in Vietnam and the economy of the country are the two major variables, and my crystal ball is murkier than most people's, so I wouldn't even hazard a guess about how those important factors will be doing by November 1972.

But if I were to lay out a program to defeat Nixon in 1972, this is how I would go about it:

First, you'd have to plan on a negative campaign. That is, the thrust of your effort would be to cause voters to vote *against* Nixon rather than *for* your candidate, whoever he might be. (This gets back to the Least Objectionable Candidate theory.) Any incumbent President in turbulent times must run on his record, or be forced to run on his record if he tries to seek another avenue. The powers of the presidency are awesome, the resources of the President are unmatchable by the party out of office, and the staff and services provided by the federal government are far too rich for the out party to match, particularly if the out party still is trying to pay off its 1968 debts.

But there is one big disadvantage to running as the incumbent: in doing so you must accept responsibility for what has happened in and to the country in the four years of your stewardship.

I'd start my campaign planning where I usually do—with polls. Starting immediately, I would try to make arrangements with the leading political polling firms, Democratic state committees, and Democratic candidates for statewide and Congressional offices to include a brief series of questions in all polls about the presidential elections. The polling firms might have to get the permission of their political clients to include the questions, but this really shouldn't be a problem. If I were running a statewide campaign for a Democratic candidate in 1972, I'd certainly want a pretty clear look at the presidential contest anyway. Even if it became necessary to pay the polling firms a few hundred dollars for adding the questions, and I don't think it would be, it still would be worth it.

These are the *kinds* of questions I'd like to see included in all polls, starting immediately, with exactly the same wording in each poll, and as close to the same demographic breakdowns as possible in each state:

PRESIDENTIAL ELECTION

1. Now I am going to ask you a series of questions about the 1972 presidential election. First of all, I am going to read you a list of names of political figures in the United States. Please tell me if you have a favorable or

unfavorable opinion of each one. If you have no opinion, or have never heard of the person, just say so.

	Favor-able	Unfavor-able	No Opinion	Never Heard of him
Richard Nixon	――	――	――	――
Spiro Agnew	――	――	――	――
Thruston Morton	――	――	――	――
Hubert Humphrey	――	――	――	――
Edmund Muskie	――	――	――	――
Edward Kennedy	――	――	――	――
Eugene McCarthy	――	――	――	――
John Lindsay	――	――	――	――
Birch Bayh	――	――	――	――
Henry Jackson	――	――	――	――
George McGovern	――	――	――	――
George Wallace	――	――	――	――
Wilbur Mills	――	――	――	――
Paul McCloskey	――	――	――	――

2. Please tell me what you consider the major *accomplishments* of the Nixon administration:

_____

3. Please tell me what you consider the major *failures* of the Nixon administration:

_____

4. Now I am going to read you a list of potential Democratic candidates for President in 1972. Please tell me which one of these you think would make the best candidate for President:
   a. Hubert Humphrey
   b. Edmund Muskie
   c. Edward Kennedy
   d. Birch Bayh
   e. John Lindsay
   f. George McGovern
   g. Henry Jackson
   h. Wilbur Mills

5. Now I am going to show you a sample ballot. Please
   mark this ballot exactly as you would if the election
   for President were being held today and these were the
   candidates:

SAMPLE BALLOT
Please check one name in each contest.

Nixon	__	Nixon	__	Nixon	__
Humphrey	__	Muskie	__	Kennedy	__
Nixon	__	Nixon	__	Nixon	__
Bayh	__	Lindsay	__	Jackson	__
Nixon	__	Nixon	__		
McGovern	__	Mills	__		

That's about all. Obviously, this isn't a survey in depth, but
it would give the Democratic National Committee, which bears the
ultimate responsibility for organizing the campaign of the Democratic candidate for President, no matter who he may be, a constant
and standardized flow of information from the various states on the
presidential election. The DNC has a computer into which this
information could be fed, and, after the computer is properly
programmed, it's just a matter of pushing a few buttons to get
current figures, comparisons, breakdowns by regions and states,
demographic breakdowns (by age groups, for example, or by race,
sex, income, education, religion, etc.)

And all for free, or practically nothing.

I can readily understand the reluctance of presidential candidates
to share their private poll information, but if they would all agree
to providing the National Committee with this kind of information,
with the understanding that all the candidates for the presidential
nomination would have access to it, they'd all benefit, and so would
the committee.

Another thing I'd start doing now, so far as polls are concerned,
would be to line up half a dozen good polling firms, zero in on the
states that need to be polled, and assign them some specific states
and dates. For example, I'd want a full-scale poll in the field about
a week after the Democratic nominee is selected, probably another

one the first week in September, and another about the second week of October. I wouldn't assign more than three or four polls to any one polling firm, because none of the firms I know of can handle a lot of states simultaneously and turn out high-quality work on time. The questionnaire should be prepared at the DNC, and the demographics selected by someone appointed to supervise polling operations for the DNC, so that the polls would be compatible and easily matched. Polling firms use various age breakdowns. My firm happens to use these: 21–30, 31–40, 41–60, over 60. We make a ten-year breakdown between 21 and 40 because those under thirty really grew up on television, those over 30 weren't as influenced in their childhood by television. In 1972, obviously, the 18–20-year-olds should be included, and I'd put them in a separate category, to measure what impact, if any, they will have in the presidential election. The breakdowns for income, education, and other demographics also should be standarized.

I wouldn't advocate any national polls, because we don't have a national election; we have a series of state elections, and there are lots of states that it would serve no useful purpose for the Democratic party to poll in 1972.

We tried to do some of this in 1968, but by the time we got going—after Labor Day—it was too late to achieve maximum effectiveness. As reported earlier, we were in the awkward position of being forced to produce our media materials before the poll results were in hand.

If the Democratic National Committee follows this outline, or something similar, it will have the best set of polls ever produced for a presidential candidate.

Another project I'd get started on early, and this is an easy one to begin if not necessarily to implement, would be the selection of target states. We wasted a lot of money in 1968 because of poor advance planning; there's no excuse for allowing this to happen again in 1972.

The target states are easy. In 1968, Nixon won thirty-two states with 301 electoral votes, Humphrey won thirteen and the District of Columbia with 191, and Wallace won five with 46.

The clear and obvious Democratic targets for 1972 are the thirteen states Humphrey won in 1968—Connecticut, Hawaii, Maine, Maryland, Massachusetts, Michigan, Minnesota, New York, Penn-

sylvania, Rhode Island, Texas, Washington, and West Virginia—
plus the states Nixon won that the Democrats have a reasonable
chance to carry in 1972.

This is the critical list, and on it I would place, in order of importance, California, Illinois, Ohio, New Jersey, Missouri, Wisconsin, Delaware, and Alaska.

Those eight states delivered 137 electoral votes to Nixon in 1968;
today, because of census reapportionment, they're worth 140. The
states Nixon carried in 1968 now total 305 electoral votes instead
of 301; Humphrey's states drop from 191 to 188; Wallace's from
46 to 45.

If the Democratic candidate can carry the thirteen states Humphrey carried in 1968, plus as few as three of the states Nixon
carried (California, Illinois, Ohio; or California, Illinois, New Jersey; or California, Ohio, New Jersey), he can accumulate the 270
electoral votes needed to win, regardless of what Nixon and any
third- or fourth-party candidate may do. I don't see this as an
impossible task.

The keystone state is California. That's the battleground for 1972.
Gainer of five electoral votes, booming it to forty-five while New
York drops back to forty-one, California is the prize that could
decide the election. Oh, sure, a Democrat could win without Cali-
fornia by carrying Humphrey's 1968 states plus, say, Illinois, Ohio,
New Jersey, Missouri, and Alaska, but it would be more difficult.

Of the states that Humphrey lost in 1968, I would say New
Jersey, Missouri, and Alaska will be the easiest to swing into the
Democratic column in 1972, closely followed by Delaware.

California, Illinois, Ohio, and Wisconsin will be tougher, much
tougher, but worth fighting for.

With the targets so clearly defined so early in the game, this is
the time to begin tooling up in the target states—for whomever the
Democratic candidate may be. Special television programs can be
developed for these states, which I will cover soon, when I get to
media preparation for 1972. Registration drives should begin at
once in Democratic strongholds in these states, among blacks and
young people and the poor. The votes aren't hard to identify, but
unless they are registered they won't do the Democratic party any
good in November 1972.

I may give the impression here that I am writing off certain states, and I am. There are some states that Nixon carried in 1968 that conceivably a Democrat could win in 1972, other than the eight I already have listed, but none in which I see the Democrats with a strong chance. Nevada, New Mexico, North Carolina, Kentucky, Tennessee possibly—but if I had my druthers I'd much rather place emphasis (i.e., money) in states where I had a better chance of winning than I do in these places. And I wouldn't bother with the Wallace states at all. It's conceivable a hawk Democrat such as Senator Jackson might pull off one or two if he wins the nomination—but I wouldn't bet on it. And who knows, at this point, whether there will be a third-party candidate (Wallace) or maybe even a fourth-party candidate (Gene McCarthy or John Lindsay)? But, for planning purposes at this stage, it really doesn't make much difference, because there is a minimum number of electoral votes required to win—270—and efforts should be directed at carrying enough states to accumulate that number of votes.

If there is a third party to the right and a fourth party to the left, it is conceivable that the election could wind up in the House of Representatives, as it almost did in 1968, but you don't base your game plan on those possibilities.

And there are at least a dozen states I'm willing to write off immediately, and avoid spending any money in at all, unless that money is raised in the state to be spent there. This may be a cold-blooded position not calculated to win friends among state chairmen and committeemen and -women, but, to tell the truth, I'd rather win the election than make friends. (It's amazing how friendly everyone gets after you've won.)

With a small budget to work on in 1972, and I guess that's another certainty, the Democratic party would, in my opinion, be making a terrible mistake if it diluted its funds instead of concentrating on the twenty to twenty-five states where it has a better-than-even chance of winning.

If this is going to be a negative campaign, and I don't see how it can be any other kind unless Nixon is not the candidate, then there are some uses the DNC computer should be used for right away. I'd begin feeding into the computer every public statement Richard Nixon has made since he became a congressman, properly coded and categorized. I'd also add the statements of Spiro Agnew and any other Republicans who might be targets of one sort or another in 1972—Republican national chairman Robert Dole, for example.

Then when I (i.e., the DNC, any of the presidential candidates, eventually *the* presidential candidate and his running mate, any other prominent Democratic speechmakers) wanted to demonstrate the inconsistencies of Nixon's actions with his words, I could just punch the right buttons on my computer and it would print out the material I needed.

This information-retrieval system can be a tremendous boon to speech writers, copy writers, film and radio producers, and local Democratic candidates. It's just a question of assembling, coding, storing, and retrieving. I assume something like this has and is being done, because the information it can provide, literally on a moment's notice, will be invaluable to the campaign.

My major interest in campaigns is political communication. This involves the use of mass media, particularly television and radio, but other media as well. When I became advertising director of the Humphrey campaign late in the '68 campaign I tried to implement some of my theories on the use of media in a presidential election, with a fair amount of success. But the shortage of time and funds caused us to fall short of our goal.

We have the time now, and I expect there will be enough money around to finance an adequate campaign—not as much as the Republicans will have, but enough to cover the necessities if it is spent properly.

I would try some new approaches to the use of media in the 1972 election, some of which can be initiated before we even know who the Democratic candidate will be.

For example, we know that California, New York, Pennsylvania, Illinois, Ohio, Michigan, and Texas are high-priority states in 1972. We won four of those states in 1968; if we had won the other three as well, Hubert Humphrey would be President today.

We also know some of the critical issues on which the 1972 election will be waged. If the war isn't over, obviously that's the major issue, and even if it is, there still may be ways of using it as an issue in the campaign. The cost of living, unemployment, poverty and welfare, taxes, education, racial tension, safety on the streets, pollution and conservation—these all will be important issues in the next presidential election.

So we find ourselves in this position:

a. We know at least some of the major issues for 1972.

b. We know the states the Democratic party must win.

c. We don't know who the Democratic candidate will be.

Now let me ask this rhetorical question: In our early media planning, is it terribly important to know who the candidate will be?

I think not.

And I hope I am not misunderstood. I am *not* saying that the campaign is bigger than the candidate, or that the candidate is incidental to the campaign. What I am saying is that there are certain things that can and should be done to help insure a Democratic victory in 1972 *regardless* of who the candidate may be.

Indeed, whoever he turns out to be should be properly grateful that someone has got a start on these projects, because he and his staff are going to be plenty busy between the time he wins the nomination and the first Tuesday after the first Monday in November.

In fact, there is no reason why the candidates could not be informed what is being done (notice I said "informed," not "consulted"; you don't produce good media by committee in consultation) on their behalf. Presumably the eventual candidate might want to scrub everything, but I doubt it if the material I envision is produced the way it should be; and even if he doesn't want to use it, it will be prepared in such a way that Democratic candidates for Senate, Congress, and state house will be able to make use of it.

Suppose I had carte blanche to organize and implement media planning and structure for the 1972 presidential election: what would I do?

First, I would take the seven big states I feel are essential to win in 1972—California, New York, Pennsylvania, Illinois, Ohio, Michigan, and Texas—and get some tough research done on *how the Nixon administration has failed to solve the problems in those states.* I would deal in hard specifics here, with problems directly related to the individual states. In New York, this could include the massive problems of welfare and drug addiction; in California, the rampant unemployment in aerospace and the erosion of natural resources; in each state, the specific local problems.

Not only would I find out what the problems are and how the Republican administration has failed to solve them, but also solutions that had been and are being presented by the Democrats. We should also note that California, New York, Illinois, and Michigan have Republican governors, and that Pennsylvania and Ohio had Republican governors until the start of 1971.

As soon as I had assembled my research, and probably concomitantly, I would engage three or four of the best television documentary producers to make a thirty-minute documentary film on each state. These films should be adaptable for use by the candidate for President as well as candidates within the state; and wherever and whenever possible, attractive local candidates can be included in the structure of the film.

By the late spring or early summer of 1972 I would have a package of half-hour documentaries for use within the major battleground states, specifically relating to their problems, revealing Republican failures and outlining Democratic programs. These films don't even have to include the Democratic presidential nominee, because they can work in his behalf no matter who he is by softening up the state and preparing it for a Democratic thrust. Remember something I noted earlier: you should never underestimate the intelligence of the American voter, or overestimate the amount of information at his disposal. We would be giving him solid chunks of anti-Nixon information preparatory to our positive campaign.

While I was producing these state documentaries, I also would be working on some *problem* (or, if you prefer, *issues*) documentaries on the major problems facing the country: lack of job opportunities, drug addiction, education, pollution and conservation, education, welfare and poverty. Again, these would be definitive studies that would document Republican failures and present Democratic programs, and they'd work for whoever the nominee might be. I can't see that there would be a sharp difference between a Humphrey, Muskie, Hughes, Bayh, McGovern, Kennedy, or Jackson program on drugs or poverty or protection of natural resources or education.

The basic footage can be filmed in the spring and early summer; by the time the candidate is nominated, he can be worked into each of the films, and there could be time and space provided for local candidate links.

These problem-oriented films could, if desired, be shown on national network television, although I would be more inclined to make local purchases within states so that you are paying only for the states you want to reach and not for states where you have no chance of winning anyway.

I'd have all these films ready to go on the air by Labor Day, and perhaps run one a week for the next five or six weeks, making them available to state committees and candidates within each state for additional showings at their convenience and expense.

As soon as the candidate is nominated, I'd begin work immediately on a biographical documentary of him and, perhaps, his running mate. This would be for use later in the campaign, say from the middle of October on.

From all these films—the state documentaries and those on problems—five-minute programs and one-minute spots also could be culled. The candidate would go into the campaign armed with the greatest assortment of television weapons any candidate for President anywhere has ever had.

What would this whole package cost? About $1 million—or something less than 8 per cent of the total Republican television time budget in 1968, around 15 per cent of what the Democrats spent on television in the past election. And there would be some offsetting gains: candidates for senator and governor might be induced to pick up part of the tab by acquiring the films they considered most useful to them in their own races and adapting them to their personal needs.

The key to the success of this project is the quality of the materials produced, as it so often is. That's why I would try to get a lock on the best film producers as early as possible, and put them to work on these films before they get so committed in other races that they don't have time to work on the presidential election. This happened in 1968, to Humphrey's detriment.

Nixon made much better use of radio than Humphrey did in 1968. For 1972, a series of low-key, factual five-minute radio programs on important issues—drugs, welfare, environment, crime, poverty, education, taxes, unemployment, etc.—can be prepared early, utilizing the best speech writers in the Democratic stable, and go on the air during the summer. The cost is low and the impact can be high.

I'd also make use of the *losing* Democratic contenders in films, perhaps a series of five-minute programs not unlike the one made with Humphrey and Ted Kennedy in 1968. These would not be for national exposure, but within the states where the losing candidate is particularly popular. For example, if Senator Jackson doesn't make it, a five-minute film of him and the Democratic nominee discussing the problems of the state of Washington should have favorable impact in that state. The same for Senator Hughes in Iowa, Senator Bayh in Indiana, Senator Kennedy in Massachusetts, Senator McGovern in the Dakotas, Senator Humphrey in Minnesota, Senator Muskie in New England. Not very expensive, and potentially very useful.

I'd get the best political time buyer available and have him begin charting the various states where we wish to make our biggest push, and outline budgets and potential time-buys in those states. Buying network time isn't as difficult in a presidential election, because the networks are, by law, forced to make equal time available to each of the presidential candidates. The time buyer's skill can best be used with the key states.

There also are some more-esoteric areas of electronic communication that I would want the Democrats to take advantage of. One is instant reaction, and the other would be the establishment of videotape and radio files.

For the 1972 presidential campaign, I would establish an "instant-reaction" electronics team, a group of television and radio specialists who could virtually instanteously capitalize on an event, a statement, a speech, a piece of news, and through electric feeds make this available to the networks and key stations throughout the country. Often these could be news material offered to the stations for use on news programs; in other cases they would be paid spots, produced in twenty-four hours or less and worked into previously purchased time.

No one knows when news that could affect the outcome of the election will break, or even when an opponent will commit a *gaffe* that could be capitalized on. Under conventional systems of producing television and radio spots, it takes days, sometimes weeks, to turn out reaction spots. Under the system I envision, these could be done in hours.

What it takes is an alert electronics team, standing by twenty-four hours a day, ready to act on literally a moment's notice. Tony Schwartz is the best man I know to handle the radio aspect of such an operation; Bill Wilson, Charles Guggenheim, Bob Squier, or Dave Garth would have no difficulty with the television side. The problem here really is not so much one of implementation, but of proper planning and having the right people ready to move when they need to move. I am convinced that the cost of such an operation would be far less than the value to be realized from it.

Candidates for years have maintained newspaper-clip files; sophisticated ones are beginning to use computer retrieval systems similar to the one I mentioned a few pages ago. But now it is time for candidates, at least for President, to establish data banks of video and audio tapes—not necessarily or exclusively of their opponents, but also of news events. These can be used for recall, to capitalize on the information already inside of everyone's brain. Consciously, we tend to forget fairly rapidly; subconsciously, we retain information for much longer periods, possibly forever. The audio/videotape banks would permit our television and radio producers to create instant recall of major events and to capitalize on both the emotionalism and the rational reactions that surrounded these events during the time they were taking place.

For example, no one who lived in New York in July 1970 is likely to forget the suffocating smog that smothered the city for a few days during the middle of that month. Utilization of news-film clips and commentaries would instantly recall those horrendous conditions, and would trigger the rage and frustration New Yorkers felt during those days.

These electronic data banks could be extraordinarily valuable in preparing television and radio materials for the 1972 presidential election—but the time to start assembling them is *now,* not after the candidate has been nominated in the middle of July 1972.

A candidate who goes into the campaign armed with this kind of backup material, and the availability of instant reaction facilities, possesses a big advantage over the candidate who doesn't, and this is the kind of thing the party apparatus can be doing prior to the election. By Labor Day 1972 the operation should be tooled up and ready to go, the material assembled, the technologists in place, the research completed, the techniques perfected.

And, needless to say, these tools can be applied as effectively by one Democratic candidate as by another. Whoever wins the nomination benefits from this kind of advance (and advanced) planning.

This whole operation requires planning, direction, and financing. The last may be the toughest, but I don't think it's a question of whether the Democratic party can afford to do it, but whether the party can afford *not* to do it. And, in the long run, I don't think the program I have outlined would cost any more than the haphazard media programs both parties have had in the past; intelligent reallocation of resources would provide maximum value for every dollar—something we have not received in past elections.

So, briefly, this is how I would go about defeating Richard Nixon in 1972:

1. Massive registration drives among the young, the poor, and the black.
2. Early and continuous comprehensive polling.
3. Early television production on state-oriented and problem-oriented documentary films.
4. Early production of radio programs.
5. Thorough utilization of losing Democratic candidates for the presidential nomination.
6. Advance planning for time buying within critical states.
7. Organization of instant-reaction operation.
8. Creation of audio/video electronic data banks.
9. Thorough planning and intelligent direction of the media program.

There's one more thing I would hope for, although we really don't have any control over this:

I wish Attorney General John Mitchell would run Nixon's campaign again.

Anyone who can manage Nixon from a fifteen-point lead to a seven-tenths-of-a-point victory in seven weeks is too good a friend to lose.

APPENDIX A

August 25, 1968

CONFIDENTIAL MEMORANDUM

To: Larry O'Brien
From: Joe Napolitan
Re: Media presentation

1. Ira and I saw the media presentation today. Another showing is scheduled at 9:30 tomorrow morning and I think it is imperative that you attend.

2. It was a disappointing showing. We saw storyboards on 12 60-second spots and one 20-second spot. Two or three were good enough to go into production at once, two or three others are usable with revisions, and the rest ranged between mediocre and terrible.

3. Not all of this is the agency's fault (although I believe their basic approach is wrong; more about this later in the memorandum). For some reason known only to themselves the Humphrey research people have not let the agency have access to polls and surveys in their possession. Lloyd Wright showed me one survey today which he said he practically had to wrestle away from the research division. It was anonymous and gave no indication of the number of interviews or where they were taken (at least the section I was able to see) but it did contain some interesting statistical information (figures only; analysis I saw was faulty). One of the interesting figures was that Wallace is taking 23 per cent of the Independent vote, 18 per cent of the Democratic vote, and only 10 per cent of the Republican vote. Another is that Humphrey is taking more than 80 per cent of the Negro vote, Nixon 6 per cent, and Wallace none.

4. The agency had made no provision for any anti-Wallace ma-

terial, and conceded they were not aware of the political nuances of the campaign. (Two of their spots for example had Negroes as narrators—an insane thing to do.)

5. My basic criticisms of the spots are these:
    1. They lacked warmth and conviction.
    2. With one or two exceptions, they fail to indicate that Humphrey is tough and decisive.
    3. They lack emotional appeal.
    4. They are burdened with statistics and figures; this is fighting emotion with logic, and it just won't work.
    5. Some were slick, and these may be useful, but I got the feeling that they might be too slick.
6. This really gets back to Step 1 of my three steps for winning this election:
    Defining the message we wish to communicate to the voter.
7. This has not been done, and, in fairness to the agency, I think it is essential that we provide them with, or work with them in developing, the messages that we wish to get across. (I intend to do a separate memorandum on this tonight.)
8. The approach, incidentally, was typically Madison Ave.: there must have been 20 people there, all set "to go to work," and none of them having the vaguest idea of what the hell they are supposed to be doing. (And I don't think there were three Humphrey votes in the whole crowd.)
9. I criticized the spot I had seen the other night. Predictably, they said they had been ordered to run that by the Vice-President's staff. (I tried unsuccessfully to find out who was giving this kind of order, or approving what was shown.)
10. My experience working with other producers and agencies has made me extremely cynical and distrustful of advertising agencies per se, and there was little in what we saw today to cause me to change my opinion. I think it would be a grave mistake to let this agency continue unfettered.
11. I make these recommendations so far as media is concerned:
    a. A very small group, and perhaps a single person with authority, be delegated to work with the agency and other producers to develop spots and films. This simply cannot be done effectively by a large committee.
    b. We take immediate steps to try to retain Charles Guggen-

heim and/or Shelby Storck to do a half-hour film (perhaps they would work on it jointly).

c. We take immediate steps to hire Tony Schwartz to produce some television and radio spots, acquainting him with the problems and turning him loose.

d. We have the agency go into immediate production on the spots that are acceptable to meet the earliest deadline dates.

e. We inform the agency that we intend to have other material produced and if it is acceptable they will place it as part of their over-all package.

12. Supervising media is a hell of a tough and important job, and it takes a tough and blunt person to do it. This assignment should be filled as quickly as possible with the best man around.

APPENDIX B

August 25, 1968

CONFIDENTIAL MEMORANDUM

To: Larry O'Brien
From: Joe Napolitan
Re: Television

1. I think these are the messages we should try to get across in our television material:

HHH the man
   Tough, firm, independent, decisive.

HHH—the record
   A leader, ahead of his times, creative, courageous.

Compare the candidates, consider the alternatives
   HHH vs Nixon and Wallace on various issues, record, experience.

Straight anti-Nixon, anti-Wallace

Party differences
   Democrats vs Republicans on critical issues: Medicare, Social Security, Aid to Education, job training, etc.

HHH programs on national problems
   Law and order
   Vietnam (HHH—man of peace, man of reason, man of responsibility)
   Marshall Plan for Cities (IF visually and dramatically presented)

Special interest targets
   Youth
   Women
   Suburbanites
   City residents
   Elderly
   Poor (delicately handled and potentially tricky)

2. I recommend this kind of package:
   a. A superbly produced 30-minute film. (This is of absolutely no value unless production is extraordinarily good.)
   b. 15-minute and 5-minute shows for fringe-time and afternoon use, some aimed at women, others regional in nature.
   c. A variety of 60's, 20's, and 10's; package of 25 or 30.

APPENDIX C

September 14, 1968

HIGHLY CONFIDENTIAL

To: Larry O'Brien
From: Joe Napolitan
Re: Campaign strategy

GENERAL COMMENTS

It is my strong belief that if this campaign continues as it has started we will lose.

Even though our media program is shaping up, and we are seeing some signs of daylight in our organization, I don't see how we can make up a 12-point gap in the Gallup Poll in seven weeks using the same campaign tactics we are now using.

I am trying to be objective about this, and I am not pessimistic by nature. Most of my political career has been devoted to helping candidates win elections that were considered unwinnable.

But every objective analysis at this point must come to the inescapable conclusion that we are losing.

The tragedy is that we have it within our means to win!

This campaign lacks bold programs.

We are playing it straight, using conventional, orthodox programs —and making no gains.

This would be fine if we were ahead. But we aren't.

We have an advantage over Nixon that we are not exploiting. (Ironically, Wallace has the same advantage and *is* exploiting it.)

The advantage we have is this:

We have nothing to lose—and the presidency to gain—by being bold.

Let me put it this way:
1. *If we continue as we are we will lose.*
2. *If we try some bold plans and they backfire, we still lose.*
3. *If we try some bold plans and they work, we may win.*

In the following pages I have outlined some simple but dramatic steps which I believe can win the election if they are implemented.

OVER-ALL STRATEGY

I believe three things are necessary to put the Vice-President in contention:
1. A sharp break with Lyndon Johnson.
2. An independent Vietnam policy that will win back votes that should be Humphrey's but which now are wavering.
3. A policy on law and order that will separate him from Nixon/Wallace and appeal to the conscience of the American voter.

Implementation of these three steps would be a dramatic breakthrough in this campaign.

Steps 1 and 2 above almost necessarily must be linked.

On the following pages I am presenting some specific thoughts for achieving these breakthroughs.

VIETNAM

Summary of the Plan
1. HHH notifies the President he is going to Paris to personally meet with Harriman and Hanoi representatives.
2. HHH announces this to the public.
3. He goes to Paris and meets with Harriman, et al.
4. HHH returns, calls a press conference, and announces that based on his conversations in Paris he is convinced that the first step on the road to peace is an immediate halt to the bombing.
5. We have people like Ted Kennedy, George McGovern, Mike Mansfield, Gene McCarthy lined up to enthusiastically endorse your position.
6. Two days later Harriman resigns and announces that he agrees with you, disagrees with the President, and intends to spend the rest of the time before the election persuading the country that your position is right.

. . . .

PRO

This would be a dramatic breakthrough that would put the stamp of leadership on the Vice-President. Obviously, it requires a hard-nosed attitude to carry it off.

But it would set to rest the fears of many persons that Hubert Humphrey does not have the courage to stand up to Lyndon Johnson.

Harriman is important to the operation, but not essential.

The biggest plus is that the move would bring back to Hubert Humphrey *millions of votes which should be his but which we cannot now claim.*

CON

The President will be unhappy. (While contemplating this, let me repeat a remark reliably attributed to Marvin Watson and made within the hearing of several persons this week: "We may not be able to elect Humphrey President but we sure as hell can stop him from being elected."

Nixon will accuse us of gimmickry, but I am not sure this hurts.

The superhawks will be upset—but I don't think we have too many of their votes anyway.

LAW AND ORDER

I think we are missing the boat on law and order for several reasons. Essentially there are two basic positions HHH can take:

   a. The same hard, tough line as Nixon/Wallace.

   b. A position to the left of Nixon/Wallace.

Before analyzing these positions, let us agree on some basic campaign strategy:

1. No matter what Humphrey says or does, he can't get to the right of Nixon/Wallace because no one will believe him.
2. The hard-line anti-Negro "law and order" vote is lost, probably irretrievably. (If we drive it away from Wallace, it is more likely to go to Nixon than HHH.)
3. In any political campaign you try to secure your strength before going after other voters. Humphrey's base of support

at this point consists basically of the non-whites: Negroes, Puerto Ricans, Mexicans. Together they represent about 10 million votes.

4. Because of his record Humphrey should be getting—but cannot now count on—the liberal and moderate-liberal votes.

5. If HHH adopts the same hard line as Nixon/Wallace he forces the voters to decide the election on other issues and, at the same time, turns off the liberal/moderate vote he should be getting. These people may not vote for Nixon or Wallace —but there is a real danger they may not vote at all.

My recommendation, therefore, is that in order to solidify the vote that should be Humphrey's he take a position to the left of Nixon/ Wallace on law and order, but with some interesting variations.

The position might be something like this:

a. HHH is for law and order; everyone is for law and order.

b. Every American deserves protection from the lunatic fringe, whether these be Black Panthers or White Ku Klux Klanners. (Note that in Humphrey's B'nai B'rith speech he even suggested legislation to prevent guerrilla bands.)

c. Maintaining law and order has become too big for local communities to support. Help from the federal government is needed.

d. *Nixon and Wallace are opposed to such federal aid.*

e. Nixon comes of the Republican party that opposed Social Security, Aid to Education, and Medicare, all on the grounds that they would cost too much. And this is the same party responsible for opposing federal anti-crime legislation on the same grounds: it would cost too much.

f. Wallace opposes federal aid because he is a strong advocate of states' rights and decentralization of the federal government.

g. A strong case can be made to show that the only effective way of fighting crime and violence in America is through federal intervention and spending—and it is possible to put Wallace and Nixon on the wrong side of this line.

h. Concomitant with advocating federal anti-crime programs and accusing Nixon/Wallace of opposing a federal role, you make a determined, emotional appeal to the conscience of America.

i. This would drive a sharp wedge between HHH and Nixon/
Wallace—and give millions of decent Americans a *reason*
for supporting HHH.

OBSERVATIONS

I feel more strongly about the Vietnam proposal than the
other—but I see no great risk in implementing either or both of
these programs.

The great unpleasantness is incurring the personal wrath of Lyndon Johnson—but if it comes to a choice between electing a President or getting a President angry, I know what I should do.

This is a time for boldness, and I think the Vice-President must
act boldly as well as talk that way.

INDEX

9 781635 617818